CHILD CUSTODY ASSESSMENTS

A Resource Guide For Legal And Mental Health Professionals

Rachel Birnbaum
Barbara Jo Fidler
Katherine Kavassalis

The paper used in this publication meets the minimum requirements of American National Standard for Information Sciences — Permanence of Paper for Printed Library Materials, ANSI Z39.48-1984.

Library and Archives Canada Cataloguing in Publication

Birnbaum, Rachel, 1954-
  Child custody assessments: a resource guide for legal and mental health professionals / Rachel Birnbaum, Barbara Jo Fidler, Katherine Kavassalis.

Includes bibliographical references and index.
ISBN 978-0-7798-1441-1

  1. Custody of children—Canada. I. Fidler, Barbara Jo, 1956- II. Kavassalis, Katherine III. Title.

KE600.B47 2007   346.7101'73   C2007-906720-4
KF547.B47 2007

Composition: Computer Composition of Canada Inc.

THOMSON
™
CARSWELL

One Corporate Plaza, 2075 Kennedy Road, Scarborough, Ontario M1T 3V4
Customer Care:
Toronto: 1-416-609-3800
Elsewhere in Canada/U.S.: 1-800-387-5164
Fax: 1-416-298-5094

Acknowledgments

Writing this book has involved many people who supported us along the way. First we thank our families for their patience, encouragement, and attentive ears.

We thank O'Neil Smith at Thomson Carswell Publishing for seeing us through this project and also seeing the value of providing a follow-up text focused on special topics. We also thank Susannah Albanese from Thomson Carswell for her helpful editing assistance. We are most grateful to our copy editor, Carol Pollock, for her excellent work, and Emily Gerhard and Dean Melamed for their administrative assistance. We also appreciate the thoughtful editorial comments from Linda Chodas, Dr. Helen Radovanovic, and Madam Justice June Maresca.

Last, but not least, we thank the children and families who provided us with guidance and humility along the way.

About the Authors

Rachel Birnbaum, Ph.D., RSW, is an associate professor at King's University College at the University of Western Ontario, where she teaches children and families, ethics and the law, and research methods. Dr. Birnbaum has practice experience in working with children and families of separation and/or divorce, and has also published in this area and presented papers on these topics both nationally and internationally. At present she is completing a master's degree in law, specializing in family law. With her coauthors, she recently published a research textbook, *Practicing Social Work Research: Case Studies for Learning* (in press), using a case-based approach. Ms. Birnbaum has also co-written *Law for Social Workers, 4th Edition* (in press). She has been President of the Ontario College of Social Workers and Social Service Workers since 2006.

Barbara Jo Fidler, Ph.D., C.Psych., Acc.FM., is a registered psychologist and accredited mediator practising in Ontario, Canada. She received her M.A. from San Francisco State University in 1980 and her Ph.D. from York University in 1986. Dr. Fidler maintains a private practice and is a founding member of Family Solutions. She provides therapeutic intervention, mediation, arbitration, parenting coordination, consultation, expert court testimony and custody/access assessment critiques. Her practice also includes marital/couple, individual (child, adolescents, and adult) and family therapy. Dr. Fidler provides training and supervision for parenting plan assessment (custody/access), parenting coordination, mediation, and parent–child contact problems, including child alienation, and has published in these and other areas. Dr. Fidler has been actively involved in the development of parenting coordination services. She was appointed to the AFCC Task Force charged with developing guidelines and standards of practice for parenting coordination. She is currently a member of the High Conflict Forum in Toronto and a frequent presenter on high-conflict families and related topics.

Katherine Kavassalis, B.A., LL.B., is a practising member of the Ontario bar. She received her B.A. from the University of Waterloo in 1979 and her LL.B. from the University of Windsor in 1982. She has practised family law since her call to the bar in 1984. In 2004, while continuing to maintain a private practice, she joined the in-house legal staff of the Office of the Children's Lawyer, Ministry of the Attorney General, in Toronto, Canada, where she represents children in family law matters. In addition to her practical experience of working with families and children in separation and divorce matters, Ms. Kavassalis has published in this area and has presented both locally and internationally. She has taught at various institutions, including the University of Western Ontario. She is currently a member of several law-related organizations, including the Family Law Advisory Committee to Legal Aid Ontario, the Family Bar Advisory Committee on Domestic Violence, the Family Rules Subcommittee on Domestic Continuing Records, and a trainer at the Advocates Society.

Preface

When we started to write this book we were excited yet full of trepidation. We come from three different disciplines (social work, psychology, and law) and often speak in different languages. We wanted our book to both address the novice custody assessor and also offer something to our experienced colleagues in the field. We hope that we have accomplished both. In fact, in the course of writing for this project, we ended up with two books; we will talk more about that later.

In this book we focus on the "how to" of child custody and access assessments in the context of the empirical and social science literature and our decades of collective practice experiences. We are not aware, in Canada, of any university courses that provide teaching in how to conduct child custody assessments, or of facilities that offer internships or practice experience (The Justice Institute of British Columbia offers an online course in this area for a fee.) The literature in the area encompasses many disciplines, textbooks, journals and organizations that often do not reach everyone. Most mental health professionals do not have access to legal databases or journals, and we believe it is very important to understand what the courts are saying about different parenting time and decision-making arrangements—joint, sole, and shared—and why. As well, it is important to understand what role custody assessors play in the judicial decision-making process. Our goal is to assemble and organize the best practices that we are aware of, along with the most relevant social science literature and applicable case law, in an effort to help our mental health and family law colleagues.

This was a challenging task. While there is much written from a theoretical perspective, little empirical research is available to support one methodology over another and/or on outcomes with respect to different parenting time arrangements. Empirical research must accompany any area of practice to provide the best guidance available for our work. Having said this, we did gather useful information from academics and practitioners with expertise in child developmental theory, conflict theory, communication theory, and risk and resiliency theory, to name a few.

The basis for our approach in this book is a developmental-ecological framework. After all, we are talking about children—their needs, hopes, fears, and challenges as they weather their parents' separation and divorce. While it is their parents' separation, and not the children's separation and divorce from their parents, the dilemma presents a struggle for children that we mental health practitioners and lawyers continue to see being played out during the subsequent child custody and access assessment process. We hope the readers find this book informative and practical in their complex and challenging work surrounding separation and divorce.

We are in the process of completing another book—*Special Practice Topics*—that examines the serious issues and allegations that often arise during the custody and access assessment process. The following topics will be covered: sexual abuse; domestic violence; relocation; assisted reproductive technology; and child alienation. As with this book, we will continue to provide the most up-to-date empirical research and social science literature in these areas, as well as a review of what the courts have to say about each area, and why.

Contents

List of Tables

Table of Cases

Table of Legislation

Chapter 1

The Evolution Of Custody Law

"We want to know in advance how cases will come out, and we want each of them to come out right." Katherine Bartlett[1]

Statistics Canada reports that fewer Canadians are divorcing. In 2002 70,155 couples divorced. This figure is down 1.3 per cent from 2001 and 1.4 per cent from 2000 (Statistics Canada, 2004). However, these figures do not include the number of common-law relationships that have dissolved, nor do they include married couples who have separated but not divorced. In custody matters regarding children under the age of 18, court proceedings were initiated in 29 per cent of the 2001 divorces and 28 per cent of the 2002 divorces (Statistics Canada, 2004). Historically, marriage and divorce rates have always fluctuated. Ambert (2005) reports that no data is available on the number of children who experience multiple parental divorces. Child custody disputes have remained constant at about 10 per cent.[2]

Recent attempts at divorce law reform in Canada began in 1986 with the introduction of "no fault" divorce. Despite attempts to reform family law throughout the country, amendments to child custody laws have remained dormant for some time. The reasons include changes in government as well as the controversy that results when the issue of child custody reform is raised.[3] Legal academics and social scientists have argued that the family law system, particularly family law reform, may not bring about the required solutions, as the law by itself cannot regulate human relationships (Bainham, 1998; Douglas, 1997; Firestone & Weinstein, 2004).

Decision-making about child custody and access matters is an increasingly complex and difficult issue for the courts. Since the 1970s, child custody determination has been predicated on the best interests of the child. The best interests test requires a court, for the most part, to choose one parent over another; to pit one against the other in a process that exposes competing parenting practices and values, along with the personal characteristics of each parent and how these attributes contribute, or not, to their child's well-being.

The purpose of this chapter is threefold. First, it will provide a framework outlining the historical roots of divorce legislation and the parallel roots of child custody and access determinations. Second, the chapter describes and explores the role of mental health professionals (social

workers, psychologists and psychiatrists), who often provide child custody and access assessments/investigations[4] to assist the court in its decision-making (Fidler & Birnbaum, 2006; Gould, 1998, 2006). Third, the
chapter highlights the conceptual frameworks that guide mental health
practitioners in determining custody and access arrangements. These
frameworks, utilized throughout the book to inform custody and access
determinations, include the following theories: attachment; developmental; risk and resiliency; systems; and conflict (Bowlby, 1969; Bronfenbrenner, 1977; Coser, 1956; Erikson, 1950, 1968; Germain & Gitterman, 1980;
Rutter, 1987, 1989; Sroufe & Waters, 1977; von Bertalanffy, 1956, 1968).

An important element in examining issues of child custody and access
decision-making is understanding the parallel development over time
between society's view of marriage and divorce and the changing status
of child custody and access decision-making. What becomes apparent is
the shifting of ideologies over the centuries. English common law, for
example, began with the "paternal doctrine," which gave absolute priority
to fathers in custody matters. This doctrine evolved over time to a presumption in favour of mothers, especially for children of "tender years."
As societal values changed, gender-neutral presumptions emerged along
with the "best interests" standard as we know it today. These presumptions led the way to the introduction of joint custody, only to revert to
maternal presumption or the primary caretaker standard and the approximation rule (Emery, Otto & O'Donohue, 2005; Kelly, 1994). A dynamic tension continues to exist between these competing presumptions
and, more recently, the role of father involvement (Kelly, 1994; Lamb,
1997).

To date, little consensus is found among the legal, mental health, and
judicial communities about what constitutes a child's best interest. In
part, this is because the basic concept is a legal one and is difficult to
translate, in practical terms, into a child's individual psychological and
developmental well-being based on social science evidence.

HISTORICAL PERSPECTIVE OF MARRIAGE AND DIVORCE

Before the Middle Ages, marriage and divorce were deemed private
matters not to be interfered with or governed by Church or State. No
evidence of Christian wedding rites is found until at least the ninth century and quite possibly later. Christians married in the earlier centuries,
but the arrangement was considered a civil order and not a rite of the
Church. A shift in the regulation of marriage and its dissolution occurred
during the tenth century (Walker, 1986), when the Ecclesiastical Courts

obtained absolute jurisdiction over marriage for Christians; it then ceased to be a private matter and became a religious one, subject to the regulation of the ecclesiastical legal system (Backhouse, 1981; Walker, 1986). The church had complex rules governing the ability to marry, and the validity of marriage was commonly challenged, thus casting doubt on the legitimacy of children born within such unions. An "illegitimate" child could not look to his parents for support in their lifetime, nor was the child capable of inheriting from their estates after their deaths. The consequences were devastating to "illegitimate" progeny, as the main source of wealth during this period was the inheritance of land.

With the Reformation, the Ecclesiastical Courts of the Catholic Church gradually lost exclusive jurisdiction over marriage. By the reign of Elizabeth I, the British parliament had established parliamentary divorce, although the procedure for obtaining such a divorce was difficult and expensive. The grounds were limited to rape, adultery, sodomy or bestiality.[5]

With the Protestant Reformation in the sixteenth century, marriage and divorce became controversial issues. Marriage, for example, was no longer viewed as sacred. This challenge first began with Martin Luther, who proposed that "marriage was not a holy sacrament, but an element of creation" (Day & Hook, 1987, p. 63). Henry VIII of England, when he was attempting to end his marriage to Catherine of Aragon, also challenged the Catholic Church's control over marriage. Before Henry VIII, the centre of authority rested with the papacy (Day & Hook, 1987) and as such, marriage was perceived to be a spiritual institution, one that inscribed women and children as the property of the husband. This view is succinctly stated in St. Paul's Epistle to the Ephesians 5:22–25: "Wives submit yourself unto your husbands, as unto the Lord. For the husband is the head of the wife, even as Christ is the head of the Church." A tradition was established that "rested on the subordination of married women, a guilt–innocence approach to divorce and the state's interest in preserving marriage" (Gettleman & Markowitz, 1974, p. 60). Divorce was allied with property rights such as the inheritance of estates by males in succession, with the focus on "legitimate" children only. The law reflected society's emphasis on a wife's subservience and her husband's rights over her. In the words of Sir William Blackstone, a legal commentator in the eighteenth century, "By marriage the husband and wife are one person in law."[6]

Early Canadian law was in fact British law, and severe laws governed divorce. For men, divorce was possible if it could be proven that the wife was an adulterer, prostitute, or convicted felon (Day & Hook, 1987). For women, obtaining a divorce was quite difficult, the major grounds at their disposal being military separation, abandonment, or conviction for a felony by the spouse (Day & Hook, 1987). Of these, and unlike her male counterpart, a woman needed to prove at least two grounds before being granted a divorce.

From a mental health perspective, many of the earlier theories constructed the pathogenic view that divorce leads to the demise of the traditional two-parent family (Fineman, 1988; Leaf, 1983; Mellinger, 1978; Wallerstein, 1984, 1991; Wallerstein & Corbin, 1989). These theoretical perspectives linked divorce to negative effects on child adjustment and psychosocial development (Amato, 1994; Kalter, Kloner, Schreier & Okla, 1989; Wallerstein, 1984, 1991; Wallerstein & Corbin, 1989). Many of these earlier studies supported the view that divorce was an inferior alternative to family life, citing differences in outcomes between separated and divorced persons and persons of other marital status. These studies included psychiatric and epidemiological surveys (Ilfeld, 1978; Leaf, 1983; Mellinger, 1978), clinical studies that compared the separated, divorced, and married or widowed on various measures of physical and emotional well-being (Coogler, Weber & McKenry, 1979; Cox, 1978; Emery, 1994), and exploratory studies that described disturbance in the divorced population (Mellinger, 1978; Wallerstein & Kelly, 1980). Consequently, North American family law focused on the pathology of family breakdown. Historically, divorce was viewed as an indication of sin and immorality (Girdner, 1986); even with the legislative changes in 1986, adultery continued to be a ground for divorce, thus continuing the historical traditions.

Origins of Child Custody Decision-Making

McDonald (1986) identified three dominant themes that illustrate how the enshrinement of custodial rights throughout history has paralleled the development of divorce legislation. All three themes share a patriarchal, property-rights–based approach in the legal system.

The first theme, the presumption of paternal superiority, originated with the child being viewed as property, with no relevant rights or feelings (Kelly, 1994). Paternal dominance, regardless of the age of the child, was equated with absolute control over the child. Men were the unquestioned heads of the household and mothers had no rights to their children. Up until the mid-nineteenth century, infanticide and child slavery were not uncommon (Bala & Clarke, 1981; Franklin & Hibbs, 1980; MacDonald, 1986).

In England, it was not until 1839 that both houses of the British parliament passed the *Infants Custody Act* based on a bill introduced by Thomas Noon Talfourd. According to the Act's provisions, a mother had a right to seek custody or access if her child was in the custody of the father or a person chosen by the father, including a guardian after the father's death. The court could now give the mother custody until the child reached seven years of age, at which age the child was returned to the father; if the child was older than seven, the mother could ask for regular access. However, if the mother was guilty of adultery, she had no rights under the legislation (Kelly, 1994; MacDonald, 1986).

Similarly, the history of child custody law in this country can be traced back to the early-nineteenth century, with Canada taking its cues from England. Although it was 1855 before Upper Canada passed legislation to equal Lord Talfourd's act, there was evidence of the judiciary's growing unease with the prevailing law before that time. For example, in 1846, Richard Snooks asked the court first to order his father-in-law to return Snooks's wife Elizabeth to him and secondly to return his seven-month-old daughter to his custody. The evidence provided at trial showed that Snooks was often intoxicated and that he regularly beat his wife and child during his drinking binges. Mr. Snooks's lawyer argued that,

> the guardianship of the children is properly with the father; and if it were not so, but the mother were allowed to remove them from him at her will and pleasure, there would perhaps be more frequent separations between husband and wife; but the knowledge [that] when she leaves her husband, she must also lose the society of her children, must frequently have the effect of inducing her to remain with him, when she would leave her home if the law were otherwise.

Eventually, this case wound its way to the Court of Appeal, where the presiding justice, John Beverley Robinson, was not swayed by Mr. Snooks's reasoning. And although Justice Robinson was aware that the *Infants Custody Act* introduced by Lord Talfourd in England had no force in Upper Canada, it influenced his thinking when he ruled that the baby's ". . . health if not its life would be endangered by depriving it of that care and of the natural food which the mother supplies to it." Neither Elizabeth Snooks nor her baby were required to return to Mr. Snooks.[7]

Beginning in the latter part of the nineteenth century and continuing into the early twentieth century, substantial changes in child custody law emerged. During this period, the "paternal doctrine," which had been fully enshrined in common law, began to erode and was replaced with a "best interests of the child" principle. Parallel to a best interest analysis was the "tender years" doctrine, which also emerged during this period. The basic assumption of the tender years doctrine was that young children (generally under the age of seven) were better off in their mother's care than their father's. In the Ontario Court of Appeal decision *Orr, Re,*[8] it was stated that courts, which made the outcome of custody matters dependent upon assumptions as to parental suitability, developed a number of rules. The court further stated that the most important of these rules was the tender years doctrine, which was described by the court as a common-sense proposition. The court stated at pp. 80–81:

> In the case of a father and mother living apart and each claiming the custody of a child, the general rule is that the mother, other things being equal, is entitled to the custody and care of a child during what is called the period of nurture, namely, until *it* attains about seven years of age, the time during which *it* needs the care of the mother more than of the father. [italics added for emphasis]

The judge also went on to state that a related presumption favoured placing older children with the parent of the same sex.

Some responsibilities and functions were typically associated with the role of the mother. These typically involved caring for husband, house, and children. The principle of the tender years doctrine was criticized because it did not serve the best interests of the child and it discriminated against men (Cochran, 1985); for example, men were not seen as being as capable as women to care for and nurture their young children. In addition, maternal presumption was criticized as "sexual stereotyping" (Cochran, 1985). Elster (1987) addresses the discriminatory and gender-biased doctrine in the following manner:

> The maternal preference rule contained the seeds of its own destruction. By resting exclusively on considerations of the child's best interest, it invited lawmakers to turn that interest into the explicit criterion for custody adjudication in each and every case. Why rest content with the rule of thumb that the interest of the child is always best served by maternal custody? Why not judge each case on its merits? (p. 9)

The second theme in child custody decision-making in Canada reflects the moral conduct of parents in family-law disputes. In the 1960s, the courts determined custody of children based on the behaviour and conduct of one or both parents; the issue of adultery, for example, could be raised against one parent by the other. In the Ontario Court of Appeal decision in *Youngs v. Youngs*,[9] Justices Robertson, Laidlaw, and Roach wrote:

> [I]t would be positively against [the children's] interest and detrimental to their welfare to permit him to associate or visit with them. He committed adultery and, after wrecking his marriage and the home life of his wife and children by his immoral conduct, he chose

deliberately to continue his wickedness after the Court adjudged him guilty.

In *Re Allan and Allan*,[10] the British Columbia Court of Appeal set aside the decision in the lower court awarding Mrs. Allan custody of the children. Relying upon the provisions of the *Equal Guardianship of Infants Act*[11] and the rule in *Re Orr*, the court held that other factors, such as the conduct of the parties, required consideration in determining the issue of child custody. Justice Sheppard found that Mrs. Allan was at fault in the breakup of her marriage, having left her husband for "no good reason." According to the court, by deciding to leave the marriage Mrs. Allan placed her own happiness ahead of the happiness of her children. She was deemed to have deserted Mr. Allan and to have violated his paternal rights by taking the children with her. Custody was awarded to the father.

In *K. v. K.*,[12] the Manitoba Court of Appeal found that the wife had deserted the husband when she moved to the city with her children. Although the wife was willing to reconcile her marriage, she found the rural isolation unbearable and wanted to remain in the city where her parents lived. The court, in 1956, refused to condone any authority in a wife to decide where she would live and raise her children. The court, quoting from an earlier British case, *Mansey v. Mansey*,[13] ruled that:

> [W]e have yet to come to the point where the wife can decide where the matrimonial home is to be, and if the husband says he wants to live in such and such a place then, assuming always that he is not doing it to spite his wife and the accommodation is of a kind that you would expect a man in his position to occupy, the wife is under the necessity of sharing that home with him. If she will not, she is committing a matrimonial offence: she is deserting him.

The earlier order granted by Judge Morkin of the Surrogate Court was set aside and the father was granted custody of the children. This judicial decision-making highlights the tensions between legal discourse and social science discourse on views of sin and immorality (Girdner, 1986). This same view is evident in the following quote from *Re Plewes*:

> Under the Infants Act, R.S.O. 1937, chap. 215, which is substantially the Infants Act, R.S.O. 1914, chap.153, the status of the mother is in some respects put upon the same plane as the status of the father as regards the child, but when they are rival claimants, the morality, fitness or ability of the father not being in serious question, the paramount right of the father appears to be as it was at common law.[14]

Over time, moral conduct, prevalent from the 1950s to the 1970s as a determining factor in child custody cases, was replaced with an examination of the parenting abilities of each parent. With increasing concern for the welfare of children and the impact of changing social attitudes to premarital and extramarital sexual relations, Canadian courts moved from placing children with the least blameworthy parent to placing them with the better parent.

The third theme influencing the determination of custody in divorce cases rested on the emotional ties of the child to the parents. Custody determinations in the 1970s were based on the best interests of the child. Goldstein, Freud & Solnit were the first influential writers (in the legal and mental health fields) to introduce the legal profession to the concept of a psychological parent in their book *Beyond the Best Interests of the Child* (1973). This principle underscored the vulnerability of the child and emphasized that continuity of relationships, surroundings, and environmental influences were critical to child development. While the children referred to were drawn mainly from child-protection and foster-care cases, the notion of a primary parent—typically the mother—reinforced a maternal presumption (Pruett, 2005).

Children's rights or the notion of children as autonomous individuals began to take centre stage in the 1970s. In 1975, in the Ontario court judgment *Brown, Re*, Stortini Co. Ct. J. stated: "[E]very child should have certain basic rights such as: the right to be wanted, the right to be healthy, the right to live in a healthy environment and the right to continuous loving care."[15]

As outlined at the outset, these three themes—paternal superiority, moral conduct of parents, and the emotional ties of the child to the parents—share common elements. The first centres on paternal dominance referring to the ownership of children: children were viewed as chattels of a male property-owner (Folberg, 1984). The second theme focuses on moral conduct as evaluated, historically, by a male-dominated judiciary.[16] The third theme shifts to a maternal presumption arising from dominant paternalistic thinking regarding the nature of "motherhood" (Boyd, 1987). The woman was relegated to child care and child nurturing, and the "tender years" doctrine prevailed.

Also important to note is that the shift in the legal discourse of child custody law paralleled the changing socio-political attitudes and the shift from an agrarian economy to an industrial economy where women became the primary child-care providers (Kelly, 1994). To this day, these same forces—social, political, and economic—continue to shape child custody law.

For example, in 1997 the Government of Canada created the *Federal Child Support Guidelines*. In order to pass this bill, a committee was established to explore changes to the *Divorce Act* that would allow for increased involvement in children's lives by both parents following divorce (Bala, 1999; Cohen & Gershbain, 2001). The debate highlighted the tensions between mothers, fathers, children's advocacy groups, lawyers, and mental health professionals, all claiming to know what was in the best interests of children. It would be naive, however, to assume that equality[17] exists for all, given the inequalities between genders that continue to remain problematic today. The discourse of equality is incommensurate with the historical roots of child custody decision-making, as it flows from a deep-seated history based on the patriarchal structure of the family.

With the enactment of no-fault divorce in 1986, legislators hoped to eliminate the burden of proving fault, and more importantly they hoped to provide validation for parents to separate without the finding of fault. The stigma was removed and divorce was now viewed as a restructuring of the family and a legitimizing of new family relationships.

This prompted a shift in the theoretical orientation of divorce from pathology towards it being seen as an opportunity for growth and development (Hetherington, 1989). In fact, researchers investigating the long-term adjustment of children to separation and divorce are finding a rich array of both resilience and vulnerability, depending on the individual resources of the child and the strengths of the parent and parent-child relationship (Amato & Keith, 1991; Emery, 1988; Galatzer-Levy & Kraus, 1999; Hetherington, 2003; Kelly & Emery, 2003). The literature related to the role of the father is equally compelling when examining the risks and resiliency factors on child and adolescent adjustment after separation and/or divorce (Amato & Gilbreth, 1999; Fabricius, 2003; Kelly & Emery, 2003; Lamb, 1997; Pruett, 2005).

Best Interests as a Defining Principle of Child Custody Law

At present, child custody law in North America is based on the legislative standard of the best interests of the child. The best interests test can be defined as a variety of factors related to the interests of the child, including, but not limited to, parents' conduct towards the children, maximum contact with each parent, and an assortment of statutory factors. The *Divorce Act*, R.S.C., 1985 c. 3 as amended, sets out the federal legislation under Section 16:

1) A court of competent jurisdiction may, on application by either or both spouses or by any other person, make an order respecting the custody of or access to any or all children of the marriage.

2) In making an order under this section, the court shall take into consideration only the best interests of the child of the marriage as determined by reference to the condition, means, needs and other circumstances of the child.

3) In making an order under this section, the court shall not take into consideration the past conduct of any person unless the conduct is relevant to the ability of that person to act as a parent of a child.

4) In making an order under this section, the court shall give effect to the principle that a child of the marriage should have as much contact with each spouse as is consistent with the best interests of the child and, for that purpose, shall take into consideration the willingness of the person for whom custody is sought to facilitate such contact.

Each province has legislation that outlines a number of factors the courts must consider when determining child custody and access matters (see Table 1). In Ontario, under section 24(2) of the CLRA the legislature decreed that the courts would consider the following factors in determining the best interests of the child:

a) the love, affection and emotional ties between the child and,

   i) each person entitled to or claiming custody of or access to the child,

   ii) other members of the child's family who reside with the child, and

   iii) persons involved in the child's care and upbringing;

b) the child's views and preferences, if they can be reasonably ascertained;

c) the length of time the child has lived in a stable home environment;

d) the ability and willingness of each person applying for custody of the child to provide the child with guidance and education, the necessaries of life and any special needs of the child;

e) any proposed plans for the child's care and upbringing;

f) the permanence and stability of the family unit with which it is proposed that the child live;

g) the ability of each person applying for custody of or access to the child to act as a parent; and

h) the relationship by blood or through an adoption order between the child and each person who is a party to the application.

Ontario's *Children's Law Reform Act* stipulates that a person's past conduct "shall be considered only if the court is satisfied that the conduct is otherwise relevant to the person's ability to act as a parent," or in accordance with subsection (24)4 of the act, regarding violence and abuse:

> In assessing a person's ability to act as a parent, the court shall consider whether the person has at any time committed violence or abuse against: (a) his or her spouse; (b) a parent of the child to whom the application relates; (c) a member of the person's household; or (d) any child, 2006, c. 1, s. 3(1).[18]

There is now legislative recognition in the definition of "best interest" of domestic violence, which has been absent and largely silent to date. However, what is still missing is the idea that domestic violence must also include emotional, sexual, and/or verbal harm as well as physical harm (Birnbaum, 2006).

What is the best interest of children? Chambers (1984) argues that flipping a coin may be equally as efficient when it comes to determining custody of children. Researchers and academics have also suggested that the standard is at best vague, discretionary, speculative, and value-laden with personal assumptions and biases (Czapanskiy, 1993; Emery, 1999a; Garrison, 1996; O'Donohue & Bradley, 1999). The present literature demonstrates that the standard leaves room for wide interpretations not only by the judiciary but also by the mental health professionals who assess and evaluate these matters (Fineman, 1987; Otto & O'Donohue, 2005).

In the final analysis, assessing the best interests of the child requires an understanding of individual and family dynamics, children's developmental ages and stages, domestic violence and all aspects of family law. The balancing of these factors can be highly subjective and difficult, if not impossible, to evaluate during child custody disputes. In *MacGyver v. Richards*, Abella J.A. stated:

> Clearly, there is an inherent indeterminacy and elasticity to the 'best interests' test which makes it more useful as legal aspiration than as legal analysis. It can be no more than an informed opinion made at a moment in the life of a child about what seems likely to prove to be in that child's best interests. Deciding what is in a child's best interests means deciding what, objectively, appears most likely in the circumstances to be conducive to the kind of environment in which a particular child has the best opportunity for receiving the needed care and attention. Because there are stages to childhood, what is in

a child's best interest may vary from child to child, from year to year, and possibly from month to month. This unavoidable fluidity makes it important to attempt to minimize the prospects for stress and instability.[19]

THE ROLE OF MENTAL HEALTH PROFESSIONALS IN CHILD CUSTODY CASES

When child custody disputes enter the legal system, mental health professionals with expertise in understanding the family are often called upon to conduct an assessment (Ash & Guyer, 1986; Fidler & Birnbaum, 2006; Gould, 1998; McCurley, Murphy & Gould, 2005; Stahl, 1994). When making child custody recommendations the mental health professional is guided by the same factors (i.e., the best interests test) as the court is when decisions are being made. The custody and access assessment is meant to offer objective and scientific evidence by providing the court with the necessary information to make a reasoned determination in the best interests of the child (Gould, 1998; Grisso, 1986).

Tippins and Wittman (2005), Grisso & Vincent (2005), Heilbrun (2001), Melton, Petrila, Poythress & Slobogin (1987) and others have echoed concerns about the role of the mental health professional in the child custody arena. In fact, some have even suggested a moratorium on child custody assessments altogether (O'Donohue & Bradley, 1999). These same concerns were also expressed in the late 1970s and early 1980s. Reppucci's (1984) statement that "based on one's view of the research, one can say we do not know enough to make any contribution, or alternatively that we have sufficient knowledge and skills so we can make a contribution" (p. 97) reflects the broad perception of "expertise" that exists.[20]

In 1990, Grisso provided guidelines for child custody assessments. He argued as to what mental health professionals could and could not do in child custody assessments given the limits of scientific information. Bala (2005) argues that the court is not the best place to make child custody determinations in the end, and that assessments by mental health professionals have been helpful to the courts. Custody disputes cannot be decided merely by the perfunctory application of established legal principles and therefore reports by mental health professionals have become increasingly more important. A mental health professional's impartial analysis of what may be an appropriate parenting plan can be quite relevant to the custody proceedings.[21] An assessor may be of assistance in the settling of a dispute between parents, evaluating the strength of a child's bond to each parent without creating loyalty conflicts, expanding the information available to the court, and assisting courts to appreciate the "common sense" importance of stability and continuity in a child's life.[22]

Additionally, an assessment by an independent mental health professional may be the best way to put the child's views and preferences before the court.[23] Courts dealing with custody and access matters have been reticent to allow children to testify. Justice Perkins in *Collins v. Petric*[24] refused a request to allow a thirteen-year-old child to testify, finding that it would be "ironic in the extreme" to cause harm to a child in order to determine the best interests of that child. Children, however, have information that is often relevant to the proceedings and to the determination of their best interests. By allowing an assessor to testify about their views and preferences, we can insure that children have a voice in the proceedings without the emotional burden of testifying.

Alternatives to the Best Interests Test

Crippen (1990), Boyd (1987), Fineman (1987), and Weitzman (1985) propose that the primary caretaker presumption should take precedence when making decisions regarding the custody of a child. They conclude that by doing so, the rights orientation of parents becomes neutralized and brings the social reality of parenting to the forefront of the best interests test. Scott (1992) and Emery, Otto and O'Donohue (2005) provide an alternative approach to the primary caretaker presumption for the resolution of child custody matters. They argue that the most effective approach to the pluralism in the family structure is to base custody decisions on the "approximation" standard. Scott (1992) argues that "the relationships between parent and child would approximate as closely as possible the pre-divorce pattern of parental responsibility in the custody arrangement" (p. 630). However, this may not differ substantively from the primary caretaker presumption, as each specifies amount of time spent with the child. Regardless of the name used to describe the standard, there is agreement that the language used should be more gender neutral (Boyd, 1987). This issue is discussed more fully in Chapter 5.

Similarly, Irving and Benjamin (1995) suggest using a language that reflects parenting language instead of the present terms, custody and access. For example, Australia is examining changes to the *Family Law Act*, 1995, and recommending clearer but rebuttable presumptions regarding custody. The presumption recommended is one in favour of equal, shared parenting as the first approach. This does not mean joint decision-making. Moreover, in cases of domestic violence, substance abuse, and child abuse, the recommendation is that the legislation be amended to a clear presumption against shared parenting. The *Children's Act 1989* in Britain similarly uses the term sharing of parental responsibility, and in Scotland, the *Children (Scotland) Act 1995*, c. 36 also refers to parental responsibilities and parental rights. In addition, Arizona, Florida, Maine and Washington in the United States focus on the "needs of children" and the responsibility of parents. In 1987 the State of Washington introduced the *Parenting Act*, which replaced the language of "custody" with "parenting." We elaborate further on this area in Chapter 5.

Irrespective of the language used to describe parenting time, the difficulties inherent in custody and access disputes are compounded when concerns arise about domestic violence. For example, abusive partners commonly resort to threats of seeking custody of their children in order to keep their partners in the relationship while continuing the abuse (Kerr & Jaffe, 1999; Bancroft & Silverman, 2002). As one judge opined on the relationship between domestic violence and custody and access:

> [A]n understanding of the theory of violence in domestic relationships and the impact of the violence on the abused spouse [*partner/ child/ren*] is essential to an understanding of the dynamics of the relationship between the batterer and the battered spouse [*partner/ child/ren*]. This in turn informs the understanding of the added complexities of a custody and access case involving a battered or abused spouse [*partner/child/ren*] [italics added for emphasis].[25]

This suggests to mental health professionals, child custody assessors, lawyers, and judges that there is neither a single child custody and access arrangement that works for all children nor a definitive criterion upon which to base custody and access arrangements, as each child and his/ her family constellation is variable and complex (Bray, 1991; Fidler & Birnbaum, 2006). The need to understand and assess the level of risk to children, or lethality involved as a result of domestic violence during separation and divorce, requires a differentiated and comprehensive assessment of the family (including a cultural and social context), as well as an understanding of domestic violence and its implications on children (physical, sexual and psychological). This will be more fully explored in Chapters 2 and 3.

Who Conducts Child Custody and Access Assessments?

In Canada, every province has legislation outlining who provides child custody assessments and how such assessments are ordered by the courts.[26] Ontario has two pieces of legislation that guide such determinations: Section 30 of the *Children's Law Reform Act*[27] and Section 112 of the *Courts of Justice Act*.[28] The decision regarding who will conduct the assessment and/or investigation depends upon the particular issue before the court requiring guidance, and the expertise available to conduct such an assessment. However, the court must be persuaded that the provision of an assessment by an expert will assist the court (namely, the judge) and will not result in prolonged proceedings.[29] A court must weigh the benefits of an assessment against the delay such an assessment would entail. Judges continue to be skeptical about the role of experts in custody and access disputes, and some are reluctant to order assessments. Justice Fleury, in the *Mantesso* decision, observed that assessments are intrusive, time-consuming, and expensive, and declined to make the requested order. Justice Granger further developed this line of thinking in his ruling in *Linton v. Clarke*,[30] where he not only dismissed the request for an assessment, but went on to state that assessments should be limited to cases in which "clinical issues" are to be determined. However, he left undefined the parameters of a clinical issue. Similarly, in declining to order an assessment in *Sheikh v. Sheikh*,[31] the court indicated that there was no evidence of pathology or any significant problem with the current custody or access arrangements. But in *Kramer v. Kramer*,[32] the court held that although assessments should not be ordered in every case, neither should they be limited to those cases where "clinical issues" are involved.

The court has to weigh the factors in any particular case when deciding whether or not an assessment should be prepared. Delay occasioned by the report may be a factor in the decision. On a motion for an investigation and report by the Children's Lawyer in *Parniak v. Carter*,[33] the court held that clinical issues are not a precondition to order an assessment. The judge went on to state that although a clinical issue may be an excellent reason for the court to obtain the assistance of an assessment, it is not the only reason to order one.

STANDARDS AND GUIDELINES

Fidler and Birnbaum (2006) have listed the guidelines and standards that mental health professionals ought to consider. These include but are not limited to:

(a) the Ontario Interdisciplinary Association of Assessor's Custody/ Access Guidelines (OIAC), endorsed by the Psychology Foundation of Ontario and revised in 1998;

(b) the Ethical Guidelines for Psychological Practice Related to Child Custody and Access, developed by the Ontario Psychological Association (OPA) in 1998 and currently being revised;

(c) the American Psychiatric Association Task Force on Clinical Assessment in Child Custody (1981);

(d) the Specialty Guidelines for Forensic Psychologists (Committee on Specialty Guidelines for Forensic Psychologists, 1991);

(e) the American Academy of Child and Adolescent Psychiatry's
     Practice Parameters for Child Custody Evaluation (AACP,1997);

(f) the American Psychological Association Guidelines for Child
     Custody Evaluations in Divorce Proceedings (APA,1994);

(g) the American Academy of Psychiatry and the Law (Ethical Guide-
     lines for the Practice of Forensic Psychiatry), adopted May, 2005;
     and

(h) The Model Standards of Practice for Child Custody Evaluation
     by the Association of Family and Conciliation Courts (AFCC
     2004, revised 2007).

The Royal College of Physicians and Surgeons of Canada and the
Ontario College of Physicians and Surgeons have no guidelines or standards for child custody assessments. The Ontario College of Social Workers and Social Service Workers (OCSWSSW) are in the process of producing child custody guidelines based on the two different statutes in
Ontario.[34]

Notwithstanding the above-noted guidelines and model standards, the
absence of any accepted uniform assessment methodology, guidelines
and/or standards of practice raises serious concerns from the point of
view of consumer protection and assessor accountability, on the one
hand, and the prevention of frivolous and vexatious complaints on the
other. Clearly, consumers must be protected and assessors must be accountable. The lack of uniformity in the various guidelines leaves the
court with broad discretion as to how to interpret child custody assess-
ments/investigations regardless of the validity of the assessment and
recommendations. As a result, when an assessment and/or investigation
and report is not in a client's favour, lawyers will often argue that it should
be dismissed on the basis that it did not follow the accepted guidelines.
Such tactics (especially when there is no valid reason for them) only serve
to exacerbate parental conflict, which in turn places children at substantial risk for psychosocial adjustment problems.

Disputes may also arise when a parent is dissatisfied with an assessor's
recommendation and retains another expert to either critique the first
assessor or offer a second opinion. These two types of reviews are often
confused by mental health professionals and by the lawyers who retain
them (Martindale, 2006). Moreover, there are no regulations and/or
standards governing critiques and second opinions/expert advice. The
social science literature is equally underdeveloped in this area (Martindale, 2006; Stahl, 1996; Greenberg, Martindale, Gould, & Gould-Saltman,
2004). From a legal perspective, the courts have provided conflicting

opinions as to how critiques and/or second opinions are to be inter-preted.[35]

Justice Wein, in *Mayfield v. Mayfield*,[36] dealt with the issue of critiques of assessments. Following the principles set out in *R. v. Mohan*,[37] Justice Wein held that a critique of an assessment might only be admitted into evidence if it meets a four-pronged test. The evidence, she stated, must be: (a) relevant; (b) not otherwise excluded; (c) given by a person properly qualified as an expert; and (d) necessary in order to assist the trier of fact. In applying this test, Justice Wein would not allow the critique to be entered into evidence, nor would she allow the evidence to be called orally. She determined that in most cases it was unnecessary or inappro-priate to have the parties bring forward evidence of a collateral critique of an assessment report. Furthermore, while a social work critique may assist counsel in cross-examining the assessor at trial, it will rarely, if ever, meet the necessity requirement for admissibility.

In a similar vein, in the case of *Huxtable v. Huxtable*,[38] the court held that a critique of an assessment by someone who had not seen any of the parties or the child is to be given little or no weight. Justice Quinn, however, in *Greenough v. Greenough*,[39] expressly rejected Justice Wein's approach to the admissibility of critiques; the justice found that critiques were helpful to the court in that they can highlight lapses in accepted methodology and, more importantly, they can highlight the significance of such lapses. In Chapters 2 and 3 we describe and review the processes, procedures and methods employed in conducting child custody and ac-cess assessments. In Chapter 4 we provide a more thorough discussion of expert opinions, critiques and second opinion assessments.

Notes

1. [1999]
2. It is difficult, if not impossible, to assess the actual number of disputed custody and access cases, as the statistics are not collected. In addition, many cases settle without proceeding to a trial. It is important to note that when we discuss disputing families, we are also referring to same-sex families.
3. For example, in 1997, a Special Joint Committee of the House of Commons and the Senate was established by the Government of Canada to examine issues of custody and access. The Committee heard submissions from various groups that all had different viewpoints regarding a child's best interest. Also, see the Federal-Provincial-Territorial Report on custody and access and child support, *Putting Children First* (November 2002).
4. It should be noted that in Canada there are both private and public services in each province that provide child custody assessments by mental health professionals. There are similar services in the United States, where they are most often referred to as child custody evaluations. The mental health professionals conducting these evaluations are also known as forensic evaluators.
5. Sheila Kieran, *The Family Matters: Two centuries of Family Law and Life in Ontario* (Toronto: Key Porter Books Limited, 1986), pg. 116.

6. Sir William Blackstone, "Commentaries on the Laws of England. In Four Books" (Oxford: Clarendon Press, 1765-1769) Book First, Ch. 15 at 442.

7. *Ibid.* at 50-51.

8. [1933] O.R. 212, [1933] 2 D.L.R. 77 (Ont. C.A.).

9. *Youngs v. Youngs* (1948), [1948] O.J. No. 343, 1948 CarswellOnt 360, [1949] O.W.N. 96 (Ont. C.A.).

10. *Allan v. Allan* (1958), 16 D.L.R. (2d) 172 (B.C. C.A.).

11. R.S.B.C. 1948, c. 139.

12. (1956), 1956 CarswellMan 68, 20 W.W.R. 449, 64 Man. R. 298, 7 D.L.R. (2d) 16 (Man. C.A.).

13. *Mansey v. Mansey*, [1940] P 139 (Eng. P.D.A.) at 140-141 as cited in *K. v. K.* (1956), 1956 CarswellMan 68, 20 W.W.R. 449, 64 Man. R. 298, 7 D.L.R. (2d) 16 (Man. C.A.) at para. 31.

14. *Plewes, Re*, [1945] O.J. No. 203, 1945 CarswellOnt 226, [1945] O.W.N. 479, [1945] 4 D.L.R. 380 (Ont. C.A.).

15. (1975), 1975 CarswellOnt 182, 9 O.R. (2d) 185, 21 R.F.L. 315 (Ont. Co. Ct.).

16. While the *Custody and Infants Act* enacted in Upper Canada in 1855 gave mothers a right to seek custody and access to their children, the statute prohibited their claims if they were guilty of adultery. No similar restriction was applied to fathers (Backhouse, 1981).

17. Thomas Axworthy in "Liberalism and Equality" and Sarah Salter in "Inherent bias in Liberal Thought" in *Equality and Judicial Neutrality*, (1987) Sheilagh Martin and Kathleen Mahoney (Eds.) discuss the requirements and philosophies of equality for the concept of justice for all to be meaningful. That is, equal treatment is accorded both man and woman.

18. *Children's Law Reform Act* R.S.O. 1990, C.C.12, s.24(2),(3),(4).

19. (1995), [1995] O.J. No. 770, 1995 CarswellOnt 90, 11 R.F.L. (4th) 432, 22 O.R. (3d) 481, 123 D.L.R. (4th) 562, 84 O.A.C. 349 (Ont. C.A.).

20. For a more thorough analysis of the debate see *Family Court Review, Vol. 43 (3)(4)*, 2005.

21. See *Weaver v. Tate* (1990), 1990 CarswellOnt 283, [1990] O.J. No. 1779, 28 R.F.L. (3d) 188 (Ont. C.A.).

22. Nicholas Bala, "Assessing the Assessor: Legal Issues" (1990) 6 C.F.L.Q. 179 at 180 and 225.

23. *Woodhouse v. Woodhouse* (1996), 1996 CarswellOnt 1906, [1996] O.J. No. 1975, 20 R.F.L. (4th) 337, 136 D.L.R. (4th) 577, 91 O.A.C. 91, 29 O.R. (3d) 417 (Ont. C.A.), leave to appeal refused (1997), [1996] S.C.C.A. No. 402, 99 O.A.C. 80 (note), 209 N.R. 80 (note) (S.C.C.).

24. (2003), 2003 CarswellOnt 2522, [2003] O.J. No. 2744, 41 R.F.L. (5th) 250 (Ont. S.C.J.) at p. 265 [R.F.L.].

25. Schnall, E.M. (1999) "Custody and access and the impact of domestic violence" Canadian Family Law Quarterly, 18, p. 27-12-13.

26. Alberta, Rules of Court, Alta. Reg 390/68, Rule 218; British Columbia, *Family Relations Act*, R.S.B.C., ch. 128, 15(1996) (Can.); Manitoba, *The Family Maintenance Act, C* C.S.M., ch. F20. 3(1997)(Can.); and the *Court of Queen's Bench Act*, C.C.S.M., ch. C280, 49(1988)(Can.); New Brunswick, *Judicature Act*, R.S.N.B., ch.1-2, 11.4 (1973)(Can.); Newfoundland, *Children's Law Act*, Nfld.R.S., ch. C-13, 36(1990); Northwest Territories, *Children's Law Act*, 29; Nova Scotia, *Judicature Act*, R.S.N.S., ch.J-4, 32F(1989)(Can.); *Maintenance and Custody Act*, R.S.N.S., ch.160, 19(1989)(Can.); Ontario, *Children's Law Reform Act*, R.S.O., ch. C12, 30(1990)(Can.); *Courts of Justice Act*, R.S.O., ch. 12, 112(1990)(Can.); Prince Edward Island, *Custody Jurisdiction and Enforcement Act*, R.S.P.E.I., ch. C-33, 4.1(1988)(Can.); Yukon, *Children's Act*, R.S.Y.T., ch. 22 43 (1986)(Can.).

27. *Children's Law Reform Act*, R.S.O. 1990, c. C.12. The court before which an application is brought in respect of custody of or access to a child, by order, may appoint a person who has the technical or professional skills to assess and report to the court on the needs of the child and the ability and willingness of the parties or any of them to satisfy the needs of the child.

28. *Courts of Justice Act*, R.S.O. 1990 c. C.43. In a proceeding under the *Divorce Act* (Canada) or the *Children's Law Reform Act* in which a question concerning custody of or access to a child is before the court, the Children's Lawyer may cause an investigation to be made and may report and make recommendations to the court on all matters concerning custody of or access to the child and the child's support and education.

29. *Mantesso v. Mantesso* (1991), [1991] O.J. No. 643, 4 F.L.R.R. 128 (Ont. Gen. Div.) *Linton v. Clarke* (1994), 1994 CarswellOnt 361, [1994] O.J. No. 2999, 10 R.F.L. (4th) 92, 21 O.R. (3d) 568, 76 O.A.C. 363 (Ont. Div. Ct.).

30. (1994), 1994 CarswellOnt 361, [1994] O.J. No. 2999, 10 R.F.L. (4th) 92, 21 O.R. (3d) 568, 76 O.A.C. 363 (Ont. Div. Ct.).

31. (2004), [2004] O.J. No. 4384, 2004 CarswellOnt 4395, 5 R.F.L. (6th) 456 (Ont. S.C.J.).

32. (2003), 2003 CarswellOnt 1228, [2003] O.J. No. 1418, 37 R.F.L. (5th) 381 (Ont. S.C.J.).

33. (2002), 2002 CarswellOnt 2311, [2002] O.J. No. 2787, 30 R.F.L. (5th) 381 (Ont. C.J.).

34. The recent professional activity in terms of revising existing guidelines and producing them where they have not existed, as well as recent professional writings, underscores the concerns and controversy pertaining to child custody assessments, both public and private.

35. See *Bryanton v. Bryanton* (2002), [2002] O.J. No. 3744, 2002 CarswellOnt 3254 (Ont. S.C.J.), *Takis v. Takis*, 2003 CarswellOnt 2358, [2003] O.J. No. 2658, 38 R.F.L. (5th) 422, [2003] O.T.C. 594 (Ont. S.C.J.), and, *Greenough v. Greenough* (2003), [2003] O.J. No. 4227, 2003 CarswellOnt 4320, 46 R.F.L. (5th) 414 (Ont. S.C.J.).

36. [2001] O.J. No. 2212, 2001 CarswellOnt 2036, [2001] O.T.C. 429, 18 R.F.L. (5th) 328 (Ont. S.C.J.).

37. [1994] 2 S.C.R. 9, EYB 1994-67655, 1994 CarswellOnt 1155, 1994 CarswellOnt 66, [1994] S.C.J. No. 36, 18 O.R. (3d) 160 (note), 29 C.R. (4th) 243, 71 O.A.C. 241, 166 N.R. 245, 89 C.C.C. (3d) 402, 114 D.L.R. (4th) 419 (S.C.C.).

38. (2001), 17 R.F.L. (5th) 82 (Ont.S.C.J.)

39. (2003), 2003 CarswellOnt 4320, 46 R.F.L. (5th) 414, [2003] O.J. No. 4227 (Ont. S.C.J.).

References

AFCC Model Standards of Practice for Child Custody Evaluation (Task Force for Model Standards of Practice for Child Custody Evaluation 2004, revised 2007).

Amato, P.R. "Life span adjustment of children to their parents' divorce" The Future of Children: Children and Divorce 4:1 (1994), 143–164.

Amato, P.R. & Gilbreth, J.G. "Non-resident fathers and children's well-being: A meta-analysis" Journal of Marriage and the Family 61 (1999), 557–573.

Amato, P. R. & Keith, B. "Parental divorce and adult well-being: A meta-analysis" Journal of Marriage and the Family 53 (1991), 43–58.

Ambert, A. "Divorce: Facts, causes, and consequences" Contemporary Family Trends (2005) The Vanier Institute of the Family website http://www.vifamily.ca/library/publications/divorce.html.

Ash, P. & Guyer, M. "Child psychiatry and the law: The functions of psychiatric evaluation in contested child custody and visitation cases" Journal of the American Academy of Child Psychiatry, 25:4 (1986), 554–561.

Axworthy, T. "Liberalism and Equality" S. Martin & K. Mahoney (Eds.) Equality and Judicial Neutrality (Toronto: Carswell, 1987).

Backhouse, C. "Shifting patterns in nineteenth century Canadian custody law" in D. Flaherty (Ed.) Essays in the history of Canadian law (Toronto: University of Toronto Press, 1981), 189–212.

Bainham, A. "Changing families and changing concepts: Reforming the language of family law" Child and Family Law Quarterly 10 (1998), 1–15.

Bala, N. "A report from Canada's 'Gender War Zone': Reforming the child-related provisions of the Divorce Act" Canadian Journal of Family Law 16:2 (1999), 163–227.

Bala, N. & Clarke, K. The Child and the Law (Toronto: McGraw-Hill Ryerson Ltd., 1981).

Bala, N. "Tippins and Wittmann asked the wrong question: Evaluators may not be 'experts,' but they can express best interests opinions" Family Court Review 43:4 (2005), 554–562.

Bancroft, L. & Silverman, J. The Batterer as Parent: Addressing the Impact of Domestic Violence on Family Dynamics (Thousand Oaks, CA: Sage, 2002).

Bartlett, K.T. "Improving the law relating to postdivorce arrangements for children', in R. Thompson & P.A. Amato (Eds.) The Postdivorce Family: Children, Parenting and Society (Thousand Oaks, CA: Sage Publishing, 1999), 71-102.

Birnbaum, R. "Rendering children invisible: The forces at play during separation and divorce in the context of family violence" in R. Alaggia & C. Vine (Eds.) Cruel but Not Unusual: Violence in Canadian Families (Waterloo: Wilfrid Laurier University Press, 2006), 267–324.

Blackstone, Sir W. Commentaries on the Laws of England in Four Books (Oxford: Clarendon Press, 1765-1769) Book First, Ch. 15, 442.

Bowlby, J. Attachment and Loss, Vol. 1: Attachment (New York: Basic Books, 1969).

Boyd, S. "Child custody and working mothers: The impact of judicial bias on family law" Equality and Judicial Neutrality (Toronto: Carswell, 1987).

Bray, J. "Psychosocial factors affecting custodial and visitation arrangements" Behavioural Sciences and the Law 9 (1991), 419–437.

Bronfenbrenner, U. "Toward an experimental ecology of human development" American Psychologist 32 (1977), 513–531.

Chambers, D.L. "Rethinking the substantive rules for custody disputes in divorce" University of Michigan Law Review 83 (1984), 480–569.

Cochran, R. "The search for guidance in determining the best interests of the child at divorce: Reconciling the primary caretaker and joint custody preferences" University of Richmond Law Review 20 (1985), 1–65.

Cohen J. & Gershbain, N. "For the sake of fathers? Child custody reform and the perils of maximum contact" Canadian Family Law Quarterly 19:1 (2001), 121–183.

Coogler, O., Weber, R. & McKenry, P. "Divorce mediation: A means of facilitating divorce and adjustment" The Family Coordinator 28 (1979), 255–259.

Coser, L. *The Functions of Social Conflict* (New York: Free Press, 1956).

Cox, F. *Stress* (Baltimore, MD: University Park Press, 1978).

Crippen, G. "Stumbling beyond best interests of the child: Re-examining child custody standard setting in the wake of Minnesota's four year experiment with the primary caretaker preference" Minnesota Law Review 75:4 (1990), 27–503.

Czapanskiy, K. "Domestic violence, the family, and the lawyering process: Lessons from studies on gender bias in the courts" Family Law Quarterly 27:2 (1993), 247–274.

Day, R.D. & Hook, D. "A short history of divorce: Jumping the broom and back again" Journal of Divorce 10:3/4 (1987), 57–72.

Douglas, K. "Child custody and access" Law and government division, Government of Canada (1997), catalogued as BP-441E.

Elster, J. "Solomonic judgements: Against the best interest of the child" The University of Chicago Law Review 54:1 (1987), 1–45.

Emery, R. "Marriage, divorce, and children's adjustment" in *Developmental Clinical Psychology and Psychiatry, Vol. 14* (Newbury Park: CA: Sage Publications, 1988).

Emery, R.E. "Changing the rules for determining child custody in divorce cases" Clinical Psychology: Science and Practice 6 (1999a), 323–327.

Emery, R. E., Otto, R.K. & O'Donohue, W.T. "A critical assessment of child custody evaluations: Limited science and a flawed system" American Psychological Society 6:1 (2005), 1–29.

Emery, R. *Renegotiating Family Relationships: Divorce, Child Custody, and Mediation* (New York, London: The Guilford Press, 1994).

Erikson, E. H. *Childhood and Society* (New York: W.W. Norton & Co., 1950).

Erikson, E.H. *Identity: Youth and Crisis* (New York: Norton, 1968).

Fabricus, W. "Listening to children of divorce" Journal of Divorce & Remarriage 32 (2003), 41–71.

Fidler, B.J. & Birnbaum, R. "Child custody disputes: Public and private assessments" Canadian Family Law Quarterly 25:2 (2006), 137–167.

Fineman, M. "Custody determination at divorce: The limits of social science research and the fallacy of the liberal ideology of equality" Canadian Journal of Women and Law 3:1 (1987), 89–110.

Fineman, M. "Dominant discourse, professional language, and legal change in child custody decision-making" Harvard Law Review 101:4 (1988), 727–774.

Firestone, G. & Weinstein, J. "In the best interests of children: A proposal to transform the adversarial system" Family Court Review 42:2 (2004), 203–215.

Folberg, J. "Custody overview" in Folberg, J. (Ed.) Joint Custody and Shared Parenting (Washington: Bureau of National Affairs. New York: Guilford Press, 1984).

Franklin, R. & Hibbs, B. "Child custody in transition" Journal of Marriage and Family Therapy 3 (1980), 285–291.

Galatzer-Levy, R.M. & Kraus, L. (Eds.) The Scientific Basis of Child Custody Decisions (New York: John Wiley & Sons, Inc., 1999).

Garrison, M. "How do judges decide divorce cases? An empirical analysis of discretionary decision making" North Carolina Law Review 74 (1996), 401–552.

Germain, C.B. & Gitterman, A. The Life Model of Social Work Practice (New York: Columbia University Press, 1980).

Gettleman, S. & Markowitz, J. The Courage to Divorce (New York: Bantam Books, 1974).

Girdner, L. "Child custody determination: Ideological dimensions of a social problem" in Julian Rappaport and Edward Seidman (Eds.) Defining Social Problems (New York: Plenum Press, 1986), 165–183.

Goldstein, J., Freud, A. & Solnit, A. Beyond the Best Interests of the Child (New York: Free Press, 1973).

Gould, J.W. Conducting Scientifically Crafted Child Custody Evaluations (Thousand Oaks, CA: Sage Publications, 1998).

Gould, J.W. Conducting Scientifically Crafted Child Custody Evaluations, 2nd Edition (Thousand Oaks, CA: Sage Publications, 2006).

Greenberg, L.R., Martindale, D.A., Gould, J.W. & Gould-Saltman, D.J. "Ethical issues in child custody and dependency cases: Enduring principles and emerging challenges" Journal of Child Custody 1:1 (2004), 7–30.

Grisso, T. "Psychological assessments in legal contexts" in William J. Curan, Louis McGarry and Saleem Shah (Eds.) *Forensic Psychiatry and Psychology: Perspectives and Standards for Interdisciplinary Practice* (1986), 103-128.

Grisso, T. "Evolving guidelines for divorce/custody evaluations" Family and Conciliation Courts Review 28:1 (1990), 35-41.

Grisso, T. & Vincent, G.M. "The empirical limits of forensic mental health assessment" Law and Human Behaviour 29:1 (2005), 1-5.

Heilbrun, K. *Principles of Forensic Mental Health Assessment* (New York: Kluwar, 2001).

Hetherington, E.M. *Coping with Divorce, Single Parenting, and Remarriage: A Risk and Resiliency Perspective* (Mahway, NJ: Erlbaum, 1999).

Hetherington, E.M. "Intimate pathways: Changing patterns in close relationships across time" Family Relations 52 (2003), 318-331.

Hetherington, E. "Coping with family transitions: Winners, losers, and survivors" Child Development 60 (1989), 1-14.

Irving, H. & Benjamin, M. *Family Mediation: Contemporary Issues* (Thousand Oaks: Sage Publications, 1995).

Ilfeld, F. "Psychiatric Status of Community Residents among Major Demographic Dimensions" Archives of General Psychiatry 35 (1978), 716-724.

Kalter, N., Kloner, A., Schreier, S. & Okla, K. "Predictors of children's postdivorce adjustment" American Journal of Orthopsychiatry 59 (1989), 605-618.

Kelly, J.B. "The determination of child custody" in *The Future of Children: Children and Divorce 4:1* (Los Altos, CA: The David and Lucile Packard Foundation, 1994), 121-142.

Kelly, J.B. & Emery, R. "Children's adjustment following divorce: Risk and resilience perspectives" Family Relations 52 (2003), 352-362.

Kerr, S.G. & Jaffe, P.G. Legal and clinical issues in child custody disputes involving domestic violence. Canadian Family Law Quarterly 17:1 (1999), 1-37.

Kieran, S. *The Family Matters: Two Centuries of Family Law and Life in Ontario* (Toronto: Key Porter Books Limited, 1986), 116.

Lamb, M.E. "The development of father-infant attachments" in M.E. Lamb (Ed.) *The Role of the Father in Child Development (3rd ed.)* (New York: John Wiley, 1997), 104-120; 332-342.

Leaf, P. "Social risk factors for psychiatric disorders: The Yale epidemiological catchment area study" Unpublished doctoral dissertation (Yale University, 1983).

Martindale, D.A. "Consultants and role delineation" The Matrimonial Strategist 24:4 (2006), 4–7.

McCurley, M.J., Murphy, K.J. & Gould, J.W. "Protecting children from incompetent forensic evaluations and expert testimony" Journal of the American Academy of Matrimonial Lawyers 19:2 (2005), 277–319.

McDonald, J. "Historical perspectives of custody and access disputes: A Lawyer's View" in R. Parry, E. Broder, E. Schmitt, E. Saunders, and E. Hood (Eds.) *Custody Disputes: Evaluation and Intervention* (Lanham, MD: Lexington Books, 1986), 9–22.

Mellinger, G. "Psychic distress, life crises, and the use of psychotropic medication" Archives of General Psychiatry 35 (1978), 1048–1052.

Melton, G., Petrila, J., Poythress, N. & Slobogin, C. *Psychological Evaluations for the Courts: A Handbook for Mental Health Professionals and Lawyers* (New York: Guilford Press, 1987).

O'Donohue, W. & Bradley, A.R. Commentary: Conceptual and empirical issues in child custody evaluations. Clinical Psychology: Science and Practice, 6:3 (1999), 310–322.

Pruett, M.K. "Applications of attachment theory and child development research to young children's overnights in separated and divorced families" Essays from the Family Court Review: An Interdisciplinary Journal (New York: Hofstra University School of Law 2005), 5–12.

Reppucci, N.D. "The wisdom of Solomon: Issues in child custody determinations" in N.D. Reppucci, L.A. Weithorn, E.P. Mulvey, and Monahan (Eds.) *Children, Mental Health, and the Law* (Beverley Hills, CA: Sage, 1984), 59–78.

Rutter, M. "Psychosocial resilience and protective mechanisms" American Journal of Orthopsychiatry 57:3 (1987), 16–331.

Rutter, M. "Pathways from childhood to adult life" Journal of Child Psychology and Psychiatry 30 (1989), 499–513.

Salter, S. "Inherent bias in Liberal Thought" S. Martin & K. Mahoney (Eds.) *Equality and Judicial Neutrality* (Toronto: Carswell, 1987).

Schnall, E.M. "Custody and access and the impact of domestic violence" Canadian Family Law Quarterly 18 (1999), 99–221.

Scott, E.S. "Pluralism, parental preference, and child custody" California Law Review 80 (1992), 615–672.

Sroufe, A.L. & Waters, E. "Attachment as an organizational construct" Child Development 48:4 (1977), 1184–1199.

Stahl, P.M. *Conducting Child Custody Evaluations: A Comprehensive Guide* (Thousand Oaks, CA: Sage Publications, 1994).

Stahl, P. "Second opinions: An ethical and professional process for reviewing child custody evaluations" Family and Conciliation Courts Review 34:3 (1996), 386–395.

Statistics Canada (1994, 2004).

Tippins, T.M. & Wittman, J.P. "Empirical and ethical problems with custody recommendations: A call for clinical humility and judicial vigilance" Family Court Review 43:2 (2005), 193-222.

Von Bertalanffy, L.V. *General Systems Theory: General Systems Yearbook 1:4* (New York: Braziller, 1956).

Von Bertalanffy, L.V. *General Systems Theory: Foundations, Development, Applications* (New York: Braziller, 1968).

Walker, T.B. "Beyond Fault: An examination of patterns of behaviour in response to present divorce laws" Journal of Family Law 10 (1986), 267–299.

Wallerstein, J.S. "Children of divorce: Preliminary report of ten-year follow-up of young children" American Journal of Orthopsychiatry 54 (1984), 444–458.

Wallerstein, J.S. "The long-term effects of divorce on children: A review" Journal of the American Academy for Child Adolescent Psychiatry 30:3 (1991), 349–360.

Wallerstein, J.S. & Corbin, S. "Daughters of divorce: Report from a ten year follow-up" American Journal of Orthopsychiatry 59:4 (1989), 593–604.

Wallerstein, J.S. & Kelly, J. *Surviving the Break-Up: How Children and Parents Cope with Divorce* (New York: Basic Books, 1980).

Weitzman, L.J. The Divorce Revolution: The Unexpected Social and Economic Consequences for Women and Children in America (New York: Free Press, 1985).

TABLE 1

A COMPARISON OF PROVINCIAL AND TERRITORIAL CUSTODY AND ACCESS LEGISLATION AND PAST PARENTAL CONDUCT AND VIOLENCE[1]

PROVINCE/ STATUTE	FACTORS – CUSTODY APPLICATIONS	FACTORS – ACCESS APPLICATIONS	ADDITIONAL FACTORS – PAST PARENTAL CONDUCT AND VIOLENCE	PARTIES
Alberta *Family Law Act* S.A. 2003, c. F-4.5	s. 18(1) In all proceedings under this Part, the court shall take into consideration only the best interests of the child. (2) In determining what is in the best interests of the child, the court shall (a) ensure the greatest possible protection of the child's physical, psychological and emotional safety, and (b) consider all the child's needs and circumstances, including (i) the child's physical, psychological and emotional needs, including the child's need for stability, taking into consideration the child's age and stage of development. (ii) the history of care for the child, (iii) the child's cultural, linguistic, religious upbringing and heritage, (iv) the child's views and preferences, to the extent that it is appropriate to ascertain them, (v) any plans proposed for the child's care and upbringing,	Factors s. 18(2)	ss. 18(2)(vi); 18(3) ; 18(4) s. 18(3) In this section, "family violence" includes behaviour by a family or household member causing or attempting to cause physical harm to the child or another family or household member, including forced confinement or sexual abuse, or causing the child or another family or household member to reasonably fear for his or her safety or that of another person, but does not include (a) the use of force against a child as a means of correction by a guardian or person who has the care and control of the child if the force does not exceed what is reasonable under the circumstances, or (b) acts of self-protection or protection of another person. s. 18(4) For the purpose of subsection (2)(b)(vi), the presence of family violence is to be established on a balance of probabilities.	

[1] Adapted from Department of Justice and Quicklaw

PROVINCE/ STATUTE	FACTORS – CUSTODY APPLICATIONS	FACTORS – ACCESS APPLICATIONS	ADDITIONAL FACTORS – PAST PARENTAL CONDUCT AND VIOLENCE	PARTIES
Alberta *Family Law Act* (cont'd)	(vi) any family violence, including its impact on (A) the safety of the child and other family and household members (B) the child's general well-being (C) the ability of the person who engaged in the family violence to care for and meet the needs of the child, and (D) the appropriateness of making an order that would require the guardians to cooperate on issues affecting the child, (vii) the nature and strength of the relationship (A) between the child and each person residing in the child's household and any other significant person in the child's life, and (B) between the child and each person in respect of whom an order under this Part would apply, (viii) the ability and willingness of each person in respect of whom an order under this Part would apply			

PROVINCE/ STATUTE	FACTORS – CUSTODY APPLICATIONS	FACTORS – ACCESS APPLICATIONS	ADDITIONAL FACTORS – PAST PARENTAL CONDUCT AND VIOLENCE	PARTIES
Alberta *Family Law Act* (cont'd)	(A) to care for and meet the needs of the child, and (B) to communicate and co-operate on issues affecting the child. (ix) taking into consideration the views of the child's current guardians, the benefit to the child of developing and maintaining meaningful relationships with each guardian or proposed guardian, (x) the ability and willingness of each guardian or proposed guardian to exercise the powers, responsibilities and entitlement of guardianship, and (xi) any civil or criminal proceedings that are relevant to the safety and well-being of the child.			
British Columbia *Family Relations Act,* R.S.B.C. 1996, c. 128 as amended	Best Interests s. 24(1) 24(1) When making, varying or rescinding an order under this Part, a court must give paramount consideration to the best interests of the child and, in assessing those interests, must consider the following factors and give emphasis to each factor according to the child's needs and circumstances: (a) the health and emotional well-being of the child including any special needs	Best Interests s. 24 (1)	s. 24(3) If the conduct of a person does not substantially affect a factor set out in subsection (1) or (2), the court must not consider that conduct in a proceeding respecting an order under this Part. s. 24(4) If under subsection (3) the conduct of a person may be considered by a court, the court must consider the conduct only to the extent that the conduct affects a factor set out in subsections (1) or (2). s. 37 On application, a court may	s. 34 mother, father and any parent (as defined in s. 1).

PROVINCE/ STATUTE	FACTORS – CUSTODY APPLICATIONS	FACTORS – ACCESS APPLICATIONS	ADDITIONAL FACTORS – PAST PARENTAL CONDUCT AND VIOLENCE	PARTIES
British Columbia *Family Relations Act* (cont'd)	for care and treatment; (b) if appropriate, the views of the child; (c) the love, affection and similar ties that exist between the child and other persons; (d) education and training for the child; (e) the capacity of each person to whom guardianship, custody or access rights and duties may be granted to exercise those rights and duties adequately. s. 24(1.1) The references to "other persons" in subsection 1(c) and to "each person" in subsection 1(e) include parents, grandparents, other relatives of the child and persons who are not relatives of the child.		(a) restrain any person from molesting, annoying, harassing, communicating or attempting to molest, annoy, harass or communicate with the lawful custody of the applicant or a child in the lawful custody of the applicant or both; and (b) require a person named in an order under (a) (i) to enter into a recognizance, with or without sureties, or to post a bond, and (ii) to report to the court or a person designated by the court, at the times and places and for the periods of time the court directs. s. 38(1) If a court makes a custody order or a separation agreement is enforceable by a court, the court may (a) order person not to enter the premises where child resides from time to time, including premises owned by person, or right to possession by person; (b) order person must not make contact or endeavour to make contact or interfere with the child or any person who has custody or access to the child, or (c) where the court concludes that person named in custody order may not comply with order under (a) or (b) court may further order person to:	

PROVINCE/ STATUTE	FACTORS – CUSTODY APPLICATIONS	FACTORS – ACCESS APPLICATIONS	ADDITIONAL FACTORS – PAST PARENTAL CONDUCT AND VIOLENCE	PARTIES
British Columbia *Family Relations Act* (cont'd)			i) enter into a recognizance, with or without sureties, in any reasonable amount that court thinks necessary ii) report to court or a person designated for period of time and at times and places as court considers necessary iii) deliver up to court, or a person designated by court, any documents that court thinks fit, or iv) transfer specific property to a trustee named by the court to be held subject to the terms and conditions specified in the order; or any combination of these. s. 45 Despite sections 44 and 48, a court may exercise its jurisdiction to make or vary an order in respect of the custody of or access to a child if (a) the child is physically present in British Columbia; and (b) the court is satisfied that the child would, on the balance of probability, suffer serious harm if the child (i) remains in the custody of the person legally entitled to	

PROVINCE/ STATUTE	FACTORS – CUSTODY APPLICATIONS	FACTORS – ACCESS APPLICATIONS	ADDITIONAL FACTORS – PAST PARENTAL CONDUCT AND VIOLENCE	PARTIES
British Columbia *Family Relations Act* (cont'd)			(ii) is returned to the custody of the person legally entitled to custody of the child, or; (iii) is removed from British Columbia.	
Manitoba *The Family Maintenance Act*, C.C.S.M. 1997, c. F.20 as amended	s. 2(1) In all proceedings under this Act the best interests of the child shall be the paramount consideration of the court. Child's views to be considered s. 2(2) Where the court is satisfied that a child is able to understand the nature of the proceedings and the court considers that it would not be harmful to the child, the court may consider the views and preferences of the child. s. 3(1) In a proceeding under this Act, the court may direct an investigation into any matter by a person who (a) has had no previous connection with the parties to the proceeding or to whom each party consents; and (b) is a family investigator, social worker or other person approved by the court for the purpose. s. 3(2) A court may direct an investigation under subsection (1) only	Best Interests s. 2(1) Factors s. 2 (2) Investigation to determine best interests s. 3	s. 39(3) In considering an application under this section, a court shall only receive evidence of the conduct of either parent if the court is satisfied that the evidence bears directly on the parent's ability to care properly for the child. s. 10(1)(c)&(d) REPEALED S.M. 1998, c. 41, s. 29 (allowed orders to restrain entrance to premises of other spouse and restraining from molesting, annoying, harassing spouse or child) s. 10.1(1) Despite the repeal of clauses 10(1)(c) (no entry to spouse's premises) and (d) (non-molestation) and Division 2 (non-molestation order by magistrate) of Part V, (a) an application for an order under any of those provisions made before this section comes into force may be continued as if those provisions remain in force; and (b) a provision of an order or interim order made under those provisions continues in force and may be revoked or varied under this Act to delete those provisions, but may not be otherwise varied.	s. 39(2)(a) either parent (biological or adoptive as defined in s. 1; or person so declared under Part II of the Act).

PROVINCE/ STATUTE	FACTORS – CUSTODY APPLICATIONS	FACTORS – ACCESS APPLICATIONS	ADDITIONAL FACTORS – PAST PARENTAL CONDUCT AND VIOLENCE	PARTIES
Manitoba *The Family Maintenance Act* (cont'd)	if satisfied that it is necessary in order to determine the best interests of the child. s. 3(3) Where a court directs an investigation pursuant to subsection (1) and a party refuses to co-operate with the investigator, the investigator shall so report to the court which may draw any inference therefrom it considers appropriate.		s. 10.1(2) Despite subsection (1), when a protection order or prevention order is made under *The Domestic Violence and Stalking Act* in respect of persons who are also parties to an order under this Act that includes a provision made under clause 10(1)(d) of this Act, (a) if the order was made by a designated magistrate pursuant to Division 2 of Part V, the order is revoked; and (b) if the order was made by a judge of the Provincial Court, that provision of the order is revoked. 10.1(3) For greater certainty, the parties referred to in subsection (2) must be the same applicant and the same respondent in both orders.	
The Child Custody Enforcement Act, R.S.M. 1987, c. C360			s. 8 Upon application, a court may make an order that any person shall not molest, annoy or harass the applicant or a child in the lawful custody of the applicant and may require the respondent to enter into such recognizance, with or without sureties, or to post such bond as the court considers appropriate. s. 14(1) Every court may punish any contempt of or resistance to its process or orders in respect of custody or of access to a child by a fine of not more than $500 or imprisonment for not more than six months or both.	

PROVINCE/ STATUTE	FACTORS – CUSTODY APPLICATIONS	FACTORS – ACCESS APPLICATIONS	ADDITIONAL FACTORS – PAST PARENTAL CONDUCT AND VIOLENCE	PARTIES
New Brunswick *Family Services Act*, S.N.B. 1980, c. F-2.2, as amended	Best Interests s. 129(2) Upon application the court may order that either or both parents, or any person, either alone or jointly with another, shall have custody of a child, subject to such terms and conditions as the court determines, such order to be made on the basis of the best interests of the child; and the court may at any time vary or discharge the order. Factors: s. 1: "best interests of the child" means the best interest of the child under the circumstances taking into consideration (a) the mental, emotional and physical health of the child and his need for appropriate care or treatment, or both; (b) the views and preferences of the child, where such views and preferences can be reasonably ascertained; (c) the effect upon the child of any disruptions of the child's sense of continuity; (d) the love, affection and ties that exist between the child and each person to whom the child's custody is entrusted, each person to whom access to the child is granted and, where appropriate, each sibling of the child and, where appropriate, each	Best Interests s. 129(2) Factors s. 1.	s. 128 Upon application of a person who is living separate and apart from his spouse a court may make an order restraining the spouse of the applicant from molesting, annoying, harassing or interfering with the applicant or any children in lawful custody of the applicant and may require the spouse of the applicant to enter into such recognizance as the court considers appropriate. s. 130(4) Notwithstanding subsection (1) and section 130.2, a court may exercise its jurisdiction to make or to vary an order in respect of the custody of or access to a child where the child is physically present in the Province, and the court is satisfied that the child would, on balance of probabilities, suffer serious harm if the child remained in the custody of the person legally entitled to custody of child, the child was returned to the custody of the person legally entitled to custody of child, or the child was removed from the Province. s. 132 (1) Where a court makes a custody order or a custody order is enforceable under this Part, the court may order that a person (a) shall not enter premises, including premises the person owns or has a right to possession of, where the child resides from time to time, or	s. 129(2) either or both parents (i.e., mother or father and any parent as defined in s. 1) or any person.

PROVINCE/ STATUTE	FACTORS – CUSTODY APPLICATIONS	FACTORS – ACCESS APPLICATIONS	ADDITIONAL FACTORS – PAST PARENTAL CONDUCT AND VIOLENCE	PARTIES
New Brunswick *Family Services Act* (cont'd)	grandparent of the child; (e) the merits of any plan proposed by the Minister under which he would be caring for the child, in comparison with the merits of the child returning to or remaining with his parents; (f) the need to provide a secure environment that would permit the child to become a useful and productive member of society through the achievement of his full potential according to his individual capacity; and (g) the child's culture and religious heritage.		(b) shall not make contact or endeavour to make contact with or otherwise interfere with either the child or any person having custody of or access to the child. s. 132 (2) Where a court is of the belief that the person named in an order under paragraph (1)(a) or (b) may not comply therewith the court may further order that the person comply with any or all of the following directions, namely (a) enter into a recognizance, with or without sureties, in such reasonable amount as the court considers necessary, (b) report to the court or person designated for such period of time, and at such times and places, as the court considers necessary and reasonable, (c) deliver up to the court such documents as the court considers fit.	
Newfoundland & Labrador *Children's Law Act*, R.S.N. 1990, c. C-13, as amended	Best Interests s. 31(1) and s. 72 Factors s. 31 (2): s. 31(2) In determining the best interests of a child for the purposes of an application under this Part in respect of custody of or access to a child, a court shall consider all the needs and circumstances of the child including	Best Interests s. 31(1) & s. 72 Factors s. 31(2)	s. 31(3) In assessing a person's ability to act as a parent, the court shall consider whether the person has ever acted in a violent manner towards (a) his or her spouse or child; (b) his or her child's parent; or (c) another member of the household; Otherwise a person's past conduct shall only be considered if the court thinks it is relevant	s. 27 parent of a child or other party. s. 69(4)(b) to (d) other party: (b) a person who has demonstrated a settled intention to treat the child as a child of his or her family; (b.1) a grandparent of the child; (c) a person who had the

PROVINCE/ STATUTE	FACTORS – CUSTODY APPLICATIONS	FACTORS – ACCESS APPLICATIONS	ADDITIONAL FACTORS – PAST PARENTAL CONDUCT AND VIOLENCE	PARTIES
Newfoundland & Labrador *Children's Law Act* (cont'd)	(a) the love, affection and emotional ties between the child and, (i) each person entitled to or claiming custody of or access to the child (ii) other members of the child's family who live with the child, and persons involved in the care and upbringing of the child; (b) the views and preferences of the child, where the views and preferences can reasonably be ascertained; (c) the length of time the child has lived in a stable home environment; (d) the ability and willingness of each person applying for custody of the child to provide the child with guidance and education, the necessaries of life and the special needs of the child; (e) the ability of each parent seeking the custody or access to act as a parent; (f) plans proposed for the care and upbringing of the child; (g) the permanence and stability of the family unit with which it is proposed that the child will live; and (h) the relationship by blood or through an adoption order between the child and each person who is a		to the person's ability to act as a parent. s. 42(1) On application, a court may make an interim or final order restraining a person from molesting, annoying or harassing the applicant or children in the applicant's lawful custody or from communicating with the applicant or children, except as the order provides, and may require the person to enter into a recognizance or post the bond that the court considers appropriate. (2) A person who contravenes a restraining order is guilty of an offence and upon summary conviction is liable, (a) in the case of a first offence, to a fine of not more than $1,000 or to imprisonment for a term of not more than 3 months, or to both; and (b) in the case of a second or subsequent offence, to a fine of not more than $10,000 or to imprisonment for a term of not more than 2 years, or to both. (3) A police officer may arrest without warrant a person the police officer believes on reasonable grounds to have contravened a restraining order. s. 40(1) Where an order is made for custody of or access to a child, a court may give the	actual care and upbringing of the child immediately before the application; and (d) another person whose presence as a party is necessary to determine the matters in issue. s. 70(1) A minor who is a parent may make an application under this Act without the need for a guardian to be appointed for the purpose and may respond without a guardian.

PROVINCE/ STATUTE	FACTORS – CUSTODY APPLICATIONS	FACTORS – ACCESS APPLICATIONS	ADDITIONAL FACTORS – PAST PARENTAL CONDUCT AND VIOLENCE	PARTIES
Newfoundland & Labrador *Children's Law Act* (cont'd)	party to the application. s. 71(1) Where possible, court will take into consideration views and preferences of child to extent that child is able to express them.		directions that it considers appropriate for the supervision of the custody or access by a person or a director of child, youth and family services under the Child, Youth and Family Services Act. s. 41(4) A denial of access is not wrongful where a) the respondent believes on reasonable grounds that the child will suffer physical or emotional harm if access is exercised; b) the respondent believes on reasonable grounds that he or she might suffer physical harm if access is exercised; (c) the respondent believes on reasonable grounds that the applicant is impaired by alcohol or a drug at the time of access; … (g) on numerous occasions during the preceding 12 months the applicant had, without reasonable notice and excuse failed to exercise the right of access; … or (i) the court thinks that the withholding of the access is, in the circumstances, justified.	

TABLE 1

PROVINCE/ STATUTE	FACTORS – CUSTODY APPLICATIONS	FACTORS – ACCESS APPLICATIONS	ADDITIONAL FACTORS – PAST PARENTAL CONDUCT AND VIOLENCE	PARTIES
Northwest Territories *Children's Law Act*, S.N.W.T. 1997, c. 14, as amended	Best Interests with a recognition that differing cultural values and practices must be respected: s. 17(1) Factors s. 17(2): (a) the love, affection and emotional ties between the child and 　(i) each person entitled to or seeking custody or access, 　(ii) other members of the child's family, and 　(iii) persons involved in the care and upbringing of the child; (b) the child's views and preferences if they can be reasonably ascertained; (c) the child's cultural, linguistic and spiritual or religious upbringing and ties; (d) the ability and willingness of each person seeking custody to, directly or indirectly, provide the child with guidance, education and necessities of life and provide for any special needs of the child; (e) the ability of each person seeking custody or access to act as a parent; (f) who, from among those persons entitled to custody or access, has been primarily responsible for the care of the child, including care of the child's daily physical and social needs,	Best Interests with respect for differing cultural values s. 17(1) Factors s. 17(2)	s. 17(3) In determining the best interests of a child for the purposes of an application under this Division in respect of custody of or access to a child, the court shall also consider any evidence that a person seeking custody or access has at any time committed an act of violence against his or her spouse, former spouse, child, child's parent or any other member of the person's household or family and any effect that such conduct had, is having or may have on the child. s. 17(4) Subject to subsection (3), a person's past conduct may be considered in an application under this Part in respect of custody or access to a child only where the court is satisfied that it is relevant to the person's ability to act as a parent. s. 23: Where an order is made for custody of or access to a child, a court may give such directions as it considers appropriate for the supervision of the custody or access by a person who has consented to act as a supervisor.	s. 20(1) a parent of a child or any other person with leave of the court (s. 20(2)).

PROVINCE/ STATUTE	FACTORS – CUSTODY APPLICATIONS	FACTORS – ACCESS APPLICATIONS	ADDITIONAL FACTORS – PAST PARENTAL CONDUCT AND VIOLENCE	PARTIES
Northwest Territories *Children's Law Act* (cont'd)	arrangements for alternative care for the child where it is required, arrangement for the child's health care and interaction with the child through, among other things, teaching, playing, conversation, reading and discipline; (g) the effect a change of residence will have on the child; (h) the permanence and stability of the family unit within which it is proposed that the child live; (i)any plans proposed for the care and upbringing of the child; (j) the relationship, by blood or though adoption, between the child and each person seeking custody or access; and (k) the willingness of each person seeking custody to facilitate access between the child and a parent of the child who is seeking custody or access.			
Nunavut *Children's Law Act (Nunavut)* S.N.W.T. 1997 c. 14, as amended	Best Interests with a recognition that differing cultural values and practices must be respected: s. 17(1) Factors s. 17 (2): (a) the love, affection and emotional ties between the child and (i) each person entitled to or seeking custody or access, (ii) other members of the child's family, and	Best Interests with respect for differing cultural values s. 17(1) Factors s. 17 (2)	s. 17(3): In determining the best interests of the child for the purposes of an application under this Division in respect of custody of or access to a child, the court shall also consider any evidence that a person seeking custody or access has at any time committed an act of violence against his or her spouse, former spouse, child, child's parent or any other member of the person's household or family and any effect that such conduct had, is having or may have on the child.	s. 20(1) a parent of a child or any other person with leave of the court (s. 20(2)).

PROVINCE/ STATUTE	FACTORS – CUSTODY APPLICATIONS	FACTORS – ACCESS APPLICATIONS	ADDITIONAL FACTORS – PAST PARENTAL CONDUCT AND VIOLENCE	PARTIES
Nunavut *Children's Law Act* (cont'd)	(iii) persons involved in the care and upbringing of the child; (b) the child's views and preferences if they can be reasonably ascertained; (c) the child's cultural, linguistic and spiritual or religious upbringing and ties; (d) the ability and willingness of each person seeking custody to, directly or indirectly, provide the child with guidance, education and necessities of life and provide for any special needs of the child; (e) the ability of each person seeking custody or access to act as a parent; (f) who, from among those persons entitled to custody or access, has been primarily responsible for the care of the child, including care of the child's daily physical and social needs, arrangements for alternative care for the child where it is required, arrangements for the child's health care and interaction with the child through, among other things, teaching, playing, conversation, reading and discipline; (g) the effect a change of residence will have on the child; (h) the permanence and stability of the family unit within which it is proposed		s. 17(4) Subject to subsection (3), a person's past conduct may be considered in an application under this Part in respect of custody or access to a child only where the court is satisfied that it is relevant to the person's ability to act as a parent. s. 23: Where an order is made for custody of or access to a child, a court may give such directions as it considers appropriate for the supervision of the custody or access by a person who has consented to act as supervisor.	

PROVINCE/ STATUTE	FACTORS – CUSTODY APPLICATIONS	FACTORS – ACCESS APPLICATIONS	ADDITIONAL FACTORS – PAST PARENTAL CONDUCT AND VIOLENCE	PARTIES
Nunavut *Children's Law Act* (cont'd)	that the child live; (i) any plans proposed for the care and upbringing of the child; (j) the relationship, by blood or through adoption, between the child and each person seeking custody or access; and (k) the willingness of each person seeking custody to facilitate access between the child and a parent of the child who is seeking custody or access.			
Nova Scotia Maintenance and Custody Act, R.S.N.S. 1989 c. 160, as amended	s. 18(5) In any proceeding under this Act concerning care and custody or access and visiting privileges in relation to a child, the court shall apply the principle that the welfare of the child is the paramount consideration. s. 19 At the hearing of an application under Section 18 or an application to vary or rescind an order respecting care and custody or access and visiting privileges, a court may request the Minister to cause a written report to be made to the court respecting the child and his parents or guardian.	Welfare of the child s. 18(5)	No existing provision.	s. 18(2) parent or guardian or other person with leave of the court (parent defined in s. 18(1).

TABLE 1

PROVINCE/ STATUTE	FACTORS – CUSTODY APPLICATIONS	FACTORS – ACCESS APPLICATIONS	ADDITIONAL FACTORS – PAST PARENTAL CONDUCT AND VIOLENCE	PARTIES

Ontario *Children's Law Reform Act,* R.S.O. 1990, c. C.12 as amended	Best Interests s. 24 (1)
	
	Factors s. 24 (2):
	(a) the love, affection and emotional ties between the child and,
	  (i) each person entitled to or claiming custody of or access to the child,
	  (ii) other members of the child's family who reside with the child, and
	  (iii) persons involved in child's care and upbringing;
	(b) the child's views and preferences, if they can be reasonably be ascertained;
	(c) the length of time the child has lived in a stable home environment;
	(d) the ability and willingness of each person applying for custody of the child to provide the child with guidance and education, the necessaries of life and any special needs of the child;
	(e) any plans proposed for the child's care and upbringing;
	(f) the permanence and stability of the family unit with which it is proposed that the child will live;
	(g) the ability of each person applying for custody of or access to the child to act as a parent; and
		Best Interests s. 24 (1)
		Factors s. 24 (2)
			s. 24(3) A person's past conduct shall be considered only,
			(a) in accordance with subsection (4); or
			(b) if the court is satisfied that the conduct is otherwise relevant to the person's ability to act as a parent.
			
			s. 23 Despite sections 22 and 44, a court may exercise its jurisdiction to make or to vary an order in respect of the custody of or access to a child where,
			  (a) the child is physically present in Ontario; and
			  (b) the court is satisfied that the child would, on the balance of probabilities, suffer serious harm if,
			    (i) the child remains in the custody of the person legally entitled to custody of the child,
			    (ii) the child is returned to the custody of person legally entitled to custody of child, or
			    (iii) the child is removed from Ontario.
			
			s. 34(1) Where an order is made for custody of or access to a child, a court may give such directions as it considers appropriate for the
				s. 21 parent of a child or any other person.

PROVINCE/STATUTE	FACTORS – CUSTODY APPLICATIONS	FACTORS – ACCESS APPLICATIONS	ADDITIONAL FACTORS – PAST PARENTAL CONDUCT AND VIOLENCE	PARTIES
Ontario *Children's Law Reform Act* (cont'd)	(h) the relationship by blood or through an adoption order between the child and each person who is a party to the application.		supervision of the custody or access by a person, a children's aid society or other body. s. 35(1) On application, a court may make an interim or final order restraining a person from molesting, annoying or harassing the applicant or children in the applicant's lawful custody and may require the person to enter into the recognizance or post the bond that the court considers appropriate. (2) A person who contravenes a restraining order is guilty of an offence and on conviction is liable to either or both a fine of $5,000 and imprisonment for a term of not more than three months for a first offence and not more than two years for a subsequent offence. (3) A police officer may arrest without warrant a person the police officer believes on reasonable and probable grounds to have contravened a restraining order. (4) Subsections (2) and (3) also apply in respect of contraventions, committed after those subsections come into force, of restraining orders made under a predecessor of this section.	

PROVINCE/ STATUTE	FACTORS – CUSTODY APPLICATIONS	FACTORS – ACCESS APPLICATIONS	ADDITIONAL FACTORS – PAST PARENTAL CONDUCT AND VIOLENCE	PARTIES
Prince Edward Island *Custody Jurisdiction and Enforcement Act,* R.S.P.E.I. 1988, c. C-33, as amended	Best Interests s. 2(a) s. 8(1) In considering an application under this Act, a court where possible shall take into consideration the views and preferences of the child to the extent that the child is able to express them.	Best Interests s. 2(a) Child's views s. 8 (1)	s. 13 Notwithstanding sections 12 and 17, a court may exercise its jurisdiction to make or to vary an order in respect of the custody of or access to a child where: a) the child is physically present in the province; and b) the court is satisfied that the child would, on the balance of probabilities, suffer serious harm if i) the child remains in the custody of the person legally entitled to custody of the child, ii) the child is returned to the custody of the person legally entitled to custody of the child, or iii) the child is removed from the province. s. 20 Upon application, the court may make an order restraining any person from molesting, annoying or harassing the applicant or a child in the lawful custody of the applicant and may require the respondent to enter into such recognizance, with or without sureties, or to post such bond as the court considers appropriate.	s. 7(3) The parties to an application under this Act in respect of a child shall include (a) the mother and the father of the child; (b) a person who has demonstrated a settled intention to treat the child as a child of his or her family; (c) a person who had the actual care and upbringing of the child immediately before the application; and (d) any other person whose presence as a party is necessary to determine the matters in issue.

PROVINCE/ STATUTE	FACTORS – CUSTODY APPLICATIONS	FACTORS – ACCESS APPLICATIONS	ADDITIONAL FACTORS – PAST PARENTAL CONDUCT AND VIOLENCE	PARTIES
Quebec *Civil Code of Quebec*, S.Q. 1991, c. 64	s. 33 Every decision concerning a child shall be taken in light of the child's interests and the respect of his rights. Consideration is given, in addition to the moral, intellectual, emotional and physical needs of the child, to the child's age, health, personality and family environment, and to other aspects of his situation. s. 34 The court shall, in every application brought before it affecting the interest of a child, give the child an opportunity to be heard if his age and power of discernment permit it.	Child's Interests s. 33 Child's Wishes s. 34	s. 606 The court may, for a grave reason and in the interest of the child, on applicant of any interested person, declare the father, the mother or either of them, or a third person on whom parental authority may have been conferred, to be deprived of such authority. Where such a measure is not required by the situation but action is nevertheless necessary, the court may declare, instead, the withdrawal of an attribute of parental authority or of the exercise of such authority. The court may also directly examine an application for withdrawal.	s. 605 either parent or a third person.
Saskatchewan *Children's Law Act*, S.S. 1997, c. C-8.2, as amended	Best Interests s. 8(1)(a) Factors s. 8(1)(a): In making, varying or rescinding an order for custody of a child, the court shall: (a) have regard only for the best interests of the child and for that purpose shall take into account: (i) the quality of the relationship that the child has with the person who is seeking custody and any other person who may have a close connection with the child; (ii) the personality, character and emotional needs of child;	Best Interests s. 9(1)(a) Factors s. 9(1)(a) In making, varying or rescinding an order for access to a child, the court shall: (a) have regard only for the best interests of the child and for that purpose shall take into account: (i) the quality of the relationship that the child has with the person who is seeking access; (ii) the personality,	s. 8(1)(b): 8(1) In making, varying or rescinding an order for custody of a child, the court shall: (b) not take into consideration the past conduct of any person unless the conduct is relevant to the ability of that person to act as a part of a child. 9(1) In making, varying or rescinding an order for access to a child, the court shall: (b) not take into consideration the past conduct of any person unless the conduct is relevant to the ability of that person to care for the child during the times that the child is in his or her care.	s. 6(1) parent (as defined in s. 2(1)(j) or other person having a sufficient interest.

PROVINCE/ STATUTE	FACTORS – CUSTODY APPLICATIONS	FACTORS – ACCESS APPLICATIONS	ADDITIONAL FACTORS – PAST PARENTAL CONDUCT AND VIOLENCE	PARTIES
Saskatchewan *Children's Law Act* (cont'd)	(iii) the physical, psychological, social and economic needs of child; (iv) the capacity of the person who is seeking custody to act as legal custodian of the child; (v) the home environment proposed to be provided for child; (vi) the plans that the person who is seeking custody has for the future of the child; and (vii) the wishes of the child, to the extent the court considers appropriate, having regard to the age and maturity of child. s. 6(5) When making an order pursuant to subsection (1), the court shall: (a) give effect to the principle that a child should have as much contact with each parent as is consistent with the best interests of the child and, for that purpose, shall take into consideration the willingness of the person seeking custody to facilitate that contact;	character and emotional needs of child; (iii) the capacity of the person who is seeking access to care for the child during the times that the child is in his or her care; and (iv) the wishes of child, to the extent that the court considers appropriate, having regard to the age and maturity of the child; and s. 6(5) When making an order pursuant to subsection (1), the court shall: (a) give effect to the principle that a child should have as much contact with each parent as is consistent with the best interests of the child and, for that purpose, shall take into consideration the willingness of the person seeking custody to facilitate that contact; (b) include in the order a condition requiring any person who has custody of a child and who intends to change the place of	23(1) On application pursuant to this subsection, a court may make an interim or final order restraining a person from: (a) molesting the applicant or a child in the lawful care or custody of the applicant; (b) annoying the applicant or a child in the lawful care or custody of the applicant; (c) harassing the applicant or a child in the lawful care or custody of the applicant; (d) communicating with the applicant or a child in the lawful care or custody of the applicant; or (e) otherwise interfering with the applicant or a child in the lawful care or custody of the applicant. (2) On an application pursuant to subsection (1), a court may require the respondent to enter into any recognizance, with or without sureties, or post any bond that the court considers appropriate. 29(1) Where a court on its own motion or on application by notice of motion is satisfied that any person has displayed wilful contempt of its orders or resistance to its process or orders with respect to custody of or access to a child, the court, in addition to any other remedy including variation of the custody or access order, may impose: (a) in the case of a first finding of contempt: (i) a fine of not more than $5,000;	

PROVINCE/ STATUTE	FACTORS – CUSTODY APPLICATIONS	FACTORS – ACCESS APPLICATIONS	ADDITIONAL FACTORS – PAST PARENTAL CONDUCT AND VIOLENCE	PARTIES
Saskatchewan *Children's Law Act* (cont'd)		residence of that child to notify, as set out in subsection (6), any person who is granted access to that child or any other person who has custody of that child of: (i) the change; (ii) the time at which the change will be made; and (iii) the new place of residence of the child.	(ii) imprisonment for a term of not more than 90 days; or (iii) both that fine and imprisonment; and (b) in the case of a second or subsequent finding of contempt: (i) a fine of not more than $10,000; (ii) imprisonment for a term of not more than two years; or (iii) both that fine and imprisonment. (2) Where the court imposes a sentence of imprisonment pursuant to subsection (1) that does not exceed 90 days, it may: (a) order that the sentence be served intermittently at those times that are specified in the order; and (b) direct that at all times when not in confinement pursuant to the order, the person comply with conditions prescribed in the order. (3) The court may order that if a person defaults in payment of a fine imposed pursuant to subsection (1) that person shall be imprisoned for a period not exceeding six months. (4) Proceedings pursuant to subsection (1) may be taken without having taken any other step for the enforcement of the order. (5) The sheriff, or any other officer or person by his or her direction or by direction of the court, may convey any person to be committed to a prison without any further	

TABLE 1

PROVINCE/ STATUTE	FACTORS – CUSTODY APPLICATIONS	FACTORS – ACCESS APPLICATIONS	ADDITIONAL FACTORS – PAST PARENTAL CONDUCT AND VIOLENCE	PARTIES
Saskatchewan *Children's Law Act* (cont'd)			warrant other than a copy of the minutes of the court certified by a judge or the registrar. (6) The keeper of the prison and all other persons whose duty it is to receive the person to be committed into custody are authorized to and shall: (a) receive the person to be committed into custody; and (b) carry out and execute the order according to its tenor and effect.	
Yukon *Children's Act*, R.S.Y. 2002, c. 31, as amended	Best Interests s. 1 and s. 30(1): Factors s. 30(1): 30(1) In determining the best interests of a child for the purposes of an application under this Part in respect of custody of or access to a child, the court shall consider all the needs and circumstances of the child including (a) the bonding, love, affection and emotional ties between the child and (i) each person entitled to or claiming custody of or access to the child, (ii) other members of the child's family who reside with the child, and (iii) persons, including grandparents, involved in the care and upbringing of the child,	s. 1 and s. 30(1)	s. 30(2) The past conduct of a person is not relevant to a determination of an application under this Part in respect of custody of or access to a child unless the conduct is relevant to the ability of the person to have the care or custody of a child. s. 36 The court may make an order restraining any person from molesting, annoying or harassing the applicant, or a child in the lawful care or custody of the applicant. s. 38 Despite sections 37 and 50, the court may exercise its jurisdiction to make or to vary an order in respect of the custody of or access to a child if (a) the child is physically present in the Yukon, and (b) the court is satisfied that the child would, on the balance of probabilities,	s. 33(1) a parent of the child or any other person (parent as defined in s. 4, i.e., father or mother of a child by birth or adoption).

PROVINCE/ STATUTE	FACTORS – CUSTODY APPLICATIONS	FACTORS – ACCESS APPLICATIONS	ADDITIONAL FACTORS – PAST PARENTAL CONDUCT AND VIOLENCE	PARTIES
Yukon *Children's Act* (cont'd)	(b) the views and preferences of the child, if those views and preferences can be reasonably determined; (c) the length of time, having regard to the child's sense of time, that the child has lived in a stable home environment; (d) the ability and willingness of each person applying for custody of child to provide the child with guidance, education, necessaries of life and any special needs of the child; (e) any plans proposed for the care and upbringing of the child; (f) the permanence and stability of the family unit with which it is proposed that the child will live, and (g) the effect that awarding custody or care of child to one party would have on the ability of the other party to have reasonable access to the child. s. 30(3) There is no presumption of law or fact that the best interests of a child are, solely because of the age or the sex of child, best served by placing the child in the care or custody of a female person rather than a male person or of a male person rather than a female person.		suffer serious harm if, (i) the child remains in the custody of the person legally entitled to custody of the child; or (ii) the child is returned to the custody of the person legally entitled to custody of the child.	

50 TABLE 1

PROVINCE/ STATUTE	FACTORS – CUSTODY APPLICATIONS	FACTORS – ACCESS APPLICATIONS	ADDITIONAL FACTORS – PAST PARENTAL CONDUCT AND VIOLENCE	PARTIES
Yukon *Children's Act* (cont'd)	s. 30(4) In any proceeding in respect of custody of a child between the mother and the father of that child, there shall be a rebuttable presumption that the court ought to award the care of the child to one parent or the other and that all other parental rights associated with custody of that child ought to be shared by the mother and the father jointly.			

Chapter 2

Methodology And Overview Of Process

"While statutes can be amended and case laws can be distinguished or overruled, we take judicial notice of the fact that children grow up only once. When a mistake is made in a custody dispute, the harmful effects are irrevocable."
Chief Justice Frank D. Celebrezze[1]

OVERVIEW OF METHODOLOGY

The Multi-Method, Multi-Source Approach

Once it has been determined that a comprehensive assessment will occur in a child custody case, a "best practice" approach is advised.[2] Inherent in such an approach is the expectation that there will be variability amongst and between assessors and disciplines. The various guidelines, models and standards of practice previously mentioned indicate that it is widely accepted that a best practice assessment involves gathering information from a variety of sources and using a number of different methods. This is referred to as the multi-source, multi-method model when applied to assessments more generally (Campbell & Fiske, 1959). The process involves hypothesis testing by seeking both convergent (supporting) and divergent (ruling out) information (Ackerman, 2001; Chisholm & MacNaughton, 1990; Leonoff & Montague, 1996; Gould, 1998, 1999; Gould & Stahl, 2000; Schutz, Dixon, Lindenberg & Rutter, 1989; Stahl, 1994).

Gathering information in this manner is important given issues of credibility (Bagby, Nicholson, Buis, Radovanovic & Fidler, 1999; Bathurst, Gottfried & Gottfried, 1997; Heilbrun, 2002; Siegel, 1996; Siegel & Langford, 1998). It is imperative that the assessor investigate concerns and allegations by obtaining different *types* of information from different *sources*, while considering alternative and sometimes competing hypotheses and both confirming and disconfirming information (Austin, 2002; Gould & Lehrmann, 2002; Gould, 1998; 2006).

Survey Literature

Conducting child custody assessments is a painstaking and time-consuming task. Survey literature includes questionnaires completed by evaluators, judges and lawyers, as well as content analyses of assessors' reports (Bow, 2006; Heilbrun, 1995). Bow summarized the survey literature by providing the average number of hours required for each step of the assessment process: parenting interviews; interviews with children; testing parents and children; parent–child observations; interviewing significant others; reviewing documents; and writing the report. There is a discrepancy in the number of hours–ranging from 10 to 88–found necessary to complete an assessment (Ackerman, Ackerman, Steffen & Kelley-Poulos, 2004; Bow & Quinnell, 2001; LaFortune & Carpenter, 1998). The hours needed to complete an assessment will depend on: (a) the specific assessor; (b) the complexity of the family circumstances (i.e., number of children, number of parties, presence of step-parents and stepchildren); (c), number of collateral sources; (d) the nature and extent of allegations; (e) the amount of court documentation; (f) the type of assessment (issue-focused or comprehensive), and in some jurisdictions; (g) the context (public or private).

In their pioneering study, now 21 years old, Keilin & Bloom (1986) reported that the average assessment was completed in 18.8 hours. In a survey conducted more than 10 years later, Ackerman & Ackerman (1996, 1997) reported an increase to 26.4 hours. Bow & Quinnell (2001) and Quinnell & Bow (2001) in subsequent studies reported an average of 24.5 to 28.5 hours spent on an assessment. All these writers have attributed the increase to more time taken to review documentation and write reports.

From our collective clinical experience of 46 years, we have found that the private comprehensive (as opposed to public and/or issue-focused) assessment typically takes between 40 and 50 hours, and sometimes more when allegations of significant potential risk to the child are present. (Johnston, Walters & Olesen (2005) report a range of 30 to 40 hours).

The increase in hours and the evident expansion in breadth and depth of methodology are likely due to the changing tide that calls for assessments to be more evidence-based (Martindale & Gould, 2004). Additionally, both legal and mental health professionals have noted a shift in which assessments are no longer as popular as they were in the 1980s. Assessments tend to involve complicated family circumstances that require more hours to assess. This complexity, coupled with the fact that child custody work often results in complaints to professional colleges (Kirkland & Kirkland, 2001; The College of Psychology of Ontario, 2007),[3] compels the assessor to leave no stone unturned, thereby increasing the number of hours required to complete the task (Fidler & Birnbaum, 2006).

Areas of Functioning Requiring Assessment

Providing recommendations for a child's residential schedule with each parent and for how major child-related decisions will be made requires a thorough assessment of numerous and related aspects of adaptive functioning. Gould (2006) provides an interview framework that includes the following categories: Individual Behaviour; Social/Dyadic; Extended Family; and Community. With the best interest standard as a foundation, these areas of functioning include:

(a) the child's adjustment (emotional/behavioural, social, academic, with respect to divorce);

(b) the quality of relative parenting capacity (parenting strengths and challenges);

(c) the psychological adjustment and health of each parent *and* the impact of these, if any, on parenting and the parent–child relationship;

(d) the quality of the parents' relationship with each other (nature and extent of conflict and cooperation, abuse and violence);

(e) the quality of the child's relationship with each parent, including the fit between the child and the parent, taking into account any special needs the child might have;

(f) the quality of the parent's relationship with any new partner or spouse;

(g) the quality of the child's relationship with other relevant family members (full, half and stepsiblings, step-parents, grandparents, etc.) and;

(h) the child's perceptions, views and preferences to the extent that these exist and can be reasonably ascertained.

Having acknowledged these components, it is important to reiterate the controversy previously alluded to in Chapter 1. That is, what assessors can and can not reliably address in child custody assessments given our lack of uniformly accepted standards and guidelines, the absence of validated methodology and standardized instruments, and the lack of empirical evidence to support various parenting time schedules and methods for decision-making.

Tippins and Whittman (2005) identify four levels of inference. Level I involves making direct and factual observations without drawing higher-order, abstracted inferences. For example, "the child cried at the office door and refused to enter the interviewing room." Level II involves providing psychological conclusions from the Level I observations: "Given the child's distress and refusal to enter the office, it is likely that he was afraid of making his absent mother angry." A Level III inference involves making conclusions about a custody-relevant variable. Here the assessor might conclude, for example, that given the child's refusal to participate and his fear of his mother, he had been unduly influenced by her. Level IV involves making recommendations about what should occur in the parenting plan based on the conclusions reached at Levels II and III: for example, a recommendation for the child to live primarily with the father and have supervised contact with the mother as a result of the undue negative influence she imposes on the child.

Tippins and Whittman concluded that inferences made at Level III should be limited to statements of risk associated with those variables, and furthermore that assessors should not make definitive recommendations at Level IV. They maintained that the evaluator's evidence fails to meet an adequate standard of reliability established by recent case law (e.g., *Daubert v. Merrill Dow Pharmaceuticals*, 1993 in the United States). In Canada, the corresponding case would be *R. v. Mohan*. The Supreme Court of Canada found four criteria for the admissibility of expert testimony: (a) relevance; (b) ability to assist the trier of fact; (c) absence of exclusionary rule, and; (d) provision by a properly qualified expert.

In response to Tippins and Wittmann (2005), other writers (Bala, 2005; Kelly & Johnston, 2005; Rotman, 2005; Stahl, 2005) agree that given the serious potential risks to children and families, accountability and a thorough methodology are imperative. These authors emphasize that assessors need to be properly trained, have familiarity with the vast literature and relevant legislation involved, and that they need to obtain continuing education to remain current. Some writers note the overuse of assessments and advise that these should be limited to more serious situations involving domestic violence, child maltreatment (physical, sexual and emotional abuse) and drug addiction (Birnbaum & Radovanovic, 1999; Jaffe, Crooks and Bala, 2005; Kelly & Johnston, 2005).

Yet notwithstanding considerable agreement with Tippins and Whittman (2005), many writers agree that we do indeed possess considerable empirical and theoretical literature in combination with our experiential knowledge that allows assessors to make recommendations. The relevant areas that child custody assessors can, do and ought to rely on to make *reasonably* informed recommendations include child development, risk and resiliency, attachment, the impact of separation and divorce and parental conflict, the impact of domestic violence, child abuse and neglect, father absence, and the contribution of fathers to child development and adjustment (Amato, 2000; Kelly & Emery, 2003; Kelly & Lamb, 2000; Lamb, 1997, 2002; Leon, 2003; Pruett, 2000; Pruett, Ebling & Insabella, 2004; Maccoby & Mnookin, 1992; Riggs, 2005; Stahl, 2005; Warshak, 2000).[4]

Similarly, Bala (2005) cogently asserts that leaving decisions in the hands of the court can be problematic as "some judges lack the expertise and experience to deal effectively and appropriately with family law cases" (p. 561). He notes that recommendations from assessors, albeit with occasional limitations, are but one important piece of evidence for the court to consider. Bala and others emphasize that assessments may assist with settlement of the dispute. The court orders assessments in the first place because it needs assistance from an expert to augment the contributions of the judge. Many believe that the benefits outweigh the risks of assessments (and of not having them),[5] providing that certain cautions are taken and that the limitations, including a discussion of the risks and benefits of various outcome alternatives, are noted in the report when making recommendations. Keeping these issues in mind, we turn to describing the assessment methodology.

OVERVIEW OF PROCESS

Setting the Stage: Appointment and Contracting

Maintaining neutrality is imperative. One-sided assessments, while previously more common, are for the most part a thing of the past. Intake and contracting will vary depending on if the assessment is public (s. 112, *Courts of Justice Act,* R.S.O., 1990 c. C. 43) or private (s. 30 *Children's Law Reform Act,* R.S.O., 1990 c. C. 12). In any case, variation exists as well, amongst private assessments and when lawyers represent one or both parents. For private assessments, referrals typically come from the lawyers involved. Assessments may be ordered by the court or agreed to by the parties. We recommend, as others do (Kirkland, Kirkland, King and Renfro, 2006), that even when consented to, court orders accompany all assessments and, further, that the assessor be specifically named in the order. This procedure protects the parents as well as the assessor from any misunderstandings later on.

When both parties are represented by lawyers,[6] the assessor will have an initial meeting or conference call with legal counsel to review the assessment mandate and process, including:

(a) clarifying specific referral questions;

(b) identification of the relevant collateral sources and court documentation;

(c) determination of how long the assessment is likely to take;

(d) establishing fees and retainer terms;

(e) establishing whether or not *ex parte* communication with counsel and the assessor are permitted;

(f) establishing procedures for disclosure and reporting; and

(g) identifying any other important issues.[7]

It is important for the lawyers to have a copy of the Parenting Plan Assessment Retainer Agreement (subsequently referred to as the Agreement)[8] in advance of the contact. The lawyers are expected to review the Agreement with their clients.[9]

Next, an intake package is sent to the parents directly or provided to them by their lawyers. The package includes a covering letter indicating intake and contracting process, a Child and Parent Intake Questionnaire, a Child Behaviour Checklist (CBCL, Achenbach & Rescorla, 2001) and the Parenting Plan Assessment Retainer Agreement.[10] Intake packages are likely to vary from assessor to assessor. The assessment begins once both intake packages are returned along with the required retainer.

Once the parents have completed the intake questionnaires and signed the agreement with their lawyers, they attend an orientation meeting, either together or separately, with the assessor.[11] During this meeting, the agreement is thoroughly reviewed. The parents are invited to ask any questions about the process and procedures.[12] Consents to release information from the various identified collateral sources may be obtained during this meeting or soon after during subsequent meetings. Finally, it is important to clarify what, if anything, the child has been told about assessment.[13] In the event this does not occur, for whatever reason, consideration should be given to gaining the agreement of both parents not to discuss the assessment with the child until the matter can be pursued further with the assessor.

Types and Sources of Information

Interviews

Semi-structured interviews will be conducted with the parents individually and, where not contraindicated, jointly. Children, unless very young (less than three or four years old), will be interviewed individually. An interview with the whole family may be especially informative. Other individuals living with the children, such as grandparents, step-parents (including common-law partners) and their children, will also be interviewed individually and in various combinations with the other family members. Collateral sources may be interviewed by telephone or in person.

An assessment is likely to require at least several interviews with each parent to adequately assess the various areas of functioning previously listed and to investigate the various allegations (Galatzer-Levy & Kraus, 1999; Gould, 2006; Stahl, 1994).[14] In addition, parents who need to feel heard should have ample opportunity to tell their stories. This is important given the high number of complaints specifically indicating parents' allegations that they did not have sufficient opportunity to convey everything they believed was important to tell the assessor. Similarly, it is important to interview a child who has been brought by each parent on different days, more than once. Even if lengthy interviews occur on the same day or two days, basing everything on these one or two occasions may be unfair, especially if the parent and/or child was upset, not feeling well, or needed time to adapt to the extremely stressful circumstances of a custody assessment; the fatigue factor cannot be overlooked either. Additionally, it may be easier for the parent to feign and/or present favourably on one given day than for many hours spread out over time.

It is usually necessary to make inquiries and even to challenge each parent's perspective based on information that has been gathered from the other parent and collateral sources. This further inquiry would not be possible if there were only one or two contacts with the parties involved. It is imperative that both parents are afforded the opportunity to respond to any relevant concerns and that these discussions be documented. Not having this opportunity poses potential concerns about a balanced and fair methodology, and consequently, may diminish the weight of the assessment evidence, as well as potentially lend support to any subsequent professional complaints.

Typically, the parents are seen for approximately the same amount of time, as are the children with each parent, to maintain neutrality, fairness and to avoid accusations of bias. However, an unequal number of hours spent or interviews conducted with each parent does not necessarily mean the assessor is biased. Sometimes, one parent has more to say than the other does, or the assessor may have more to ask of one parent based on the allegations and concerns expressed by the other parent or perhaps even the parent advancing the allegations. However, too large a gap in hours spent with each parent would be a potential concern. Also, the fewer the total number of hours dedicated to each party, the more significant the discrepancy in hours may be. To avoid any confusion or misunderstanding as to why the assessor spent more, or fewer, hours with each parent, it is advisable to document the reasons for the discrepancy, the procedures used, and the number of interviews and/or time spent with each parent.

Written Self-Report Questionnaires and Checklists

As previously noted, in addition to obtaining information during interviews, self-report written information from behaviour checklists, structured questionnaires and surveys may be obtained from parents and older children. If these are completed outside the assessor's office, the parent should be asked if they had anyone assisting them. While they may be standard to the extent that the assessor always uses them, typically these materials do not have reliability or validity but often provide important information. Some of these may be published, for example, the Spousal Assault Risk Assessment Guide (SARA), 1998; The Warshak Parent Questionnaire (Warshak, Second Edition, (WPQ-2), 2004),[15] the Abuse Observation Checklist (Jaffe, Lemon & Poisson, 2003). Others, such as the assessor's own intake questionnaires, may not be published.

Intake materials typically completed by each parent include the following information:

(a) demographic data;

(b) the parents' individual, marital and separation histories;

(c) the parents' knowledge of their children's developmental history;

(d) the parents' knowledge of their children's behaviour and adjustment;

(e) each parent's perception of their own and the other parent's parenting before and after the separation; and

(f) the parents' perceptions of their own and the other parent's relationship with the children, the parents' proposals and concerns, etc.

(See Appendices 3 and 3A for sample intake questionnaires completed by each parent. Slightly adapted forms are used for step-parents.)

Having these written responses, however, does not mean that questionnaires should be relied on exclusively. The assessor may also cover the same material, or at least some of it, during interviews. The parents are unlikely to feel heard if their input has been limited to written responses. In addition, information obtained face-to-face is in many respects more informative, given that considerable communication is conveyed nonverbally. Written responses may flag areas requiring further inquiry. Note that some parents express themselves better in writing, while others do so orally. Keeping these considerations in mind, written responses from each parent provide the assessor with a different *type* of information from the same *source*, thereby providing the opportunity to examine consistencies and inconsistencies within the same source of data.

Observations

Structured and unstructured observations of the parents with their children are mandatory. Where it is relevant, siblings, step-parents and grandparents may also be included. These observations provide important information related to the parents' relative parenting abilities and the quality of the child's relationship with each parent, as well as any step-parents, and full, half and stepsiblings (Hynan, 2003; Schutz, et al., 1989). Invariably, observations will occur in the assessor's office. The survey literature indicates that home visits are conducted about one third of the time (Bow & Quinnell, 2001; Keilin & Bloom, 1986).[16] The timing or specific day of the observation is an important consideration. An observation of a particular circumstance or situation may be useful in addressing specific concerns and/or allegations. For example, observing the transitions of the child from one parent to the other, of the child before and after these transitions, or of the child from the parent to the daycare staff may be extremely informative. Seeing the child on a Monday morning in the home where he/she spent the previous weekend may be especially useful. This allows the child, who may not spend much time with that parent, to have settled in, and may be especially informative when there are allegations that the child does not want to spend time with that parent.

Observations may also occur in public places, such as a restaurant or a park, at the child's school and/or daycare centre. While the parents are not usually present for these, there may be circumstances in which a parent would or could be observed with the child at the park or daycare centre. Irrespective of location, more than one observation of each child with each parent—typically at least two—will increase the reliability and validity of the assessment. For reasons already mentioned, if home visits are not carried out, at least two office visits are advised.

Third-Party Information (Collateral Sources)

Obtaining information from third parties is integral to any assessment in light of problems related to credibility, impression management, and the frequently reported allegations of a serious nature (Heilbrun, 2001; Melton, Petrila, Poythress & Slobogin, 1997). Collateral source data adds another layer of important information. In addition, the AFCC Model Standards and Guidelines (AFCC 2004, revised 2007) state that the assessor should disclose reliance on uncorroborated information while formulating custody and access recommendations.

Irrespective of whether or not the assessment has been court-ordered, parents are routinely asked to sign releases of consents for all professional third parties. Although this is specifically addressed in most orders and/or retainer agreements and is discussed with the lawyers initially, determining which specific sources will be contacted may not always be a straightforward process. Initially, the lawyers and then the parents provide a list of potential collateral sources; in addition, the Parent and Child Intake Questionnaires often inquire about any and all previous professional contacts the children and parents have had. In the event of a dispute about which of these sources the assessor will ultimately obtain information from, or a parent refusing to consent to the release of the collateral information, the assessor will make the ultimate determination. The assessor must explain clearly the reason why the collateral is being contacted and how the information will be used.

A best practice assessment will routinely include information obtained from both professional and personal sources by way of letters, reports, and written responses to predetermined questions, as well as in-person and/or telephone interviews. Psychometric instruments, measures and behaviour checklists, such as the Teacher Rating Form (Achenbach and Rescorla, 2001), the Conners Rating Scale for teachers (CRS; 1997), or Attwood's Australian Scale for Asperger's Syndrome (Attwood, 1996) may also be completed by third parties such as teachers and daycare providers. Contact with collateral sources with whom the parents and children have had direct contact is likely to have more importance than those who have only indirect information (Kirkland, McMillan IV & Kirkland 2005). Care must be taken not to stigmatize the child while gathering collateral information.

Using a semi-structured interview protocol in combination with additional questions, where relevant for the specific source, is advised to increase both the reliability and validity of an assessment.[17] Complications can result from obtaining only verbal reports from informants, with either an assessor misstating in either direction an informant's report, or the informant later stating that he or she did not say what the assessor reported. Consequently, and more recently, it is common (although not uniform) for assessors to require that the information be provided in writing. A list of questions would then be provided to the informant. The assessor may choose to follow up with that informant in either a telephone or face-to-face meeting based on the written responses.[18] Detailed notes are carefully taken during these meetings. However, if the collateral source does not provide a letter or report, it is prudent for the assessor to ask the collateral source to review and confirm the assessor's written summary of his or her verbal report prior to releasing the report.[19]

Collateral sources must be advised in advance that while the assessor may use discretion when reporting, ultimately their report carries absolutely no guarantee of confidentiality and accordingly, any reports and letters provided, or notes taken by the assessor, become part of the file and court record should the file be requested by one or both parties or by the court. It is common for assessors to neglect to explain this adequately to the collateral sources, who may later claim that they did not understand the limits of confidentiality. Many assessors require that the collateral source sign a waiver or release indicating the terms of their involvement, including the absence of any guarantee of confidentiality, without which the collateral is not interviewed (Gould, 2006). While it is the court that will ultimately determine the weight of any evidence, the assessor must in some sense weigh (consider bias, relevance, congruence with other data) the collateral information during this process of hypothesis testing and generating any opinions.

Austin (2002) speaks of conceptualizing collateral sources in terms of graduating concentric circles, with the most subjective sources closer to the centre and the more objective sources placed in the outer circles. He recommends that an assessor include a representative cross-section of all of these collaterals. Moving from the centre outward, the collateral sources might include relatives, extended family, nannies, friends, co-workers, neighbours, church members, pediatricians, other health care professionals, psychologists, child protective service workers, teachers, tutors, daycare personnel, therapists, piano teachers, and coaches. The more independent or objective the source, the less potential bias there is likely to be, however, this information may not be especially robust (Austin, 2002; Gould & Lehrmann, 2002). The more subjective the source, the more robust the information is likely to be, although it is also more likely to be biased (Austin, 2002). The greater the degree to which the assessor finds that the convergence of information across these various sources, along with the other obtained data, either supports or does not support a hypothesis, the greater sense of certainty that the information obtained from any one collateral source is useful.

Ackerman (2006) advises that "recency" and frequency of the contacts are informative. For example, different weight is likely to be attributed to a pattern of assault than to a single incident when the parent was a teenager, or to repeated psychiatric hospitalizations in comparison with a single hospitalization followed by compliance with a treatment program and emotional stabilization. Although the information obtained from the more personal third parties closer to the centre, such as friends and relatives, is likely to have limited value due to the subjective nature of those reports, sometimes these sources provide useful information. The weight afforded to a relative's report that includes both positive and negative information is likely to be greater than one in which the relative speaks only favourably about, or worse, idealizes the parent on behalf of whom they are reporting. Negative reports from relatives and friends, while uncommon, do occur and can be especially informative.

Similarly, a professional source, such as a therapist, considered potentially more objective than a personal source, may in fact not be objective at all. Regrettably, it is extremely common to obtain reports from therapists who only sing the praises of their clients and have little or no insight (or choose not to share it) into their client's challenges and participation in the parental conflict. Moreover, it is remarkable how common it is to obtain reports from therapists condemning their clients' former spouses and, worse yet, making recommendations about custody and access without having ever met the other parent or the children. Of course, these biased reports should be given little to no weight.

In addition, the assessor may wish to consider making recommendations after all the information is collected about the suitability of the child continuing to see a therapist who is clearly biased and in turn doing more harm than good. These practices on the part of therapists may be grounds for "advices" and "cautions" and subsequent undertakings for supervised practice determined by professional disciplinary bodies (College of Psychologists of Ontario, 2007).

Court Documentation

Court documentation will be obtained from the lawyers directly and may include: affidavits; motion records; previous court orders pertaining to custody and access; restraining orders; and any third-party reports (e.g., hospital records and reports, criminal records, employment records) that have already become part of the court record. During the initial contact with the lawyers, the assessor should identify the relevant documentation that exists and, further, who will be providing these to the assessor. Each lawyer may provide his or her "own" material, or one lawyer may provide all of it. In any case, the covering letter listing the enclosed documents should be copied to the lawyer on the other side, because otherwise the assessor has no way of knowing if indeed all of the materials were provided. In addition, during the initial contact with counsel, the presence of any other relevant records or reports that may not have been part of the record to date should be canvassed.

Psychological Tests, Self-Report Inventories and Checklists[20]

Psychological testing is another source of information frequently used in child custody assessments with parents, and to a lesser extent with children (Ackerman & Ackerman, 1996; Bow, Gould, Flens & Greenhut, 2006; Hagen & Castagna, 2001).[21] Quinnell & Bow (2001) report survey results indicating that testing is ranked as moderately important (fourth and sixth among 10 main procedures). They also report that testing is no longer the primary procedure with respect to forensic assessments in general. Quinnell and Bow (2001) and Heilbrun (1992) have noted that testing answers psychological but not legal questions. Accordingly, the assessor must supplement other procedures to create hypotheses to be further tested with all of the other obtained data during a custody assessment.

No psychological tests have predictive validity relating to parenting capacity, specific parenting time schedules, and/or sole custody compared with joint custody. Notwithstanding, psychological tests may be used to rule out psychopathology and to assess personality characteristics (Bow et al., 2006). More specifically, test results are likely to provide useful information relevant to: (a) credibility; (b) malingering; (c) impulse control; (d) anxiety and depression; (e) self-esteem; (f) sociability; (g) paranoia; (h) coping mechanisms; (i) response to rules and authority; (j) narcissism; (k) empathy, and; (l) other personality characteristics and traits that may impact parenting capacity and the quality of a child's relationship with his or her parents (Ackerman & Ackerman, 1997; Flens, 2005; Caldwell, 2005; Calloway, 2005; Erard, 2005; Gould, 2005; Otto, Edens & Barcus, 2000).

Psychological testing in child custody assessments has not gone without criticism (Brodzinsky, 1993; Erickson, Lilienfeld & Vitacco, 2007a; Melton, et al., 1997). One cannot overlook the reported problems related to insufficient training, inappropriate test selection, misuse, and overuse. For example, Bow and his colleagues reported:

(a) insufficient training and base-level knowledge;

(b) lack of knowledge regarding appropriate cut-offs and reading level required for specific tests;

(c) failure to determine reading level before administration;

(d) failure to use context-specific normative data when available;

(e) failure to verify computer keypad data entry;

(f) reliance on hand scoring; and

(g) administration of tests in an uncontrolled environment contrary to test administration requirements (Bow, Flens, Gould & Greenhut, 2005; Bow et al., 2006).

In addition, computer-generated interpretive reports (CGIR),[22] while frequently used, have been met with considerable criticism (Bow et al., 2005; Gould, 2005; Otto & Butcher, 1995).[23] Although not a majority, some assessors continue to insert the computer-generated statements contained in the MMPI-2 report into their custody reports (nine per cent), while a larger number (22 per cent) insert statements with slight modifications (Bow et al., 2005). The admissibility of these computer-generated statements is questionable given that assessors would be unable to explain how the interpretive statements were generated, as they do not know the cut-off scores for stem statements. Additionally, publishers do not make this information available. Not having this knowledge may be contrary to the APA codes of ethics (Flens, 2005).[24]

Underwager and Wakefield (1993) provide numerous examples quoted directly from assessment reports illustrating how test results have been misused, leaving the reader rather alarmed that such practices actually exist. They astutely note that any mistaken conclusions in a clinical setting may be managed and addressed given that the client is seen over time and the treatment plan can be adjusted. They caution that incorrect decisions made in a forensic context (a "one-shot deal"), on the basis of psychological test data may lead to serious and potentially irreversible consequences relating to child custody.

Careful attention in selecting reliable and valid instruments is imperative.[25] The tests ultimately selected must reliably measure the *functional* abilities relevant to the questions posed for assessment purposes. Flens (2005) notes that "evaluators should focus their attention and assessment efforts on functional abilities that bear directly upon the attributes, behaviours, attitudes and skills that published research suggests are reliably associated with effective parenting and co-parenting" (p. 15). The more relevant the measures are to the ultimate questions, the more solid the foundation upon which the assessor's opinions and recommendations are ultimately based. As previously mentioned, the reader will note that admissibility of evidence for court purposes requires an assessment of,

(1) relevance;

(2) necessity in assisting the trier of fact;

(3) to be provided by an expert; and

(4) that there is no exclusion to preclude admission of the evidence.[26]

Heilbrun (1992) and more recently Otto et al. (2000) have developed criteria that can be used to determine a test's appropriateness for use in a forensic (i.e., custody/access or parenting plan) assessment. These criteria cover seven key areas and are listed in Table 2 below.

Table 2

Criteria for the Selection of Psychological Tests in Child Custody Assessments

(Adapted from Otto et al., 2000)

(1) the assessor's qualifications to use the instrument;

(2) whether or not the test is commercially published;

(3) the availability of a test manual;

(4) demonstrated adequate levels of reliability (± 0.08) and validity;

(5) the validity of the test for its intended purpose;

(6) the existence of peer reviews relating to the instrument;

(7) the ability to draw an acceptable level of inference from the construct to the relevant psycho-legal question (i.e., parenting capacity, the parent–child relationship, the fit between the parent and child).

Further assisting the selection and knowledge of the instruments are two resources that provide critical reviews of most published psychological tests.[27] In addition, assessors using psychological tests should stay current with the literature debating the use of tests—some in particular—and must be familiar with the various relevant guidelines, ethical codes and standards of practice.[28] Clarity about the court and/or lawyers' specific referral questions is imperative when selecting appropriate tests. While some tests may be administered routinely (MMPI-2), other tests are used selectively when a specific concern may be raised in the area the test purports to measure. Appendix 5 provides a list of tests commonly used in assessments.

Measures of cognitive functioning and intelligence may be used to evaluate a parent's abilities to academically support and stimulate their children. In addition to revealing a person's IQ, these data may provide relevant information about how parents process information and their flexibility in thinking (Gould, 1998). The assessor may wish to consider using the Substance Abuse Screening Inventory-3 (SASSI-III; Miller, 1997) to address allegations relating to alcohol use and dependency, or the Australian Scale for Asperger Syndrome (Attwood, 1996) for concerns about Asperger Syndrome, or the Hare Psychopathy Checklist (PCL-R, Hare, 1991) in response to allegations of sociopathic behaviour. The Child Abuse Potential Inventory-IV (CAPI-IV, Milner, 1986) may be used to investigate allegations of physical abuse, while the Parenting Stress Index (PSI, Abidin, 1995) may be used when abuse, neglect, maltreatment of children and/or poor parenting are alleged. When domestic violence is a concern, the assessor should consider using assessment protocols and structured interviews that screen specifically for familial violence.[29]

Although the survey literature indicates that intelligence tests are commonly used (Ackerman & Ackerman, 1997; Hagen & Castagna, 2001; Heilbrun, 1992; Quinnell & Bow, 2001), the custom of routinely doing so is debated. While some recommend using these tests routinely (Ackerman, 2006), others advise that they be used only when there is a question about intellectual competence and the ability to meet the child's needs (Gould, 2006). Gould (2006) notes that adult intelligence measures such as the WAIS-III are invaluable given that they have established reliability and validity and continue to be researched and updated; have been used in many forensic settings; have been proven to be admissible in court; and provide a screening for learning disabilities and neurological impairments in both children and adults.

In their survey study, Quinnell and Bow (2001) report that parenting inventories such as the Parent–Child Relationship Inventory (PCRI, Gerard, 2004) and the Parenting Stress Index (PSI, Abidin, 1995) have been used more frequently in recent years. Parents may also complete behaviour checklists such as the Child Behaviour Checklist (CBCL, Achenbach & Rescorla, 2001) or the Conners' Parent Rating Scale-R (L) (CPRS, Conners, 1997). These checklists and inventories provide information relating to the parent's perception of their children's behaviour and their academic, social and emotional adjustment, along with the nature and degree of their own stress as it relates to parenting and their children, their relationship with their child, and their parenting strengths and challenges.

Children can and do behave differently in different environments. The results from checklists completed by the parents may be informative about the extent to which the parents' perceptions are similar or different. In addition, parents may have difficulty differentiating their own symptoms from those of their child. Parents may have a stake in presenting their children as doing very well and as being free of problems, or in other situations, presenting their children to be suffering, and symptomatic (Johnston et al., 2005). For example, a parent not wanting the parenting arrangement to change to shared custody may report the child as healthy and symptom-free, thereby justifying the status quo and not "upsetting the apple cart," while the parent proposing the change may report that the child is suffering and maladjusted, attributing this to the child not seeing that parent enough.

The question often arises as to whether or not both parents need to complete all of the same measures. It is generally accepted that a parallel methodology be used for both parents. However, in the case of testing, while some tests are routinely administered to both parents, it may not always be necessary for all the tests to be administered to both. If allegations regarding alcohol use, for example, have been alleged against one parent only and it is stipulated that it is not a concern for the other, the assessor may be able to justify testing only one parent for this. Notwithstanding their discretion in such matters, to ensure transparency, assessors need to acknowledge differences in methodology from one parent to the other, along with the reasons for these variations, and document these in their report.

Keilin and Bloom (1986) found that the majority of clinicians in the assessment of children used no single instrument. Subsequent survey studies replicated these earlier findings, noting that intelligence tests (e.g., Weschler Intelligence Scale for Children, WISC-R, 1991) and projective measures such as the Thematic Apperception Test (TAT, Murray & Bellak, 1973), the Children's Apperception Test (CAT, 1974; Bellak & Bellak, 1992), the Rorschach Comprehensive System (Exner, 1993), the Bender Visual Motor Gestalt Test (Bender, 1946) and various forms of the Sentence Completion were commonly used (Ackerman & Ackerman, 1997). Bow and Quinnell's survey indicates a decline in the testing of children from that previously reported in the Ackerman study from 92 per cent to 61 per cent (Bow & Quinnell, 2001; Quinnell & Bow 2001).

Lee and Olesen (2001) state that testing of children provides useful information about cognitive ability, information-processing styles (e.g., rigid, flexible) and operations, developmental level, reality testing and emotional factors, including self-esteem and sense of identity, interpersonal skills, coping style, emotional control and vulnerability. Others warn that there are data indicating that the Rorschach has shown severe maladjustment in children (and adults) who were actually psychologically healthy (Erickson, Lilienfeld & Vitacco, 2007b).

When parents and/or collateral sources express specific concerns about a child's emotional adjustment, the assessor may wish to consider using measures that tap the child's self-esteem (Piers-Harris Children's Self-Concept Scale, Piers, 1984), degree of anxiety (How I Feel Questionnaire, Stait-Trait Anxiety Inventory, STAIC, Spielberger, 1973), or depression (Children's Depression Inventory, CDI, Kovacs, 1992). These psychometric measures may provide further appreciation for the degree of the child's difficulties compared with other children of the same age and gender. In addition, when a child is reticent to elaborate, questions on these measures may be used as clinical interviewing tools augmenting the semi-structured interview.

68   METHODOLOGY AND OVERVIEW OF PROCESS

The survey literature consistently indicates that for adults The Minnesota Multiphasic Personality Inventory-2 (MMPI-2),[30] a test of personality and psychopathology (Butcher, Graham, Ben-Porath, Tellegen, Dahlstrom & Kaemmer, 2001) is the most commonly used psychological test, with estimates as high as 90 per cent (Ackerman & Ackerman, 1997; Hagen & Castagna, 2001; Keilin & Bloom, 1986; Otto et al., 2000). While recognizing that the MMPI-2 is not a test of parenting or parent–child relationships per se, writers indicate that it can contribute valuable information relating to personality and adaptive functioning that may then be considered with all of the other obtained data (Erard, 2005; Caldwell, 2005). More specifically, Caldwell maintains that the MMPI-2 results may shed light onto five areas of functioning relevant to child custody decisions, namely: attachment; antisocial behaviour; temper control; alienation; and chemical abuse and dependence.

In addition, the survey literature indicates that the Millon Multiaxial Inventory-III (MCMI-III), also a test of personality and psychopathology, is frequently used, with estimates as high as 60 per cent of the time.[31] The MCMI-III was first published in 1994 to coordinate with the fourth edition of the Diagnostic and Statistical Manual of Mental Disorders (DSM-IV) (Millon, Davis & Millon, 1997). Notwithstanding its popularity, questions regarding the interpretation and applicability of the MCMI-III results to custody-disputing parents have been raised and hotly debated (Dyer & McCann, 2000; Hynan, 2004; McCann, 2002; Rogers, Salekin & Sewell, 1999). Some writers note that the MCMI-III has limited validity to begin with, and consequently, they recommend against its use in forensic evaluations (McCann & Dyer, 1996; Retzlaff, 1996; Rogers, Salekin & Sewell, 2000).

Another important criticism is that the MCMI-III was developed on a clinical psychiatric population and intended for use with such individuals, not custody-disputing parents. In fact, the MCMI-III test manual states that ". . . the MCMI-III is not a general personality instrument to be used for normal populations or for any other purpose other than diagnostic screening or clinical assessment" (p. 5). Consequently, Hynan (2004) argues that the results tend to indicate pathology where there may be none and thus the test is not appropriate for custody evaluations. He also notes that there appears to be a gender bias against female parents, given that they are likely to score significantly more pathologically on certain scales than men, when there is no corresponding validity for these results in prevalence rates.

Others, though, maintain that both the MMPI-2 and the MCMI-III are applicable because the normative samples include a significant number of high-conflict married individuals undergoing therapy, experiencing marital problems and/or undergoing divorce (Gould, 2006; Millon, 1994; McCann & Dyer, 1996). It has been noted that personality disorders are common in high-conflict custody litigants, with estimates as high as 60 per cent (Johnston, 1988; Siegel & Langford, 1998). Also noteworthy is that high-conflict families are a minority, comprising approximately 10 to 25 per cent (Maccoby & Mnookin, 1992) of the divorcing population, and the rate of personality disorders is about 10 per cent in the normal population. Moreover, both the MMPI-2 and the MCMI-III have context-specific normative data of parents participating in custody assessments (Bathurst, et al., 1997; Halon, 2001; Lampel, 1999; McCann, Flens, Campagna, Vollman, Lazzaro & Connor, 2001). Utilizing tests that have comparison groups allows the assessor not only to understand each parent, but also to compare the parent with the normative group, the context-specific group (custody litigants, psychiatric population, etc.) and with the other parent.

The assessor needs to consider malingering and deception, which can be either intentional or unintentional. This is often referred to as the respondent's "response style." The literature on the MMPI-2 and MCMI-III, each of which has several validity scales, indicates that custody litigants are prone to present favourably and minimize problems by exhibiting what is commonly referred to as a "fake good" response style, a finding that is not unexpected given the context (Baer, Wetter, Nichols, Greene & Berry 1995; Bagby, et al., 1999; Bathurst et al., 1997; Halon, 2001; Strong, Greene, Hoppe, Johnston & Olesen, 1999). Given this common finding, assessors need to be careful not to over-interpret elevations on the validity scales (Erickson, Lilienfeld & Vitacco, 2007b). It is important then to rely on the normative data we now have on custody litigants when considering the extent of defensiveness exhibited by the parties. The Paulhus Deception Scales (Paulhus, 1998) is another validity test that has been identified as useful with forensic populations.

Researchers have found that the "fake good" response style comprises two factors. One is "impression management," which involves a conscious and deliberate attempt to present favourably due to the circumstances and the context of the custody dispute. Here, the parent's responses to the true/false items may indicate a favourable but inaccurate characteristic, or deny an unfavourable but accurate characteristic. The second response style is referred to as "self-deceptive enhancement," wherein the parent actually believes and is overly confident that they have the favourable characteristics (Bagby & Marshall, 2004; Siegel & Langford, 1998; Strong, Greene, Hoppe, Johnston & Olesen, 1999). These individuals are described as having poor insight and narcissistic qualities, and they are easily angered when confronted, these being more stable and unintentional qualities.

The efficacy of projective tests (e.g., The Rorschach, TAT, projective drawings, sentence completion), while used frequently by assessors, remains debatable (Brodzinsky, 1993; Erard, 2005, 2007; Erickson, Lilienfeld & Vitacco, 2007a, 2007b; Calloway, 2005; Gould, 2005; Otto, et al., 2000).[32] Underwager and Wakefield (1993) maintain that tests like the House-Tree-Person (HTP) and the Kinetic Family Drawings (KFD) are often over-interpreted and misinterpreted. At best, psychological tests lacking adequate reliability and validity, if used, should be deployed as clinical assessment tools to engage the respondent and augment the semi-structured interview protocol.

Some argue that the Rorschach does not meet legal standards of admissibility (Grove, Barden, Garb & Lilienfeld, 2002; Wood, Nezworski, Garb & Lilienfeld, 2001). Erickson, Lilienfeld & Vitacco (2007a) go as far as to assert that its use is "unwise at best and unethical at worst." Others refute these claims and maintain that the scientific basis of the test has been generally well established and has been upheld in court (Erard, 2007; Medoff, 2003; Meyer, 2000; Meyer et al., 2001; Ritzler, Erard & Pettigrew, 2002).[33]

Unlike the MMPI-2 and the MCMI-III, the Rorschach has not been normed on a sample of custody litigants. However, there are some preliminary studies, primarily paper presentations and dissertations, which have examined the Rorschach protocols of custody litigants, some comparing them with other samples (Bonieskie, 2000; Hoppe & Kenney, 1994; Lee, 1996). Reported characteristics differentiating custody litigants to varying degrees from non-patient controls include cognitive simplicity, withdrawal from affect, potentially poor impulse control, coping deficits and pathological narcissism, disturbances in self-esteem and problems with reality testing (Hoppe & Kenney, 1994).

Proponents of the Rorschach test maintain that using the Exner Comprehensive System (CS) (Exner, 1993) for scoring and interpreting the Rorschach (and not other, unvalidated methods for interpretation) can yield useful information, including that relating to internal resources, thinking style, affect style and impulse control, stress management, interpersonal functioning, and coping styles (see Calloway, 2005 and Erard, 2005; 2007 for further elaboration).[34] Calloway (2005) reports that a comparison of each parent's Rorschach results in custody cases can provide useful insights into how the parents relate to one another emotionally, and their respective contributions to the oftentimes, dysfunctional dynamic, including the parental conflict.

In addition, writers note the contribution of the Rorschach to the extent that it counters the proverbial impression-management problems previously discussed that exist with objective personality inventories like the MMPI-2, which are based entirely on the parents' self-reports (Calloway, 2005; Erard, 2005; Meyer, 2001, Meyer & Archer, 2001; Johnston et al., 2005). These writers are careful to note, though, that while the Rorschach may yield qualitatively different and useful information than that obtained from self-report objective tests like the MMPI-2, the administration, scoring and interpretation of the Rorschach requires highly specialized skills and training. In addition, it adds substantially to the hours and cost of an assessment, which for some is prohibitive. Moreover, given the complexity in scoring and interpreting, regular and frequent use is advised to ensure the assessor remains familiar with the demands of the test. Foundation training as well as continuing education is imperative given that new research data are published regularly.

Unlike the projective and personality tests discussed, there is a group of assessment instruments that purport to assess constructs directly relevant to child custody decision-making. These include:

(a) the various Bricklin instruments for both parents (Parent Perception of Child Profile, Bricklin & Elliot, 1991 and the Parent Awareness Skills Survey, PASS, Bricklin 1990), and

(b) for children, the Bricklin Perceptual Scales, BPS; Bricklin 1990 and the Perception of Relationships Test, PORT, Bricklin 1989;

(c) the Ackerman-Schoendorf Parent Evaluation of Custody Test (ASPECT)[35] (Ackerman & Schoendorf, 1992), and

(d) the Custody Quotient (Gordon & Peek, 1988).

While custody-specific tools were used by many, although not the majority, in the past (Ackerman & Ackerman, 1997), their usage appears to have declined due to significant psychometric and conceptual limitations present in these tools (Bow & Quinnell, 2001; Flens, 2005; LaFortune & Carpenter, 1998; Otto, et al., 2000).[36]

In conclusion, the various guidelines and standards, in combination with the substantial literature, consistently indicate that it is imperative that assessors recognize and document throughout that psychological test results are but one source of information to be treated as hypotheses for further testing along with all of the other obtained assessment information. Test selection must include measures that are both relevant to the outcome variables—that is, parenting capacity, quality of parent–child relationship, goodness of fit between parent and child—and have adequate reliability and validity. Consideration of cultural factors as well as an examination of the norm-referenced group is important, given that most tests, with the exception of the MMPI-2, the MCMI-III and the PSI do not have published norms relevant to custody litigants.[37] The assessor needs to acknowledge each test's limitations. Findings should always be presented as probability statements with the notation that these findings reflect characteristics of a comparable group of individuals who provided similar responses. Accordingly, individual differences are always a possibility, indicating that although the individual scored similarly to the group, that individual may not in fact be like the group. Psychological tests, then, when selected and used properly, are likely to assist the child custody assessor in making best interest recommendations.

In this chapter, we provided an overview of a best practice approach to conducting child custody assessments. We summarized the survey literature and contracting phase of the work. We described the multi-method, multi-source methodology, specifically the information gathering stage of the work, information obtained from interviews, written self-report questionnaires and checklists, parent-child observations, third-party information, court documentation, and psychological tests, inventories and checklists. In our discussion of psychological testing we highlighted the advantages and disadvantages of specific tests and discussed issues related to the misuse and selection of appropriate tests. Numerous appendices were provided to assist the assessor.

Notes

1. [Wonderly, 423, N.E.2d 420, 427 (Ohio 1981)]

2. For further elaboration see the previously cited guidelines and model standards and child custody texts by Ackerman (2006), Gould (2006), Lenoff & Montague (1996), Schutz, Dixon, Lindenberg & Rutter (1989), and Stahl (1994, 1999).

3. The Kirkland survey of 61 board members (representing 39 boards) of the Association of State and Provincial Psychology Boards (56 per cent response rate), indicated that 2,413 complaints had been filed between 1990 and 1999. Complaints related to child custody work were the fastest growing and most frequent next to those related to sexual misconduct. The survey indicates that 27 of these complaints (less than one per cent) were reported to be in formal fault. The Bulletin of the College of Psychology of Ontario indicates that between January and February 28, 2007, there were 48 complaints (39 in the same period in 2006). Eleven of these were related to custody/access and child welfare (six in the same period in 2006). The nature of complaint occurring most frequently for all complaints were bias (four), followed by quality of services (two), failure to fulfill the terms of agreement with user (one), failure to respond to a request in a timely manner (one), false or misleading statements (one), and inadequate data to support conclusions (one), leaving one unstated.

4. See Appendix A (pp. 62–63) in Gould, Kirkpatrick, Austin & Martindale (2004) for suggested references/citations by topic.

5. Without assessments, we would have no choice but to resort to one-size-fits-all presumptions that are insensitive to the individual needs of children (see Kelly and Johnston, 2005 and Greenberg, Gould-Saltman & Schnider, 2006) compared with Emery, Otto & O'Donohue, 2005 for further elaboration of this debate).

6. If one or both parents are self-represented, the assessor contracts directly with the parents or sometimes with the lawyer and other unrepresented parent. With the self-represented parent's consent, best obtained in writing, the assessor may have *ex parte* contact with the other lawyer. If a lawyer represents the child, the lawyer will be included in the referral and contracting process.

7. Appendix 1 contains a sample checklist for the conference call with counsel.

8. Also known as a Statement of Understanding or Retainer Agreement.

9. Some maintain that given that there is always a court order for the assessment, it is unnecessary for the parents to also sign a service agreement indicating their consent to participate, as they may not in fact be willing participants, and further, because the court order necessarily provides for the release of the obtained information to the court, the

lawyers and the other parent. Notwithstanding, based on our experience and knowledge of the expectations of regulatory bodies, we believe it is prudent for the parents to sign the agreement, which includes not only waivers with respect to lack of confidentiality and the release of information, but also the various details pertaining to process, procedure, mandatory reporting of suspected abuse, and the assessor's retainer, fees, and office policies, much of which is typically not contained in the orders in our jurisdiction.

10. Appendix 2 contains the Parenting Plan Assessment Retainer Agreement.

11. Based on personal preference and/or the presence of domestic violence, assessors vary with respect to the initial orientation meeting and whether or not both parents attend together or separately.

12. If the parents have yet to sign the agreement, preferring to meet first with the assessor for the orientation/contracting meeting, the parents are asked to return to their respective lawyers for execution of their consent.

13. We have found that if the parents have not already told the child about the assessment (and the assessor would want to know at some point what they have told the child, and why), they usually want some guidance from the assessor as to how to explain the assessment to the child.

14. The previously cited surveys indicate increases from 2 hours reported in 1986 to 4.7 hours reported in the 1996 and to 7 or more hours in the 2001 study. Somewhat surprisingly, hours with children were fewer and had declined by 2001 (1.5 hours in 1986; 2.7 hours in 1996; and 1.6 hours in 2001).

15. This questionnaire obtains written parent reports on the child's development, behaviour and adjustment from birth to the present (available from www.wpqonline.com).

16. Our impression is that home visits may be more common in the Greater Toronto Area (GTA) than the survey literature indicates. We have found these to be particularly informative. Location, though, may make these visits impractical and costly. Furthermore, consistent with our practice, the hours required for two home visits (one in each home) and two office observations (one with each parent–child dyad) are inconsistent with the survey literature that reports an average range from 1.6 to 2.6 hours for parent–child observations.

17. See Appendix 4 for a sample semi-structured interview protocol.

18. See Gould (2006) for a sample consent form, "Collateral Data Form" (adapted from Martindale, 2003), and pre-determined interview questions, "Collateral Interview Questions" form.

19. In fact, when acting as a collateral source (e.g., a therapist for a parent or child) and when we do not provide our own written report, we require that the assessor allow us to review the summary for the assessment report prior to its release.

20. See Appendix 5 for a list of tests typically used with children and adults in child custody assessments.

21. Social workers or psychiatrists would need to refer to either a psychologist or psychometrist for the testing component of their assessment, a common practice in Ontario.

22. Computer-generated reports are available for many tests, most notably the MMPI-2, the MCMI-III, the Rorschach and the various Weschler Scales (intelligence measures).

23. The 2007 AFCC Model Standards of Practice for Child Custody Evaluation (AFCC 2004, revised 2007) states: "Evaluators shall exercise caution in the use of computer-based test interpretations and prescriptive tests. In reporting information gathered, data obtained and clinical impressions formed and in explaining the bases for their opinions, evaluators shall accurately portray the relevance of each assessment instruct to the evaluative task and to the decision-making process. Evaluators shall recognize that test data carry an aura of precision that may be misleading. For this reason, evaluators shall not assign to test data greater weight than is warranted, particularly when opinions expressed have been formatted largely on some other bases (section 6.6, p.84).

[24.] The CPA Code of Ethics and Standards of Practice parallels the American ones.

[25.] When speaking about psychological testing, reliability refers to the consistency of results (e.g., across time, situation and assessor), while validity refers to whether or not the test measures what it's supposed to, that is, the accuracy of the test. Otto et al. (2000) state ". . ..the reliability of a measure limits its validity, tests with poor reliability are tests with poor validity, and tests with unknown reliability are tests with unknown validity" (p. 334).

[26.] See *R. v. Mohan* at p.23.

[27.] See for example, *Buros Mental Measurements Yearbook* and *Tests in Print*, www.unl.edu/buros.

[28.] These include the CPA (2000) and APA Ethical Principles of Psychologists and Code of Conduct (1992), the Standards for Educational and Psychological Testing (1999), published by the American Educational Research Association, American, American Psychological Association, National Counsel on Measurement in Education, and The APA Guidelines for Computer-Based Tests and Interpretations. See also Anastasi A. & Urbina, S. (1997) for more information about psychological testing.

[29.] Examples include those by Austin (2000); Drozd, Kleinman & Olesen (2000); Jaffe, Lemon & Poisson (2003); and the DOVE (Ellis & Stuckless, 2006).

[30.] The MMPI has been in existence for more than 60 years and has been examined in more than 15,000 articles and books to date (Ackerman, 2006).

[31.] Further elaboration of the use of the MMPI-2 may be found in Ben-Porath et al., (1995) and Pope, Butcher & Seelen (2000) and for the use of the MCMI-III in forensic assessments in McCann & Dyer, 1996. The Personality Assessment Inventory (PAI-Morey, 1991) is another personality measure assessors may choose to use.

[32.] See entire Volume 2 of Journal of Child Custody (2005) devoted to psychological testing in child custody assessments and Volume 45:2 of the Family Court Review (2007).

[33.] See white paper and attached bibliography both supporting and critical of the Rorschach published by the Board of Trustees of the Society for Personality Assessment, 2005, also available online at www.personality.org. Note that critics (Erickson, Lilienfeld & Vitacco, 2007b) claim this is a biased advocacy paper.

[34.] For example, one indice of the CS, the Coping Deficit Index (CDI), identifies coping limitations in terms of stress overload, maturity, inner resources and interpersonal skills. The response style of over- or under-incorporation (based on several ratios and frequencies) describes indices processing information by detailed and careful scanning of the stimulus field or by hasty and haphazard scanning, neglecting critical components of the stimulus field. The Affective Ratio, which relates to interest in emotional stimuli and the FC: CF + C ratio, which describes the willingness to make emotional responses and the extent of emotional control, may assist in the assessment of how emotions are expressed and managed. See Caldwell (2005) and Erard (2005) for further elaboration including case examples.

[35.] The ASPECT is a protocol completed by the assessor (not the parent) that incorporates scores, impressions and findings from various sources of information including test results, interview data, observations, etc.). Quinnell & Bow (2001) reported the BPS was used with children eight per cent of the time, while five years earlier it was used 34.8 per cent of the time (Ackerman & Ackerman 1996). About the Bricklin Scales, Otto et al. (2000) state: "Although these tests have good face validity (i.e., their item content makes sense and appears to assess factors relevant to child custody decision making), significant questions remain regarding their utility, and their appropriateness for use in custody evaluations at the present time" (p. 317). They go on to say: "In essentially every published review of these custody assessment instruments, concerns about their reliability and validity have been identified, and the need for research has been made clear. Unfortunately, child custody evaluators continue to wait for that research" (p.

336). LaFortune and Carpenter (1998) warn that "the validity of these measures is unestablished at best and seriously flawed at worst" and that their use "cannot be recommended" (p. 222).

[36.] The interested reader is referred the Journal of Child Custody, 2 (Volume 1/2) for further discussion regarding this debate and controversy (Ackerman, 2005a, 2005b; Bricklin & Halbert, 2004; Connell, 2005).

[37.] See Abidin, Flens, and Austen (2006) for PSI custody litigation norms.

References

Abidin, R.R. *Parenting Stress Index (PSI), Third Edition* (Odessa, FL: Psychological Assessment Resources, Inc. 1995).

Abidin, R.R., Flens, J.R. & Austin, W.G. "The Parenting Stress Index (PSI" Forensic uses and limitation" (Chapter 11, pp. 297-328), in R. P. Archer (Ed.), *Forensic uses of clinical assessment instruments* (Mahwah, NJ: Erlbaum, 2006).

Achenbach, T.M. & Edelbrock, C. *Manual for the Child Behavior Checklist 4-18* (Burlington, VT: Queen City Printers, 1991).

Achenbach, T.M. & Rescorla, L.A. *Manual for the ASEBA School-Age Forms & Profiles* (Burlington, VT: University of Vermont, Research Center for Children, Youth & Families, 2001).

Ackerman, M. J. *Clinician's Guide to Child Custody Evaluations, Third Edition* (Hoboken, NJ: John Wiley & Sons, Inc., 2001).

Ackerman, M.J. *Clinician's Guide to Child Custody Evaluations, Third Edition* (New Jersey: John Wiley and Sons, Inc., 2006).

Ackerman, M.J. & Ackerman, M.C. "Child custody evaluation practices: A 1996 survey of psychologists" Family Law Quarterly 30:3 (1996), 565–586.

Ackerman, M.J. & Ackerman, M.C. "Child custody evaluation practices: A survey of experienced professionals (revisited)" Professional Psychology: Research and Practice 28 (1997), 137–145.

Ackerman, M.J. "The Ackerman-Schoendorf scales for parent evaluation of custody (AS-PECT): A review of research and update" Journal of Child Custody 2:1/2 (2005a), 179–194.

Ackerman, M.J., Ackerman, M.C., Steffen, L.J. & Kelley-Poulos, S. "Psychologists' practices compared to the expectations of family law judges and attorneys in child custody cases" Journal of Child Custody 1:1 (2004), 41–60.

Ackerman, M.J. & Schoendorf, K. *ASPECT: Ackerman–Schoendorf Scales for Parent Evaluation of Custody manual* (Los Angeles: Western Psychological Services, 1992).

AFCC Model Standards of Practice for Child Custody Evaluation (Task Force for Model Standards of Practice for Child Custody Evaluation 2004, revised 2007).

Amato, P.R. "The consequences of divorce for adults and children" Journal of Marriage and Family Therapy 62:1 (2000), 269–288.

Anastasi, A. & Urbina, S. *Psychological Testing, 7th Edition.* (Upper Saddle River, NJ: Prentice Hall, 1997).

Attwood, D. *Australian Scale for Asperger's Syndrome.* (Petrie, Queensland, 1996).

Austin, W.G. "Assessing credibility in allegations of marital violence in the high-conflict child custody case" Family and Conciliation Courts Review 38:4 (2000), 462–477.

Austin, W. "Guidelines for utilizing collateral sources of information in child custody evaluations" Family and Conciliation Courts Review 40:2 (2002), 177–184.

Baer, R.A., Wetter, M.W., Nichols, D.S., Greene, R. & Berry, D.T.R. "Sensitivity of MMPI-2 validity scales to underreporting of symptoms" Psychological Assessment 7:4 (1995), 419–423.

Bagby, R.M., Nicholson, R.A., Buis, T., Radovanovic, H. & Fidler, B.J. "Defensive responding on the MMPI-2 in family custody and access evaluations" Psychological Assessment 11:1 (1999), 24–28.

Bagby, R.M. & Marshall, M.B. "Assessing underreporting response bias on the MMPI-2" Assessment 11:2 (2004), 115–126.

Bala, N. "Tippins and Wittmann asked the wrong questions: Evaluators may not be 'experts,' but they can express best interests opinions" Family Court Review 43:4 (2005), 554–562.

Bathurst, K., Gottfried, A.W. & Gottfried, A. E. "Normative data for the MMPI-2 in child custody litigation" Psychological Assessment 9 (1997), 205–211.

Bellak, L. & Bellak, S. *Children's Apperception Test* (CAT 1974) (1992).

Bender Visual Motor Gestalt Test (New York: The American Orthopsychiatry Association Inc., 1946).

Birnbaum, R. & Radovanovic, H. "Brief intervention model for access-based postseparation disputes" Family and Conciliation Court Review 35 (1999), 504–513.

Bonieskie, L.M. "An examination of personality characteristics of child custody litigants on the Rorschach" Dissertation Abstracts International 61:6-B (2000), 3271.

Bow, J. N. "Review of Empirical Research on Child Custody Practice" Journal of Child Custody 3:1 (2006), 23–50.

Bow, J.N. & Quinnell, F.A. "Psychologists' current practices and procedures in child custody evaluations: Five years after American psychological association guidelines" Professional Psychology: Research and Practice 32:3 (2001), 261–268.

Bow, J.N., Flens, J.R., Gould, J.W. & Greenhut, D. "An analysis of administration, scoring, and interpretation of the MMPI-2 and MCMI-II/III in child custody evaluations" Journal of Child Custody, 2:4 (2005), 1–22.

Bow, J.N., Gould, J.W., Flens, J.R. & Greenhut, D. "Testing in child custody evaluation-selection, usage and Daubert admissibility: A survey of psychologists" Journal of Forensic Psychology Practice 6:2 (2006), 17–38.

Bricklin, B. *Perception of Relationships Test Manual* (Furlong, PA: Village, 1989).

Bricklin, B. *Bricklin Perceptual Scales Manual* (Furlong, PA: Village, 1990a).

Bricklin, B. *Parent Awareness Skills Survey Manual* (Furlong, PA: Village, 1990b).

Bricklin, B. & Elliott, G. *Parent Perception of Child Profile Manual* (Furlong, PA: Village, 1991).

Bricklin, B. & Halbert, M. *A Fully Explicated Evidence-to-Conclusions Model for Two Child Custody Tests, the PORT and BPS* (Furlong, PA: Village Publishing, Inc., 2003).

Brodzinsky, D.M. "On the use and misuse of psychological testing in child custody evaluations" Professional Psychology: Research and Practice 24:2 (1993), 213–219.

Butcher, J.N., Graham, J.R., Ben-Porath, Y.S., Tellegen, A., Dahlstrom, W.G. & Kaemmer, B. *Minnesota Multiphasic Personality Inventory-2: Manual for Administration, Scoring, and Interpretation, Rev. Ed.* (University of Minnesota Press: Minnesota, 2001).

Caldwell, Jr., A.B. "How can the MMPI-2 help child custody examiners?" Journal of Child Custody 2:1/2 (2005), 83–118.

Calloway, G.C. "The Rorschach: Its use in child custody evaluations" Journal of Child Custody 2:1/2 (2005), 143–158.

Campbell, D.T. & Fiske, D.W. "Convergent and discriminant validation by the multitrait-multimethod matrix" Psychological Bulletin 56 (1959), 81–105.

Chisholm, B. & MacNaughton, H.C. *Custody/Access Assessments: A Practice Guide for Lawyers and Assessors* (Toronto: Carswell, 1990).

Connell, M. "Review of "The Ackerman-Schoendorf scales for parents evaluation of custody" (ASPECT)" Journal of Child Custody 2:1/2 (2005), 195–209.

Conners, C. Keith. *Conners' Teacher Rating Scale, Revised (L)* (North Tonawanda, NY: Multi-Health System Inc., 1997).

Conners, C. Keith. *Conners' Parent Rating Scale, Revised (L)* (North Tonawanda, NY: Multi-Health System Inc., 1997).

Dyer, F.J. & McCann, J.T. "The Millon Clinical Inventories, research critical of their forensic application, and Daubert criteria" Law and Human Behavior 24:4 (2000), 487–497.

Ellis, D. & Stuckless, N. "Domestic violence, dove, and divorce mediation" Family Court Review, 44:4 (2006), 658–671.

Emery, R.E., Otto, R.K. & O'Donohue, W.T. "A critical assessment of child custody evaluations" American Psychological Society, 6:1 (2005), 1–29.

Erad, R. "Picking cherries with blinders on: A comment on Erickson et al. (2007) regarding the use of tests in family court" Family Court Review 45:2 (2007), 175–184.

Erard, R.E. "What the Rorschach can contribute to child custody and parenting time evaluations" Journal of Child Custody 2:1/2 (2005), 119–142.

Erickson, S.K., Lilienfeld, S.O. & Vitacco, M.J. "A critical examination of the suitability and limitations of psychological tests in family court" Family Court Review 45:2 (2007a), 157–174.

Erickson, S.K., Lilienfeld, S.O. & Vitacco, M.J. "Failing the burden of proof: The science and ethics of projective tests in custody evaluations" Family Court Review 45:2 (2007b), 187–192.

Exner, J.E. The Rorschach: A Comprehensive System, 3rd Ed., Vol. 1 (New York: Wiley, 1993).

Fidler, B.J. & Birnbaum, R. "Child custody disputes: Private and public assessments" Canadian Family Law Quarterly 25:2 (2006), 137–167.

Flens, J.R. "The responsible use of psychological testing in child custody evaluations: Selection of tests" Journal of Child Custody 2:1/2 (2005), 3–30.

Galatzer-Levy, R.M. & Kraus, L. (Eds.). The Scientific Basis of Child Custody Decisions (Toronto: Wiley & Sons, 1999).

Gerard, A.B. Parent-Child Relationship Inventory (PCRI) Manual (Los Angeles, CA: Western Psychological Services, 1994).

Gordon R. & Peek, L. A. The Custody Quotient (Dallas, TX: Willmington Institute 1988).

Gould, J.W. Conducting Scientifically Crafted Child Custody Evaluations (Thousand Oaks, CA: Sage Publications, 1998).

Gould, J.W. "Scientifically crafted child custody evaluations: Part One: A model for interdisciplinary collaboration in the development of psycho-legal questions guiding court-ordered child custody evaluations" Family and Conciliation Courts Review 37:1 (1999), 64–73.

Gould, J.W. "Use of psychological tests in child custody assessment" Journal of Child Custody 2:1/2 (2005), 49–70.

Gould, J.W. Conducting Scientifically Crafted Child Custody Evaluations, 2nd Ed. (Sarasota, Florida: Professional Resource Exchange, Inc., 2006).

Gould, J.W. & Lehrmann, D. "Evaluating the probative value of child custody evaluations" Juvenile and Family Court Journal 53:2 (2002), 17–30.

Gould, J.W., Kirkpatrick, H.D., Austin, W.G. & Martindale, D.A. "Critiquing a colleague's forensic advisory report: A suggested protocol for application to child custody evaluations" Journal of Child Custody: Research, Issues, and Practices, 1:3 (2004), 37–64.

Gould, J.W. & Stahl, P.M. "The art and science of child custody evaluations: Integrating clinical and forensic mental health models" Family and Conciliation Courts Review 38:3 (2000), 392-414.

Greenberg, L.R., Gould-Saltman , D.J., & Schnider, R. "The problem with presumptions-A review and commentary." Journal of Child Custody, 3:3/4 (2006), 139-172.

Grove, W. M., Barden, R. C., Garb, H. N. & Lilienfeld, S. O. "Failure of Rorschach-comprehensive-system-based testimony to be admissible under the Daubert-Joiner-Kumho standard" Psychology, Public Policy, and Law 8:2 (2002), 216–234.

Hagen, M.A. & Castagna, N. "The real numbers: Psychological testing in custody evaluations" Professional Psychology: Research and Practice 32:3 (2001), 269–271.

Halon, R.L. "The Millon Clinical Multiaxial Inventory-III: The normal quartet in child custody cases" American Journal of Forensic Psychology 19:1 (2001), 57–75.

Hare, R.D. The Hare Psychopathy Checklist-Revised Manual (Toronto: Multi-Health Systems, Inc., 1991).

Heilbrun, K. "The role of psychological testing in forensic assessments" Law and Human Behaviour 16:3 (1992), 257.

Heilbrun, K. "Child custody evaluations: Critically assessing mental health experts and psychological tests" Family Law Quarterly 29:1 (1995), 63–78.

Heilbrun, K. Principles of Forensic Mental Health Assessment (New York: Kluwer Academic/ Plenum Publishers, 2001).

Hoppe, C. & Kenney, L. "A Rorschach study of the psychological characteristics of parents engaged in child custody/visitation disputes" Paper presented at the 102nd Annual Convention of the American Psychological Association (Los Angeles, August, 1994).

Hynan, D.J. "Parent-child observations in custody evaluations" Family Court Review 41:2 (2003), 214–223.

Hynan, D. "Unsupported gender differences on some personality disorder scales of the Millon Clinical Multiaxial Inventory–III" Professional Psychology: Research and Practice 35 (2004), 105–110.

Jaffe, P., Crooks, C.V. & Bala, N. "Making appropriate parenting arrangements in family violence cases: Applying the literature to identify promising practices" Department of Justice Canada, September 7, 2005.

Jaffe, P., Lemon, N. & Poisson, S. *Child Custody and Domestic Violence* (Thousand Oaks, CA: Sage, 2003).

Johnston, J. R. & Campbell, L. E. G. *Impasses of Divorce: The Dynamics and Resolution of Family Conflict* (New York: Free Press, 1988).

Johnston, J.R., Walters, M.G. & Olesen, N.W. "Clinical ratings of parenting capacity and Rorschach protocols of custody-disputing parents: An exploratory study" Submitted for publication in the Journal of Child Custody 2:1-2 (2005), 159–178.

Keilin, W. & Bloom, L. "Child custody evaluation practices: A survey of experienced professionals" Professional Psychology 17 (1986), 338–346.

Kelly, J.B. & Emery, R. "Children's adjustment following divorce: Risk and resilience perspectives" Family Relations 52 (2003), 352–362.

Kelly, J.B. & Johnston, J.R. "Commentary on Tippins and Wittmann's "empirical and ethical problems with custody recommendations: A call for clinical humility and judicial vigilance" Family Court Review 43:2 (2005), 233–241.

Kelly, J.B. & Lamb, M.E. "Using child development research to make appropriate custody and access decisions for young children" Family and Conciliation Courts Review 38:3 (2000), 297–311.

Kirkland, K. & Kirkland, K.L. "Frequency of child custody evaluation complaints and related disciplinary action: A survey of the association of state and provincial psychology boards" Professional Psychology: Research and Practice 32:2 (2001), 171–174.

Kirkland, K., Kirkland, K. E., King, G. D. & Renfro, G. J. "Quasi-Judicial Immunity for Forensic Mental Health Professionals in Court-Appointed Roles" Journal of Child Custody 3:1 (2006), 1–22.

Kirkland, K, McMillan IV, E.L. & Kirkland, K.L. "Use of collateral contacts in child custody evaluations" Journal of Child Custody 2:4 (2005), 95–110.

Kovacs, Maria. *CDI* (North Tonawanda, NY: Multi-Health Systems, 1992).

LaFortune, K. A. & Carpenter, B. N. "Custody evaluations: A survey of mental health professionals" Behavioural Sciences and the Law 16 (1998), 207–224.

Lamb, M.E. "The development of infant-father attachments" in *The Role of the Father in Child Development, 3rd Ed.* (New York: Wiley, 1997), 104–120, 332–342.

Lamb, M.E. "Infant-father attachments and their impact on child development" in C.S. Tamis-LeMonda & N. Cabrera (Eds.) *Handbook of Father Involvement: Multidisciplinary Perspectives* (Mahwah, NJ: Erlbaum, 2002a), 93–117.

Lamb, M.E. "Noncustodial fathers and their children" in C.S. Tamis-LeMonda & N. Cabrera (Eds.) *Handbook of Father Involvement: Multidisciplinary Perspectives* (Mahwah, NJ: Erlbaum. 2002b), 169–184.

Lamb, M.E. & Kelly, J.B. "Using the empirical literature to guide the development of parenting plans for young children: A rejoinder to Solomon and Biringen" Family Court Review 39 (2001), 365–371.

Lampel, A.K. "Use of the Millon Clinical Multiaxial Inventory-III in evaluating child custody litigants" American Journal of Forensic Psychology 17:4 (1999), 19–31.

Lee, M. "The use of the Rorschach in child custody evaluations" Paper presented at the 2nd Child Custody Symposium of the Association of Family and Conciliation Courts, Washington, DC. (1996).

Leon, K. "Risk and protective factors in young children's adjustment to parental divorce: A review of the research" Family Relations 52 (2003), 258–270.

Leonoff, A. & Montague, R.J. *Guide to Custody and Access Assessments* (Toronto: Thomson Canada Ltd., 1996).

Maccoby, E. & Mnookin, R. *Dividing the Child: Social & Legal Dilemmas of Custody* (Mass: Harvard University Press, 1992).

Martindale, D.A. "Custody Evaluations and Risk Management" Printed materials distributed in conjunction with presentation offered in Cincinnati, Ohio, on September 20, 2003. Available through the American Academy of Forensic Psychology.

Martindale, D. A. "Reporter's foreword to the Association of Family and Conciliation Courts' Model standards of practice for child custody evaluation" Family Court Review 45:1 (2007), 58–69.

Martindale, D.A. & Gould, J.W. "The forensic model: Ethics and scientific methodology applied to custody evaluations. Journal of Child Custody 1:2 (2004), 1–22.

McCann, J.T. "Guidelines for forensic application of the MCMI-III" Journal of Forensic Psychology Practice 2:3 (2002), 55–69.

McCann, J.T. & Dyer, F.J. *Forensic Assessment with the Millon Inventories* (New York: Guilford, 1996).

McCann, J.T., Flens, J.R., Campagna, V., Collman, P., Lazzaro, T. & Connnor. E. "The MCMI-III in child custody evaluations: A normative study" Journal of Forensic Psychology Practice 1 (2001), 27–44.

Medoff, D. "The scientific basis of psychological testing" Family Court Review 41:2 (2003), 199–213.

Melton, G.B., Petrila, J., Poythress, M.G. & Slobogin, C. *Psychological Evaluations for the Courts: A Handbook for Mental Health Professionals and Lawyers, 2nd Ed.* (New York: Guilford, 1997).

Meyer, G. J. "On the science of Rorschach research" Journal of Personality Assessment 75 (2000), 46–81.

Meyer, G.J. & Archer, R.P. "The hard science of Rorschach: Legal citations during the past 50 years" Journal of Personality Assessment 69 (2001), 486–502.

Meyer, G.J., Finn, S.E., Eyde, L.D., Kay, G.G., Moreland, K.L., Dies, R.R. et al. "Psychological testing and psychological assessment: A review of evidence and issues" *American Psychologist 56*:2 (2001), 128–165.

Morey, L.C. *Personality Assessment Inventory (PAI)* (Lutz, FLA: Psychological Assessment Resources, Inc., 1991).

Miller, Glenn. *SASSI–3: Adult form*. SASSI Canada Inc. (1997).

Millon, T. *Millon Clinical Multiaxial Inventory-III (MCMI-III) Manual* (Minneapolis: National Computer Systems, 1994).

Millon, T., Davis, R. & Millon, C. *Millon Clinical Multiaxial Inventory–III (MCMI-III) Manual: 2nd Ed.* (Minneapolis, MN: NCS Pearson, Inc., 1997).

Millon, T., Davis, R. & Millon, C. *Millon Multiphasic Personality Inventory–III: Manual, 2nd ed.* (Minneapolis, 1997).

Milner, J. S. *CAP Inventory Form VI*. U.S.A. (1986).

Murray, H.A. & Bellak, L. *Thematic Apperception Test (TAT)* (San Antonio, TX: Psychological Corporation, 1973).

O'Donohue, W. & Bradley, A.R. Conceptual and empirical issues in child custody evaluations. Clinical Psychology: Science and Practice 6:3 (1999), 310–322.

Otto, R.K. & Butcher, J.N. "Computer-assisted psychological assessment in child custody evaluations" Family Law Quarterly 29:1 (1995), 79–96.

Otto, R.K., Edens, J.F. & Barcus, E.H. "The use of psychological testing in child custody evaluations" Family and Conciliation Courts Review 38:3 (2000), 312–340.

Otto, R.K. & Edens, J.F. "Parenting Capacity" Chapter 7 in Thomas Grisso *Evaluating Competencies: Forensic Assessments and Instruments, 2ⁿᵈ Ed.* (New York: Plenum, 2003), 229–307.

Paulhus, D. *Paulhus Deception Scales* (North Tonawanda, NY: Multi-Health Systems, 1998).

Piers, E. "The Way I Feel About Myself, Piers-Harris 2, 2002" *Children's Self-Concept Scale: Revised Manual* (Los Angeles, CA: Western Psychological Services, 1984).

Pruett, K. *Fatherneed: Why Father Care is as Essential as Mother Care for Your Child* (New York: The Free Press, 2000).

Pruett, M., Ebling, R. & Insabella, G. "Critical aspects of parenting plans for young children: Interjecting data into the debate about overnights" Family Court Review 42:1 (2004), 39–59.

Quinnell, F.A. & Bow, J.N. "Psychological tests used in child custody evaluations" Behavioural Sciences and the Law 19 (2001), 491–501.

Retzlaff, P. "MCMI-III diagnostic validity: Bad test of bad validity study" Journal of Personality Assessment 66 (1996), 431–437.

Riggs, S.A. "Is the approximation rule in the child's best interests? A critique from the perspective of attachment theory" Family Court Review 43:3 (2005), 481–493.

Ritzler, B., Erad, R. & Pettigrew, G. "A final reply to Grave and Barden: The relevance of the Rorschach Comprehensive System for expert testimony" Psychology, Public Policy, and Law 8 (2002), 235–246.

Rogers, R., Salekin, R.T. & Sewell, KW. "Validation of the Millon Clinical Multiaxial Inventory for Axis II disorders: Does it meet the Daubert standard?" Law and Human Behaviour 23 (1999), 425–443.

Rogers, R., Salekin, R.T. & Sewell, K.W. "The MCMI-III and the Daubert standard: Separating rhetoric from reality" Law and Human Behavior 24:4 (2000), 501–506.

Rotman, A. S. "Commentary on "Empirical and ethical problems with custody recommendations: A call for new family court priorities" Family Court Review 43:2 (2005), 242–245.

Schutz, B., Dixon, E., Lindenberger, J. & Rutter, N. *Solomon's Sword: A Practice Guide to Conducting Child Custody Evaluations* (San Francisco: Jossey Bass, 1989).

Siegel, J. "Traditional MMPI-2 validity indicators and initial presentation in custody evaluations" American Journal of Forensic Psychology 13:3 (1996), 55–63.

Siegel, J. & Langford, J. "MMPI-2 validity scales and suspected parental alienation syndrome" American Journal of Forensic Psychologist 16:4 (1998), 5–14.

Society for Personality Assessment "The status of the Rorschach in clinical and forensic practice: An official statement by the Board of Trustees of the Society for Personality Assessment" Journal of Personality Assessment 85 (2005), 219–237 (available online: http://www.personality.org).

Spielberger, C. Stait-Trait Anxiety Inventory for Children, (STAIC, 1973).

Stahl, P. *Conducting Child Custody Evaluations* (CA: Sage Publications, 1994).

Stahl, P. *Complex Issues in Child Custody Evaluation* (New York: Sage Publications, 1999).

Stahl, P.M. "The court: A response to Tippins and Wittmann" Family Court Review 43:2 (2005), 260–265.

Strong, D.R., Greene, R.L., Hoppe, C., Johnston, T. & Olesen, N. "Taxometric analysis of impression management and self-deception on the MMPI-2 in child custody litigants" Journal of Personality Assessment 73 (1999), 1–18.

Tippins, T.M. & Wittmann, J.P. "Empirical and ethical problems with custody recommendations: A call for clinical humility and judicial vigilance" Family Court Review 43:2 (2005), 193–222.

Underwager, R. & Wakefield, H. "Misuse of psychological tests in forensic settings: Some horrible examples" American Journal of Forensic Psychology 11:1 (1993) Website www.ipt-forensics.com.

Warshak, R.A. "Blanket restrictions: Overnight contact between parents and young children" *Family and Conciliation Courts Review 38*:4 (2000), 422–445.

Wood, J.M., Nezworski, M.T., Garb, H. & Lilienfeld, S. "Problems with the norms of the Comprehensive System for the Rorschach: Methodological and conceptual considerations" Clinical Psychology: Science and Practice 8 (2001), 397–402.

Appendix 1

Checklist For Conference Call With Counsel

1. Brief overview of the case in terms of need for assessment of custody, access, or both, and specific referral questions, such as: number of children; names and ages of children; involvement of step-parents, if applicable; presence of allegations of domestic violence, child maltreatment, substance abuse, etc. Each counsel to give a *brief* overview of the case.

2. Has counsel reviewed the Assessment Retainer Agreement? Are there any questions or concerns?

3. Reiterate that feedback to all (in some combination) with detailed parenting plan recommendations will be provided in writing, and that no comprehensive report is to be undertaken unless they are unable settle on the basis of the recommendations.

4. Come to agreement regarding court documentation to be reviewed, and who will send which documentation; reminder that counsel to provide other counsel with copy of covering letter setting out what is sent so that all parties know what is sent.

5. Determine what portion of fees and retainer each party is paying.

6. Define terms around subsequent contact with counsel during assessment—*ex parte* or not.

Appendix 2

Parenting Plan Assessment Retainer Agreement

RE: _____

General

1. It is hereby agreed that _____ is retained to act as Assessor with respect to the following issues:

   (i) custody of and access to the child(ren) of the marriage;

   (ii) parenting arrangements for the child(ren).

2. This signed agreement serves as acknowledgement that both parents and counsel have reviewed and accepted the Assessor's qualifications as adequate to perform the Assessment.

3. The manner in which fees are paid (detailed further on) has been determined by either the Court, or through negotiations among the parties and their lawyers. Although the Assessor's fees are not paid by the Court, the assessment is done for the Court. Regardless of the source of remuneration, I am impartial and as an Assessor I am expected to operate as though the Court employs me.

4. Reasonable steps are taken to minimize the distress associated with the assessment process. Nevertheless, though approximately 90 per cent of the cases in which I am involved are resolved without judicial intervention, I must presume there will be a trial and conduct myself accordingly. As an Assessor I am expected to secure verification of assertions made by those I am assessing. This means that information you provide will be questioned and, at times, you may feel as though you are being interrogated rather than interviewed. In order to perform the Court function, I must be an examiner and not a therapist. Your cooperation will be expected as verification of assertions made by you is sought. You will also be given the opportunity to respond to relevant assertions made by the other parent.

Procedures

5. It is further understood and accepted that [Assessor] shall per-

form all functions regarding the interviewing processes such as all interviews and home visits and contacts with collateral sources with the exception of psychological testing of the parents and possibly the children. A duly qualified registered psychologist shall undertake and interview, administer, interpret and provide feedback in relation to any psychological testing of the parents and children and interpret any psychological testing. There shall be an initial orientation meeting (one meeting if both parents are present, two meetings if the parents are seen individually).

6. The parents shall be seen individually, and possibly jointly. Depending on the age of the children, a family meeting may be conducted to introduce the children to the assessment process. In addition, the child(ren) shall be seen individually, together with their siblings and observed during a home visit and with each parent during office visits.

7. Step-parents and common-law partners shall be seen individually and together with their new partner or spouse. Step-parent's and common-law partner's children may be seen individually, with their siblings, the other children and/or during family meetings, office observations and home visits in various combinations.

8. Individuals being evaluated agree to authorize me to obtain information from professional collateral sources (e.g., teachers, coaches, therapists, pediatricians, physicians, etc.), who in my judgment may have information bearing on the subject of the assessment. In most cases, information needed from professionals will be obtained by telephone interview and/or by a review of their written reports.

9. Individuals who are advocates for one party may provide information in writing and/or be interviewed on the telephone or in person (e.g., grandparents, other relatives, co-workers, friends, neighbours, etc.). Each parent will provide a list of people from whom they wish the Assessor to obtain information. The Assessor will determine which of these third parties shall be involved. It is the parents' responsibility to advise these individuals that the information they provide is not confidential, and further that they are required to sign a form indicating that they consent to their information being revealed to any of the individuals involved in the assessment. Letters from any third parties providing information shall be mailed (not faxed) directly to the Assessor and shall not be provided by the parents or their counsel. The Assessor may contact these people for clarification and/or additional information.

10. Assessments typically take between 40 and 50 hours and between three and four months to complete. This may vary from family to family.

11. The Assessor is not to be contacted in cases of emergency that would require the services of a lawyer, physician, nor should the assessor, who is not equipped to handle such situations, be contacted for assistance in case of an emergency. You may contact your lawyer, physician, the police, a child welfare agency, the nearest hospital or other appropriately trained professional.

12. Out-of-session contact (casual waiting-room conversation, telephone calls, e-mails, etc.) should be avoided. It is to your disadvantage to communicate information to the Assessor in an informal manner. Telephone, voice mail, and e-mail (only when agreed to in advance) should be limited to scheduling appointments and addressing other procedural matters. Information concerning matters pertinent to the assessment itself should *not* be communicated by telephone or voice-mail, unless determined otherwise by the Assessor.

Obtaining Additional Information

13. Documents you wish me to consider must be delivered in a manner that ensures safe transfer into my custody. Under no circumstances are the parties to make unannounced visits to my offices to deliver documents. I do not accept any substantive information from parties by fax and/or email, unless agreed to otherwise and prior to sending materials. Material may be provided by mail, courier, or at a previously scheduled meeting. Any and all items submitted to me should be clearly identified with your name. All materials you provide become part of the file and cannot be returned. Please be sure to make copies for yourself in advance of providing me with the material.

Confidentiality and Consent to Release Information

14. This signed agreement serves as the parents' informed consent for [Assessor] to obtain information from the Court, counsel and both parents AND for [Assessor] to provide information received from all sources to the Court, counsel and the other parent.

15. Once there is a Court order for the assessment, or it has been consented to by the parties, I endeavour to avoid *ex parte* communications with the lawyers representing the parties. Agreements regarding the terms pertaining to *ex parte* communications

will be discussed with the lawyers during the initial conference call.

16. Thus, there is no confidentiality or privilege in a custody/access assessment. Any and all of the information provided by each parent may be shared with the other parent and with others in the assessment (including where necessary and appropriate, children and collateral sources). By presenting information to others, verification of information provided can be sought and the other party can be afforded the opportunity to respond to allegations that may have been made.

17. Statements made by children may be cited in the feedback and/ or Report. Do not tell your child(ren) that what they say to the Assessor is confidential. It is not.

18. Any and all office/clerical staff who become involved in aspects of your assessment receive instruction in matters relating to confidentiality.

19. In the event the Assessor is required to resort to small claims court and or a collection agency to retrieve payment, the party waives the right of confidentiality to the extent that identifying information is required for the claim.

Allegations of Abuse/Neglect

20. I am required by law to report to the proper authority and/or child welfare agency if I have a 'reasonable suspicion' that a party may harm himself or herself or the other parent, or that a child is being abused, harmed or neglected. Any report on our part must not be interpreted as support for the individual who has made the allegations, or as an indication that I disapprove of the alleged actions of the person accused. It must not be inferred that my reporting of such allegations suggests I find them credible.

Feedback and Reporting

21. The Assessor shall prepare written Parenting Plan Recommendations, the form of which has been outlined in our initial orientation meeting. These recommendations shall be provided along with a complete list of the sources of information, a summary of the psychological tests administered and verbal feedback of the findings and conclusions to both counsel and the parents when the assessment is completed.

22. The recommendations and findings may provide a basis for a settlement. The parents are advised to obtain independent legal advice, preferably before the assessment commences, but in any event, before a final agreement is reached, to ensure they are fully informed of their legal rights and obligations and the legal implication of such an agreement.

23. If the parents are unable to arrive at a settlement on the basis of the verbal feedback and written recommendations (i.e., the Parenting Plan Recommendations), a comprehensive assessment Report shall be provided upon request.

24. The initial retainer will not cover the costs of the comprehensive Report. When a Report is requested, the Assessor shall advise both parties of the request and the amount of the retainer required for the Report. The Assessor shall begin the Report when the full retainer has been received. Copies of the Report shall be distributed to both counsel, both parents, and the Court.

Fees

25. The hourly rate shall be $_____ per hour plus GST. The assessment fees shall be paid as follows: _____.

    A _____ hour retainer is requested prior to the initiation of the assessment. Additional retainers will be requested by the Assessor to complete the assessment as required. The Assessor is not obliged to proceed until such retainers are paid.

26. Fees are applied to all time expended in any/all professional activities, including administrative matters associated with the assessment process and/or arising from the assessment process. This includes fees charged retroactively from the time that our services are initially requested and the file is opened. This also includes disbursements paid to collateral sources for verbal and/or written reports and agency/hospital reports. Note that insurance companies may not cover fees paid for custody/access assessments.

27. There is considerable cost to opening the file and continuing scheduling issues with both the parents and collateral sources as required. A non-refundable administrative fee of $_____ payable by each parent, or in accordance with the proportions that they have agreed to, will be applied once the referral has been accepted. Accordingly, there will be no further charges for the

Assessor and administrative assistant's time in connection with setting up the process and ongoing scheduling.

28. There may be times when an individual being assessed will be required to pay fees for time expended by the Assessor in obtaining and reviewing information that the individual would have preferred not obtained or reviewed. Similarly, there may be times when parties will be required to pay fees in connection with the evaluation of a third party that the financially responsible party or parties would have preferred not evaluated.

29. Record-keeping requirements make it necessary to log each email, telephone call and/or message and make a record of even the briefest telephone call. For this reason there will be a minimum fee (five minutes @ $_____ hr) charged for every phone and email contact, with exceptions made for brief contacts made about scheduling.

30. Regular statements detailing the date, service, time and hourly rate will be provided.

31. Fees are not refunded for services rendered if completion of the assessment becomes either impossible or unnecessary.

32. The fee for a comprehensive Report, if required, shall be shared as have been the assessment costs, unless otherwise agreed to and determined *at the start* of the Assessment, or as determined differently by the Court.

33. The Court may apportion the costs of the assessment and/or the Report subsequent to the completion of either or both.

34. In the event interim accounts are sent out to the parents, payment shall be due when rendered.

35. Interest shall be charged on all accounts outstanding after 30 (thirty) days from the time the account is rendered.

36. The parties shall be billed for an appointment in which there are fewer than 24 (twenty-four) business hours' notice prior to cancellation. If an appointment is scheduled for 8 a.m., after 4:00 p.m. or on the weekend, the Assessor requires 48 (forty-eight) business hours' notice prior to cancellation. The parties shall each be responsible for bills arising from his/her respective cancellations.

37. The Report and/or Parenting Plan Recommendations shall not be released until all outstanding professional fees and disbursements related to the assessment have been paid in full.

Post-Assessment Developments

38. Services may not end at the time that Parenting Plan recommendations and verbal feedback are provided, or even after a comprehensive report is provided. Post-assessment services may include time spent with the parents and/or counsel reviewing and responding to correspondence, for telephone contact and meeting, for preparation for and attendance at discoveries, for preparation for and attendance as fact or expert witness at trial, travel for same, etc.

39. Fees for all post-assessment services will be billed at the rate of $_____. In the case of a Section 30 Assessment, the parents shall be responsible for these fees in the same manner they were for the Assessment, unless other arrangements have been consented to in advance, or if the Court has ordered in advance that the responsibility for these fees be apportioned in some other manner. If the Assessment is not ordered by the court, (i.e., a Section 30), the party requesting the services shall be responsible for the fees unless other arrangements have been consented to in advance or the Court has ordered in advance that the responsibility for these fees to be apportioned in some other manner. In the event both parties are requesting services, the fees shall be paid in the same manner as the Assessment fees.

40. Prior to submitting any statements regarding what [Assessor] may have said during the assessment feedback into affidavit and/or motion material, counsel and/or the parties shall obtain written confirmation from the Assessor that the statements are indeed accurate.

41. Your signature below indicates: (1) that you have received, read, understand and will abide by my policies and procedures; (2) that you are waiving privilege (i.e., that you consent to the appropriate disclosure of the information contained in my file concerning this matter); and, (3) that you are authorizing the release by me of information, including my Parenting Plan recommendations and any written reports, to the Court, the lawyers for both parities, and the children's lawyer if appointed.

DATED at _____, this _____ day of _____, 20___

| _____ | _____ | _____ |
| Witness | Father | Date |

| _____ | _____ | _____ |
| Witness | Mother | Date |

Appendix 3

Child Questionnaire

(Use back if necessary.)

Your name and relationship to child: _____

Child's name: _____ Birthdate: _____
           Last First Middle

Age: _____ Sex: _____ Grade: _____

Child's school: _____ Teacher's Name: _____

FULL School Address & Phone Number: _____

Board: _____

List all schools child has attended and the reasons for changes:

_____

_____

List all residential moves for the child and the reasons for the moves:

_____

_____

_____

With whom does the child live? _____

Why is the child living with this parent? _____

_____

How long has this living arrangement been in effect? _____

How old was the child at the final separation? _____

How often does the child see the other parent? _____

_____

What is the most recent court order regarding custody/access?

_____

If the child's time with the other parent is different now from what it was before, list previous visitation arrangements, including dates, and reasons for the changes:

_____

_____

List other significant caregivers, their phone numbers, ages, and the amount of time per week they spend with the child (e.g., babysitters, grandparents, other relatives):

_____

_____

PREGNANCY:

Was the pregnancy planned? yes no (circle one) If no, explain:

_____

How old were you when the child was born? _____

Complications:

Excessive vomiting _____ Hospitalization required _____
Excessive staining or blood loss _____ Threatened miscarriage _____
Infection(s) (specify) _____
Toxemia _____
Operation(s) (specify) _____
Other illness(es) (specify) _____
Smoking during pregnancy _____ average no. cigarettes per day _____
Alcohol consumption during pregnancy _____ describe if beyond oc-
casional drink:

_____

Medications taken during pregnancy _____
X-ray studies during pregnancy _____
Duration of pregnancy _____ weeks

Delivery:

Type of labour: Spontaneous _____ Induced _____
Forceps: high _____ mid _____ low _____
Duration of labour: _____ hours
Type of delivery: Vertex (normal) _____ breech _____ Caesarean __

Complications:

Cord around the neck _____ Cord presented first _____
Haemorrhage _____ Infant injured during delivery _____
Other (specify) _____
Birth weight _____

    Appropriate for gestational age (AGA) _____
    Small for gestational age (SGA) _____

Post-Delivery Period (While in Hospital):

Respiration: immediate _____ delayed (if so how long) _____
Cry: immediate _____ delayed (if so how long) _____
Mucus accumulation _____ Apgar score (if known) _____
Jaundice _____ Rh factor _____ transfusion _____
Cyanosis (turned blue) _____ Incubator care _____ No. of days ___

Suck: strong _____ weak _____ Infection (specify) _____
Vomiting _____ diarrhea _____
Birth defects (specify) _____

Total number of days baby was in the hospital after delivery: _____

INFANT–TODDLER PERIOD:

Were any of the following present, to a significant degree, during the first two years of life?
If so, describe.

Did not enjoy cuddling _____
Was not calmed by being held and/or stroked _____

Colic _____
Excessive restlessness _____
Diminished sleep because of restlessness and easy arousal _____
Frequent headbanging _____
Constantly into everything _____
Excessive number of accidents compared to other children _____

DEVELOPMENTAL MILESTONES:

If you can recall, record the age at which your child reached the following
developmental milestones.

*I cannot recall exactly, but to the best of my
recollection it occurred*:

	AGE	EARLY / AT THE NORMAL TIME / LATE
Smiled	___	___ / _____ / ___
Sat without support	___	___ / _____ / ___
Crawled	___	___ / _____ / ___
Stood without support	___	___ / _____ / ___
Walked without assistance	___	___ / _____ / ___
Spoke first words besides "ma-ma" and "da-da"	___	___ / _____ / ___
Said phrase	___	___ / _____ / ___
Said sentence	___	___ / _____ / ___
Bowel-trained, day	___	___ / _____ / ___
Bowel-trained, night	___	___ / _____ / ___
Bladder-trained, day	___	___ / _____ / ___
Bladder-trained, night	___	___ / _____ / ___
Rode tricycle	___	___ / _____ / ___
Rode bicycle (without training wheels)	___	___ / _____ / ___
Buttoned clothing	___	___ / _____ / ___
Tied shoelaces	___	___ / _____ / ___
Named colours	___	___ / _____ / ___
Named coins	___	___ / _____ / ___
Said alphabet in order	___	___ / _____ / ___
Began to read	___	___ / _____ / ___

COORDINATION:

Rate your child in the following skills:

	GOOD	AVERAGE	POOR
Walking	_____	_____	_____
Running	_____	_____	_____
Throwing	_____	_____	_____
Catching	_____	_____	_____
Tying shoelaces	_____	_____	_____
Buttoning	_____	_____	_____
Athletic abilities	_____	_____	_____

COMPREHENSION AND UNDERSTANDING:

Do you consider your child to understand directions and situations as well as other children his or her age? _____ If not, why not? _____

_____

How would you rate your child's overall level of intelligence compared to other children?
Below average _____ Average _____ Above average _____

SCHOOL:

Has your child been diagnosed through the school or by private educational/developmental evaluation as any of the following?

Gifted and talented	yes	no	(circle one)
Learning disabled	yes	no	
Mentally retarded	yes	no	
Emotionally disturbed	yes	no	
Physically handicapped	yes	no	
Developmentally delayed	yes	no	

Has your child received any special education or tutoring services?

yes   no   (circle one)

If yes, provide details: _____

Rate your child's school experiences related to academic learning.

	GOOD	AVERAGE	POOR
Nursery school	_____	_____	_____
Kindergarten	_____	_____	_____
Current grade	_____	_____	_____

To the best of your knowledge, at what grade level is your child functioning in the following areas:
Reading _____ Spelling _____ Arithmetic _____

Has your child ever had to repeat a grade? If so, when _____

Does your child's teacher describe any of the following as significant classroom problems?

        Doesn't sit still in his or her seat _____
        Frequently gets up and walks around the classroom _____
        Shouts out; doesn't wait to be called upon _____
        Won't wait his or her turn _____
        Does not cooperate well in group activities _____
        Typically does better in one-to-one relationships _____
        Doesn't respect the rights of others _____
        Doesn't pay attention during storytelling _____

Describe briefly any *other* classroom behavioural problems _____

_____

_____

PEER RELATIONSHIPS:

Does your child seek friendships with peers? _____
Is your child sought by peers for friendship? _____
Does your child play primarily with children his/her own age?
_____ younger _____ older _____ same
Describe briefly any problems your child may have with peers:

_____

_____

HOME BEHAVIOUR:

All children exhibit, to some degree, the kinds of behaviour listed below. Check those that you believe your child exhibits *at home* to an excessive or exaggerated degree when compared to other children his or her own age.

        Hyperactivity (high activity level) _____
        Poor attention span _____

Impulsivity (poor self-control) _____
Low frustration level _____
Temper outbursts _____
Sloppy table manners _____
Interrupts frequently _____
Doesn't listen when being spoken to _____
Sudden outbursts of physical abuse of other children ____
Acts like he or she is driven by a motor _____
Wears out shoes more frequently than siblings _____
Heedless of danger _____
Excessive number of accidents _____
Doesn't learn from experience _____
Poor memory _____
More active than siblings _____

INTERESTS AND ACCOMPLISHMENTS:

What are your child's main hobbies and interests?

_____

What are your child's areas of greatest accomplishment?

What does your child most enjoy doing?

_____

What does your child most dislike doing?

_____

MEDICAL HISTORY:

If your child's medical history includes any of the following, please note the age when the incident or illness occurred and any other pertinent information.

Childhood diseases (describe any complications):

_____

Operations: _____

_____

Hospitalization for illness(es) other than operations: _____

_____

Head injuries: _____

_____ With unconsciousness _____ Without unconsciousness

Convulsions _____

With fever _____ Without fever _____

Coma _____

Meningitis or encephalitis _____

Immunization reactions _____

Persistent high fevers _____ highest temperature ever recorded __

Eye problems _____

Ear problems _____

Poisoning _____

PRESENT MEDICAL STATUS:

Present height _____ present weight _____

Present illness(es) for which the child is being treated

_____

Medication child is taking on an ongoing basis _____

Appendix 3A

Parent Questionnaire

(Use back if you require more space.)

BASIC DATA:

Date: _____ Name: _____

Address: _____

_____

Postal Code: _____

Phone: (H) _____ (W) _____

Age & date of birth: _____ Occupation: _____

Employer's name and address:

_____

_____

Work hours: _____

Holidays (No. of weeks per year; when taken):

_____

Name persons (give ages) who live in your home:

_____

_____

_____

Lawyer's name and *full* address: _____

_____

YOUR FAMILY:

Your mother's name: _____ Age: _____ Occupation: _____

Address: _____

Your father's name: _____ Age: _____ Occupation: _____

Address: _____

List your siblings and their ages, occupations, and addresses:

_____

	Circle one:	
Has anyone in your family (parents or siblings) abused drugs or alcohol, now or in the past?	YES	NO
Has anyone in your family:		
Been in psychotherapy?	YES	NO
Been hospitalized for emotional reasons?	YES	NO
Received medication for emotional reasons?	YES	NO
Has anyone in your family been arrested? Convicted?	YES	NO
Has anyone in your extended family been investigated for physical or sexual child abuse? If so, which?	YES	NO

_____

Were your parents:		
Ever separated?	YES	NO
If yes, when? _____		
Your age at time of separation _____		
Ever divorced?	YES	NO
If yes, when? _____		
Your age at time of divorce _____		
Ever remarried?	YES	NO
If yes, when? _____		
Your age at time of re-marriage_____		

Date and age when you moved out of your parents' home? Why did you move? _____

EDUCATION AND WORK HISTORY:

Highest level of school completed: _____

Did you receive special education services?   YES   NO

Did you leave any educational program prior to completion: YES NO

If yes, explain:

_____

DETAILED WORK HISTORY:

Job Title   Place of Employment   Salary   Hours   Dates/Reason Left

_____

_____

_____

_____

PERSONAL AND HEALTH INFORMATION:

Do you have a religious affiliation? YES (Name it): _____ NO

Do you belong to a congregation? YES NO

    If yes, how often do you attend services? _____
    When was the last time you attended services? _____

List any and all mental health professionals you have had contact with:

(*Include full addresses and postal codes*)

Date   Agency/Person   Reason   Hospitalization

_____

_____

_____

_____

_____

Has a physician ever prescribed you medication for an emotional problem?

    YES   NO   (If yes, give date, name of physician, address, and name
of medication.)

_____

_____

_____

Have you ever been charged, arrested and/or convicted?   YES   NO

    (If yes, explain.)

_____

_____

_____

Have you ever been under investigation by the police or children's aid
society or child protection agency?   YES   NO

Do you drink alcohol at all?   YES   NO

If you answered yes to the above question, complete form titled "Michigan Alcohol Screening Test" attached to this questionnaire.

Do you currently have, or have you previously had, a chronic or recurrent
health problem or physical handicap?   YES   NO

If yes, give details:

_____

Are you currently on any prescribed medications?   YES   NO
If yes, provide medication, dosage, reason, and name of physician:

_____

Do you use any drugs or medications other than as prescribed?
                                                    YES   NO
If yes, explain:

_____

List dates and reasons for any hospitalizations you have had:

_____

_____

RELATIONSHIP WITH THE OTHER PARENT:

Date you met: _____ Date of Cohabitation: _____ Marriage: _____

Date of final separation: _____

If more than one separation, list dates and durations:

_____

_____

Reasons for the final separation:

_____

_____

List residences while with former spouse:

_____

_____

_____

PREVIOUS MARRIAGES, COMMON-LAW AND/OR SERIOUS RE-LATIONSHIPS:

Date, Nature of Relationship, Reason for Separation/Divorce, Children:

_____

_____

_____

INFORMATION REGARDING OTHER PARENT:

Do you have any of the following concerns about the other parent:

Alcohol abuse	yes no
Drug abuse	yes no
Emotional abuse of children	yes no
Physical abuse of children	yes no
Sexual abuse of children	yes no
Sexual behaviour	yes no
Physical health	yes no
Criminal behaviour	yes no
Potential for violent behaviour	yes no
Potential for suicide attempt	yes no
Child-snatching	yes no

If yes, explain:

_____

_____

_____

Is the other parent likely to express any of these concerns about you?

YES   NO   If yes, give details:

_____

_____

_____

Does the other parent drink alcohol at all?   YES   NO

If yes, describe use:

_____

What I do best as a parent is:

_____

_____

_____

My significant concerns about parenting are:

_____

_____

_____

My hopes/goals for parenting in the future are:

_____

_____

_____

My significant concerns about my relationship with the other parent are:

_____

_____

_____

My significant hopes/goals for my relationship with the other parent are:

_____

_____

_____

During the relationship important decisions were made about: _____

_____ By Other Parent   By Me   Jointly

- A) Household finances
- B) Purchases of family property
- C) Children's education
- D) Children's health care
- E) Children's religious training
- F) Children's extracurricular activities

Are you able to discuss family issues openly with each other? YES _____
NO _____

Comments regarding your ability to make decisions about the children cooperatively.

_____

_____

_____

Have there been any incidents of verbal abuse?	YES _____	NO _____
In the past six months?	YES _____	NO _____
Or at any time in the relationship?	YES _____	NO _____
Have there been any incidents of physical abuse?	YES _____	NO _____
In the past six months?	YES _____	NO_____
Or at any time in the relationship?	YES _____	NO _____

Give specifics regarding the above:

_____

_____

_____

Appendix 4

Collateral Semi-Structured Interview Protocol[1]

PERSONAL SOURCES

1. How long have you known the mother/father/child?

2. How frequently do you have (or have you had) contact with the mother/father/child?

3. When was the last time you had contact with the mother/father/child and for what reason?

4. How would you characterize your relationship with the mother/father/child?

5. Please describe what you have observed of the mother's/father's parenting, using specific situations or examples that you have directly observed of the mother/father with the child.

6. Describe what you have observed about how the mother/father disciplines the child.

7. Describe your observations of the mother's/father's use of force such as slapping, physical or verbal threats, hitting, pushing or any other like behaviour.

8. Do you have any concerns about the mother's/father's parenting skills?

9. Based on your direct observations, if any, describe how the parents communicate with each other.

10. What has the mother/father said to you about the other parent?

11. What is your understanding of what the parent has told the child about the other parent?

12. What is your understanding of the child-related tasks each parent did prior to the separation and to what extent?

13. Is there anything else you think is important for us to know, given our mandate?

14. Is there any other person you think would be useful for me to talk with? If yes, who? What is their phone number?

PROFESSIONAL SOURCES
Physicians, Therapists, Other Health Care Professionals:

1. Who are the individuals in the family you have had direct contact with?

2. How long have you known each?

3. In what capacity have you known each?

4. How often (many times) have you seen each?

5. How would you describe the child's relationship with each parent? (Pursue behavioural observations.)

6. Describe each parent's parenting strengths and challenges, with specific behavioural examples?

7. What is the parental relationship like in terms of cooperation, communication and conflict? Please provide specific examples.

Educators

1. How long have you taught/known this child?

2. Academic adjustment? (strengths and challenges)

3. Social/peer adjustment? (strengths and challenges)

4. Emotional and behavioural adjustment? (strengths and challenges)

5. Has the child talked to you about the family circumstances? If so, what has he/she said?

6. Do you have any specific concerns? Why?

7. Describe each parent's contact with the school? For what events, activities, reasons?

8. Do you have any other information you think might be important for me to know given my mandate?

9. Do you have any specific concerns about either parent? Why?

10. If you have made any suggestions to either parent, how did they react and what did they do (how responsive, open were they)?

---

[1] Combined and adapted from Ackerman (2006), Austin (2002), Gould (2006), Kirkland, McMillan & Kirkland (2005) and Stahl (1994).

Appendix 5

Tests Used In Child Custody Assessments

CHILDREN:

Wechsler Intelligence Scale for Children-Fourth Edition: Integrated (WISC-IV Integrated, Wechsler, 2004)
Rorschach (Exner Comprehensive System, Exner, 1993)
Children's Depression Inventory (CDI; Kovacs, 1992)
Piers-Harris Self Esteem Inventory (Piers & Harris 2002)
Stait-Trait Anxiety Inventory for Children (STAIC, Spielberger, 1973)
Thematic Apperception Test (TAT; Murray & Bellak, 1973)
Children's Apperception Test (CAT, Bellak & Bellak, 1992)
Bricklin Instruments:
    Perception of Relationships Test (PORT; Bricklin, 1989)
    Bricklin Perceptual Scales (BPS; Bricklin, 1990)
Sentence Complete Tests (various formats)
House-Tree-Person (HTP)
Kinetic Family Drawing

ADULTS:

Wechsler Adult Intelligence Scale-Third Edition (WAIS-III; Wechsler, 2001)
Millon Multiaxial Personality Inventory-3 (MCMI-III; Millon, Davis & Millon, 1997)
Minnesota Multiphasic Personality Inventory-2 (MMPI-II; Butcher, Graham, Ben-Porath, Tellegen, Dahlstrom & Kaemmer, 2001)
The Personality Assessment Inventory CPAI (Morey, 1991)
Beck Depression Inventory-II (BDI-II; Beck, 1996)
Rorschach (Exner Comprehensive System, Exner, 1993)
Thematic Apperception Test (TAT; Murray & Bellak, 1973)
Parent Child Relationship Inventory (PCRI; Gerard, 2004)
Parenting Stress Index (PSI; Abidin, 1995)
Substance Abuse Screening Inventory-3 (SASSI-3; Miller, 1997)
Child Abuse Potential Inventory (CAPI-IV; Milner, 1997)
Psychopathy Checklist-Revised (Hare, 1991)
Ackerman-Schoendorf Parent Evaluation of Custody Test Scales (AS-PECT; Ackerman & Schoendorf, 1992)

Custody Quotient (Gordon & Peek, 1989) (used but a research tool and
    creator does not recommend for use in custody evaluations)
Bricklin Instruments:
    Parent Perception of Child Profile (PPCP, Bricklin & Elliot, 1991)
    Parent Awareness Skills Survey (PASS, Bricklin, 1990)

Chapter 3

Deconstructing Clinical Assessments

"High conflict families are like a bowl of chocolates. You never know what you're going to get."[1] Winston Groom.

In Chapter 2 we addressed general guidelines for interviews and observations and the different sources of information. In this chapter, we review the clinical assessment of parents and children during interviews and observations. More specifically, we discuss: (a) how we evaluate and investigate the parents' relationship; (b) each parent's adjustment; (c) the extent to which this adjustment impacts parenting; (d) parenting capacity; (e) the children's adjustment and special needs; and (f) the quality of the parent–child relationship. All of these factors are relevant to making custody and access recommendations. This chapter concludes with a discussion relating to the disclosure and written report of the assessment findings and recommendations.

CLINICAL ASSESSMENT OF PARENTS AND CHILDREN

How parenting and the quality of parent–child relationships (including attachment) are precisely assessed and subsequently reported varies considerably. Based on our experience and review of other assessments, an adequate assessment of parenting skills is neglected in many child custody assessments. Parenting is multi-dimensional, and these various dimensions need to be explored and investigated in custody cases. The parenting capacity literature addresses parenting dimensions that are often conceptualized on a continuum (Budd, 2001; Kuehnle, Coulter & Firestone, 2000; Steinhauer, 1983). Examples of these dimensions, each containing numerous behavioural manifestations, include:

   (a) communication (effective vs. ineffective);

   (b) differentiated self (differentiation vs. fusion);

   (c) perceptions of child (accurate vs. inaccurate);

   (d) affective involvement (warm vs. cold);

   (e) control (permissive vs. intrusive); and

(f) expectations (reasonable vs. unreasonable).

While guidelines and authoritative texts have identified the child's attachment to each parent as critical to child custody decisions, there is considerable confusion about what attachment is, variability about how to assess it, and in some cases, incorrect application of the principles (Byrne, O'Conner, Marvin & Whelan, 2005).[2] While standardized measures of attachment exist,[3] these have not been validated for use specifically in child custody assessments. Furthermore, using these measures requires specialized training and equipment and is time-consuming, thus adding considerably to the time required for and the cost of an assessment.

The assessor needs to understand the various *types* of attachment, each differentiated from the other to some extent. These are secure or insecure, and if insecure they can be avoidant, resistant/ambivalent/preoccupied or disorganized (Main & Hesse, 1990). Both the *type* and *level* of the attachment, rather than one or the other, needs to be assessed. Additionally, the *quality* of the attachment needs to be distinguished from its *strength*. For example, a close attachment may be beneficial, but it can also be harmful if the parent and child are "enmeshed" and the child is unable to demonstrate age-appropriate autonomy and/or needs to tell that parent what he or she needs to hear. The assessor must ask, "How is the closeness expressed and how does it affect the child?"

Although evidently quite common, it is not enough to simply observe the parent–child dyad in low- or no-stress play situations, and on that basis alone conclude the presence of a good, healthy and/or positive relationship and/or attachment (Byrne et al., 2005). In this circumstance, it may not be the attachment at all, but rather other aspects of parenting, such as the parent's ability to support the child at play that is being observed. Thus, to understand attachment, the parent–child dyad must be assessed under mild stress and/or in the face of disruptions while the child's and parent's reactions are observed. Stated differently, the attachment system needs to be activated or challenged similarly to how it occurs in the more formal Strange Situation (SS), a structured research assessment procedure formally employed with 12- to 20-month-old infants (Byrne et al., 2005; Cassidy & Shaver, 1989; Calloway, Grace & Lee, 2006; Marvin, Cooper, Hoffman & Powell, 2002). For example, how does the child cope with the real-life experience of distress and/or separation from each parent? How does the child react when that parent returns? To what extent is the child able to use the parent as a secure base to "refuel" and then return to independent exploration? Does the child explore independently at all?

In addition, the type of attachment, secure or insecure, is not determinative to later functioning (Marvin et al., 2002). While a secure attachment is a protective factor (i.e., resilience) and an insecure attachment a risk factor for subsequent problems, the latter is not synonymous with pathology, just as the former does not ensure adaptive functioning free of pathology. One form of insecure attachment, referred to as "Insecure-Disorganized," when compared with secure and other forms of insecure attachment, has been strongly related to risk for psychopathology (Greenberg, 1999).

It is important to note that attachment is but one element of the parent–child relationship, and stands separate from other important components, such as providing for instrumental needs, discipline and teaching. In addition, the parent's own attachment[4] has been shown to be highly predictive of child adjustment, behaviour and attachment (Hesse, 1999; van Ijzendoorn, 1995). In other words, inquiries into how the parent perceives his/her childhood and early relationships, and not only parent–child observations, are central to understanding the quality of the parent–child relationship (Schmidt, Cuttress, Lang, Lewandowski & Rawana, 2007). Note that both the Adult Attachment Interview (AAI) and the Strange Situation (SS) are research tools, and as such should not be used for clinical work without considerable training. Notwithstanding this caveat, incorporating questions from these tools into the child custody assessment protocols is likely to provide an abundance of relevant information related to child development and parent–child relationships that can then be considered with all of the other information obtained during the assessment. We will return to the application of attachment to child custody decisions in Chapter 5.

A growing trend supported in practice guidelines, standards and models for assessments is to uniformly utilize standard, semi-structured assessment and observation protocols (Ackerman, 2005; AFCC Model Standards 2004, revised 2007; Gould, 1998, 1999, 2006). Doing so allows for flexibility depending on the family circumstances. Using congruent or parallel methods both for interviews and observations will demonstrate neutrality and increase the reliability and validity of the assessment (Austin & Kirkpatrick, 2004; Gould, 1998; Schutz et al., 1989; Stahl, 1994).[5] This is important not only to ensure reliability within the assessment (so that each parent receives the same questions and the assessor is comparing "apples with apples"), but also to ensure reliability between assessments should the process be replicated. In addition, use of congruent methods permits the assessor to accumulate his/her own sample of responses. Common responses in this particular sample of high-conflict families involved in custody assessments can then be distinguished from those that are uncommon, taking into account other relevant factors including culture, context and the unique family circumstances.

The assessor must exercise caution when arriving at opinions and conclusions about what is considered to be preferred parenting. Unlike situations that may be found in child protection assessments, in child custody work it is not uncommon for both parents to have demonstrated minimum standards or parenting that is "good enough." Indeed, there is a wide range of acceptable parenting, and custody litigants should not be held to a higher standard than any other parent, including the assessor. Furthermore, parenting tends to be value-laden. Ethnic and cultural lifestyle, as well as religious practice and/or factors must be taken into account in any assessment of parenting capacity and parent–child relationships. Clearly, each parent has strengths and challenges. Recommendations should consider how the child would benefit from the strengths and opportunities, similar and different, that each parent may offer. In addition, the ability and willingness of each parent, who may not have had a previous opportunity, to learn new parenting skills, is important to assess. Especially informative is each parent's ability to reflect realistically (i.e., insight) about not only what they do well, but also about their regrets and what they may be able to improve. How open is the parent to new ideas and direction? Having these characteristics in general indicates that the parents may also have the same tendencies where the rearing of their children is concerned (Fidler & Birnbaum, 2006).

CLINICAL INTERVIEWS WITH PARENTS

The contracting-orientation meeting with the parents has already been described. Next, each parent is seen for several interviews. Generally, the format involves moving from more open-ended to specific inquiry. Table 3 lists the categories of inquiry with the parents in the sequence in which they typically unfold. Variations may occur and the assessor may end up moving back and forth between content categories. We have found that keeping parents to the content category where possible and appropriate assists with the overall organization of the voluminous material obtained during the assessment. The assessor can guide the parent back to the topic at hand, noting that the other topics will be covered in due course. The ability of the parent to remain on track, to take direction, and the extent to which he or she reverts to irrelevancies or interminable blame and criticism of the other parent are relevant to the assessment findings and conclusions.

Table 3

Parent Interviews: General Areas of Inquiry

- Open-ended inquiry: What does the parent think is most important for the assessor to know?

- Parenting plan proposals and plan of care

- Individual history (family of origin, academic, social, employment, criminal, mental health, social and previous marriages, relationships)

- Marital history

- Relevant history since the separation

- Parenting assessment protocol

- Wrap-up, response to allegations made by the other parent, miscellaneous questions

---

Appendix 6[6] provides a sample standard, semi-structured interview protocol for each area of inquiry during the parent interviews. During the first interview, each parent is asked what they believe is most important for the assessor to know, given the task of making best interest parenting plan recommendations. Next, the parents are asked to explain their respective plans of care (i.e., parenting plan proposals for a parenting-time schedule and for making major child-related decisions) and why they believe their proposal is best for the child. Details of the parents' work schedules and proposals for before and after school and/or daycare are important to obtain. The parents are also asked to disclose any concerns they have about the children and any allegations against the other parent. After these areas have been sufficiently investigated, the focus turns to history.

Standard marital and separation histories are obtained. The marital, separation and individual histories contribute to an assessment of each parent's general health and adjustment, interpersonal functioning, parenting and relationship with the other parent, including the nature and extent of parental conflict. Some assessors choose to obtain the marital and separation histories in a joint meeting, while others prefer individual meetings. This decision will depend on the circumstances of each case, as joint interviews may be contraindicated, as well as on the assessor's training and comfort level. If a joint meeting occurs, the assessor should be sure to provide the parent with an opportunity to supply additional information during a subsequent individual interview.[7] Next, the parents provide their individual histories in response to the semi-structured interview protocol.

The above-noted histories are followed by further assessment—specifically of both parenting and parent–child relationships—obtained during interviews and observations also utilizing the standard, semi-structured parenting assessment protocol. Generally, the protocol includes:

(a) the pregnancy, delivery/labour and developmental history for each child;

(b) the parents' perceptions of each child and their relationship with each child;

(c) the parents' perceptions of their own and the other parent's parenting practices, strengths and challenges;

(d) if and how the separation was explained to the children; and

(e) attitudes towards the other parent, involvement of new partners, etc.

As noted, it is important to explore the vicissitudes of parenting, including but not limited to:

(a) the parent's knowledge of and ability to support appropriate developmental growth in the child (availability, refueling, autonomy);

(b) boundaries;

(c) enmeshment;

(d) parentification;

(e) intrusive parenting;

(f) responsiveness;

(g) attentiveness;

(h) empathy;

(i) attunement for both distress and non-distress situations;

(j) verbal and nonverbal affection;

(k) parenting style (authoritative, authoritarian, permissive);

(l) control patterns;

(m) discipline techniques (setting limits, follow-through, flexibility, explanations given, age-appropriate expectations, degree and kind of reinforcement and praise, patience);

(n) education and stimulation (manner, style);

(o) language (age-appropriate, infantilizing, pseudo-mature, relating to child as adult);

(p) ability to manage more than one child at a time;

(q) attachment/bond;

(r) communication skills;

(s) tone of interactions (calm/relaxed, anxious/strained, chaotic/orderly, fun/serious); and

(t) how conflict situations are handled by the parents, children and siblings.

One or two additional individual interviews are conducted with each parent towards the conclusion of the assessment, and usually after the assessor's observations have been conducted (see below), to address areas yet to be covered, including issues or concerns that may have arisen during the observations. It is imperative for the parents to know when they are having their last interview. They are explicitly asked if there is anything else they want to say or think the assessor needs to know. It is good practice to document specific questions asked. Such documentation may either preempt or if not, address any objections made by one or both parents that amount to false claims about the process. Furthermore, the parents' final remarks can be informative. Do they focus on the child's needs, or do they reiterate yet again their blame and denigration of the other parent? If they have not done so already, these final interviews provide each parent with an opportunity to respond to the other parent's concerns and allegations. It is not uncommon for parents to become defensive and even angry in response to pointed questions about their behaviour and the other parent's allegations. It may be useful to remind them (previously reviewed with them during the orientation/contracting meeting and also covered in the Parenting Plan Assessment Retainer Agreement) that while their defensiveness is understandable, the pointed inquiry affords them a final opportunity to respond to allegations. In addition, it can be explained that the inquiry, albeit difficult for them, is required for a best practice methodology and that more concerns may arise out of not having this opportunity than out of having it in terms of the basis upon which the recommendations are derived and, subsequently, the weight given to the recommendations by the court.

PARENT–CHILD OBSERVATIONS

Appendix 7[8] provides a sample standard, semi-structured protocol for home and office parent–child observations. Typically, at least four observations are conducted; one in each parent's home plus two office observations, with the child brought on a different day by each parent. During each of these four observations, the child, depending on his/her age, is usually interviewed individually, as set out in a later section of this chapter.

With a younger child, the assessor may choose to activate the attachment system by observing the child's and parent's reactions when the parent leaves the room and then returns. The assessor may also choose to leave the child briefly and return and observe the child's reactions. Depending on the issues, concerns and circumstances, the assessor may choose to orchestrate additional observations of the transitions between parents from home to home and/or from parent to daycare. Incidental observations of parents and child in the waiting area of the assessor's office or in the community may prove to be very informative as well.[9] With the door open, the assessor may observe from his/or her office while the parents wait with their children, or a receptionist can be trained to observe and note (not interpret) behavioural observations. Observations of the seating arrangements, parent behaviour (e.g., punctuality, limit-setting, affection, reaction to sibling conflicts, reaction to separation from the child), child behaviour and appearance (e.g., how they are dressed, activity level, emotions, statements, reaction to separation from the parent, ability to play independently) and the parent–child interactions may be useful. In the latter case, this method should be noted in the Sources of Information document.

Taking the idea originally from Schutz et al. (1989), both age-appropriate structured and unstructured (spontaneous) observations of each child with each parent, and with all children and each parent reap rich data about relative parenting abilities and the quality of the parent–child relationships. In doing these more structured observations, a comparison may be made between what the parents *reported* about their parenting style and approach (i.e., their intellectual awareness) and what they *actually do* in a real-life, albeit contrived situation. The spontaneous interactions may involve free-play and/or having lunch or a snack, for example. The structured tasks require the parent and child to engage in three different types of age-appropriate, structured tasks:

(1) cooperative (e.g., drawing a picture of your family doing something together, building a Lego house, planning a vacation);

(2) teaching (e.g., explaining a card or board game, or how to write a cheque); and

(3) problem-solving (e.g., discussions about rules for an adolescent, or about a child's refusing to clean up her toys or do homework).

These tasks do not take much time and provide a wealth of observational data relevant to various dimensions of parenting.

FAMILY INTERVIEWS

A family interview may be arranged to set the stage for the child's involvement in the assessment. Deciding whether or not a family interview should occur and then determining the protocol for the meeting requires consideration of several factors, for example, the child's age and comprehension. Not all assessors feel comfortable with or are adequately trained to conduct a family interview. Some believe it is unnecessary and that it places too much pressure on the children (Ackerman, 2006). In our view, this interview is not only informative but may also assist the child in feeling more comfortable about the whole process. Of course, having the entire family in one room may not be appropriate, depending on the circumstances, such as the level of parental conflict, including domestic violence. Both indications and contraindications need to be considered carefully when deciding on whether to proceed with a family meeting.

The family portion of the interview may be as brief as 15 to 30 minutes or it may be longer. While the value of having a semi-structured interview protocol at the assessor's disposal cannot be overstated, flexibility is equally important to the extent that the assessor must select from a repertoire of questions relevant to different scenarios and circumstances. More specifically, the interview will necessarily depend not only on the age and comprehension of the children more generally, but also on what they already know, if anything, about the separation/divorce and the assessment. Inquiry is made into the children's understanding of why they are present and the role of the assessor.

Knowing in advance what the children have been told will determine the course of this inquiry. If the children are aware of the assessor's role in making recommendations to the court, the assessor may explain that while their feelings and ideas are important to know, children do not make these decisions; rather, adults do. The assessor may further add that if the parents cannot make these decisions, the assessor will make a recommendation to the judge about what is best for the children and then the judge will decide. Alternatively, if the parents have agreed not to burden their younger children with the fact they are disputing custody, the assessor may choose to talk more generally about making things as good as possible for the children, by doing a "check-up," or assisting their family through the various changes (e.g., mom and dad living in two homes because of the separation, etc.) so that things can be as good as possible for the children.

During the family meeting, the parents will be asked to give the child permission to be honest with the assessor and not to be worried about hurting the parents' feelings. The children will be advised that they can speak with their parents about what is discussed during interviews, but they are not obliged to do so. They are encouraged to ask the parents to stop asking them questions and/or to ask the assessor to do so. Finally, the lack of confidentiality is reviewed with the child in an age-appropriate manner.

If there is more than one child, the siblings may be seen together to aid in their comfort level and gain rapport before each sibling is seen individually. If the joint sibling interview does not seem necessary, the children may be seen individually right away. Interviewing the children for the first time with both parents waiting on-site may address any concerns one or both parents may have about the other parent being the first to bring the children, or which home visit was conducted first.

CLINICAL INTERVIEWS WITH CHILDREN

Give me your evidence and don't be nervous or I'll have you executed on the spot.

[Lewis Carroll, Alice's Adventures in Wonderland, 1865]

Information obtained from the child is an integral part of the assessment. The child interview results in one type of information from one source. This information is then further investigated or crosschecked with data obtained from other sources, such as the parents and third parties. Table 4 lists the general areas of review and inquiry covered during this interview. A standard, semi-structured interview protocol that includes a full repertoire of questions is available in Appendix 8.[10] This forms the basis of the interview, with the assessor asking many of these questions routinely, while others are chosen depending on the circumstances. Additional questions not in the protocol may be asked.

Table 4

Child Interview Protocols and Areas of Review and Inquiry

- Rapport-building and socializing stage

- Introducing the assessment and limits of confidentiality (don't make false promises)

- Basic data questions (name, age, date of birth, grade, etc.)

- Lessons, activities, peers and school

- Academic, social and emotional adjustment (feelings, self-esteem, anxiety, fears, drugs, alcohol, etc.)

- Perceptions, feelings and knowledge about separation/divorce

- Perceptions and feelings about current situation (each home, parenting time arrangements, logistics of two homes, time with and apart from each parent)

- Perceptions and feelings about family functioning (related to parents, parents' relationship and siblings)

- Perceptions of relationships with each parent and parenting

- "Fantasy" questions (e.g., three wishes, desert island, dreams, nightmares)

- Future-oriented questions

The child interview allows for a general assessment of the child's emotional, academic, social and behavioural functioning and adjustment, including any special needs. Is there any indication of maltreatment, physical or sexual abuse or neglect? Information about the child's coping skills and adaptive functioning (temperament, ability to change, reactions to change and transitions, how resilient or vulnerable the child is) is important to obtain, along with a sense of what the child's life, adjustment and experiences were like both before and since the separation and what the child knows, if anything, about the reasons for the separation. What are the child's strengths and challenges? In addition, the assessor needs to query the child's feelings and perceptions about the family, the parenting received from each parent and the relationships he or she has with each parent, sibling, and step–parent. A child may inform the assessor's understanding of specific parenting behaviours, such as showing affection, setting reasonable limits, giving routine care, emotional support, attention to safety, etc.

Understanding a child's adjustment generally and specific to separation/divorce will necessarily depend on the child's gender, current age and age at separation, and time elapsed since the separation. For effective and reliable interviewing, the assessor needs to have a good working knowledge of both the clinical literature and empirical research on children's comprehension, memory and cognitive development, along with developmentally informed interviewing techniques, an understanding of children's testimony and the suggestibility and accuracy of their statements, the ability to assess for coaching and undue influence, and knowledge of the various guidelines for reliable interviewing.[11]

Wakefield (2006) reviews 24 sources including books, articles and various guidelines and recommendations made for child interviews. In at least half or more of these sources, the following are recommended:

(a) avoiding bias and exploring alternate hypotheses or explanations;

(b) videotaping interviews;

(c) interviewing the child alone unless the child is too young to separate from the parent;

(d) building rapport at the outset;

(e) using a practice interview;

(f) setting ground rules;

(g) using open-ended questions;

(h) encouraging free narrative, and if specific questions are used, pairing them with open questions;

(i) avoiding pressure, coercion, suggestion, leading and repeated questions; and

(j) not reinforcing specific responses.

Avoiding play, fantasy and imagining is recommended in 10 of the 24 sources. Fantasy means different things to different assessors, and although it is debated, the use of such a tool can be effective, depending on how and when it is used by the assessor.

Typically, children four years of age and older are interviewed. The child's age and cognitive development will determine the manner and extent of the interview. The assessor must first determine the child's cognitive ability, including his or her level of comprehension. (See Appendix 9 for further information relevant to how children think.)

What the child knows or does not know about the separation/divorce will also determine the assessment protocol. As previously mentioned, discussions with the parents (either during the orientation/contracting period or the initial individual interviews) regarding what if anything they have told the child about both the separation/divorce and the assessment are critical prior to interviewing the child.

Developing rapport with the child is the first step as it assists to establish trust and a supportive environment. The child is encouraged to talk as much as possible at his or her own pace while the assessor remains neutral (nonjudgmental) with respect to what the child is reporting (Crossman, Powell, Principe, & Ceci, 2002). Also, the assessor's role should be explained to the child. In addition, the child's role should be clarified; their input is important and will be considered, however, their preferences, if any, are only part of what the assessor considers when making his or her recommendations.

Children frequently respond by saying, "I don't know," irrespective of whether they know or not. It is helpful to assist the child at the outset to differentiate "I don't know" from "I don't understand the question" or "I don't want to say." The assessor should assist the child in differentiating these responses at the outset in a practice interview. For example, to clarify a correct "I don't know" response, the assessor might ask: "What is my cat's name?" For "I don't understand," the assessor might ask, "Do you feel *treckalocious* today?" In addition, the child needs to be given explicit permission to correct and/or disagree with the assessor. The assessor can test this out by asking what the child would do if she called him/her the wrong name.

Although the child must be told in no uncertain terms that there is no confidentiality, it may be informative to explore specifically what if anything the child is uncomfortable about revealing and why. Sometimes with discussion it turns out the child really does want the parents to know but he/she does not know how to tell them. The child may want help doing this or may give the assessor permission to do so on his/her behalf. Even though the file including the child's specific statements can ultimately be released, the assessor may exercise discretion during the verbal disclosure and in the written report by including general statements and trends as opposed to specific information identifying the child as the source. However, sometimes using the child's direct quotes can be important and revealing (e.g., in cases of alienation), as these speak for themselves and require little interpretation, if any, by the assessor.

Open-ended or free narrative questions, as opposed to closed questions that require a response to multiple choices or either a yes or no, are likely to reap the most accurate information. Focusing on specific questions would then follow these. Leading or suggestive questions should be avoided (Poole & Lamb, 1998). (See Appendix 10, "Question

Types and Examples.") Play and drawings,[12] sentence completion measures and/or games (e.g., Gardner's "Thinking, Feeling, Doing Game," or "Life") may be useful clinical tools to engage some children. Caution, though, needs to be exercised when interpreting the meaning and significance of drawings and play behaviour, as there is little if any empirical data that links these outcomes (Martindale, 2006; Wakefield, 2006).

Interviewing Children: Practice Tips

- First develop rapport.
- Use the child's words, not yours.
- Be reassuring: "Is it hard to talk about that?" "I can see you are struggling with that." "Try. . . it's okay to talk here."
- Use short, simple questions rather than run-on sentences with multiple questions.
- Try to finish one topic at a time instead of shifting back and forth between topics.
- Try not to move back and forth in chronological time.
- Give some indication or signal of a shift in topics.
- Allow time (count to 10) before you rephrase or ask the question again, or go on to new question (avoid offering a possible answer; rephrase instead).
- Children may answer even though they don't understand. Check to see if they understand the words and question by asking the same question in a somewhat different way another time. Check by asking a nonsense question and see if they react appropriately.
- Avoid pronouns, use specific names.
- Never ask the child to guess.
- Avoid "Do you remember. . .?"
- Don't ask "why" questions (child perceives blame, responsibility).
- Use other "wh" questions (What do you and your dad do together that you like?) vs. questions requiring a yes/no response (Do you and your dad have fun together?).
- Avoid leading, suggestive and repeated questions.

CHILDREN'S VIEWS AND PREFERENCES

Considerable debate exists regarding the role and weight that children's participation and preferences should receive in child custody decisions (Smart, 2002; Wallerstein, Lewis & Blakeslee, 2000; Wallerstein & Tanke, 1996; Warshak, 2003). Tapp and Henaghan (2000) from New Zealand have concluded in their work with children of separation and/or divorce that "[b]eing heard develops feelings of self-esteem, competence and relatedness which are vital to a citizen in a democracy." Smith, Taylor and Tapp (2003) challenge the assumption that children are not competent enough to be involved in decision-making about their family. Child development literature has also demonstrated that when children are actively involved in problem solving and given recognition that their ideas are important and are being heard, their confidence grows, as does their self-esteem (Baumrind, 1975; 1991). Furthermore, academic scholars such as Smart (2003), Butler, Scanlon, Robinson, Douglas and Murch (2002), Thomas and O'Kane (1998), and Moloney (2004, 2005) from the UK, along with Cashmore (2003a; 2003b) from Australia, and Smith, Taylor and Tapp (2003) from New Zealand, all advance the argument that from a practice and policy point of view, children and youth are important and competent social actors in their parents' separation and/or divorce and should have a voice in the decisions that affect their lives. This point of view appears in part to be a reaction to decades of making decisions without considering the views of children (Smart, 2003).

Children's voices alone, these writers point out, are not necessarily determinative of the issues, but rather allows children to be involved and to feel heard; their views are then taken into account in the final decision-making. Most conclude that children should not be asked directly which parent they wish to live with. Children's input then is not to dominate but to be afforded the appropriate balance and weight.

When it comes to child custody decisions, some believe that children's voices are not heard enough (Bruch, 2001a; Davies, 2004; Smart, 2002; Smith, Taylor & Tapp, 2003; Walker, Brantley & Rigsbee, 2004), while others caution that the risks associated with bringing the children into the middle of the parental conflict may cause more harm than good (Crossman, Powell, Principe & Ceci, 2002; Emery, 2003; Greenberg, Gould-Saltman & Schnider, 2006; Warshak, 2003). While some children may be able to solve problems and make rational decisions about some areas of their lives, such as extracurricular activities, these same children may not be mature enough emotionally to provide reasoned opinions and make rational decisions relating to their parents' custody dispute. In addition, while recognizing the importance of their feeling heard, many note that children do not have rights and control over many decisions, such as those relating to school, health care, discipline and extended family, and therefore should not have ultimate control over their custody and access arrangements. In addition, the accuracy of children's reports and the degree to which they may have been influenced are important considerations we return to further on.

Irrespective of this debate, consideration of a child's views and preferences is one of several criteria included in every legal best interest standard and thus germane to child custody assessments. Furthermore, in 1989 the United Nations adopted the *Convention on the Rights of the Child*,[13] which recognizes the right of children to be heard in proceedings that affect their future. The recommendations made in the parliamentary Report of the Special Joint Committee on Child Custody and Access, *For the Sake of the Children* (Ottawa: Parliament of Canada, 1998), reflect similar sentiments.

Having a competent and trained assessor interview the child to obtain his/her true views and preferences is generally accepted as preferable to having a child testify directly, given the negative impact doing so is likely to have on the child (Bala 2004). While an assessment stands distinct from therapy, the motto "Do no harm," or perhaps more realistically, "Minimize risk," prevails. Understanding the child's feelings, thoughts and perceptions are important, however not at the expense of compromising the child's adjustment by embedding the child even further into the battlefield of their parents' conflict exacerbating feelings of disloyalty, guilt and an overburdened sense of responsibility.

Social work, psychiatry and psychology professional standards and ethical codes of practice as well as child custody guidelines uniformly indicate it is *not* appropriate to ask a child to choose between his/her parents. Rather, and in the absence of the child's speaking outright about his/her preferences, a child's views and preferences can be ascertained indirectly by assessing his/her overall adjustment and the parent–child relationships, using all of the sources of information. The reports of the child are then treated as hypotheses to be tested further with the other obtained data.

A thorough review of memory development and children's testimony is beyond the scope of this chapter. In addition to the references cited in endnotes 10 and 11, Crossman, Powell, Principe, and Ceci (2002) provide an informative summary review of the literature. Briefly, they note that the accuracy of what a child reports necessarily depends on the ability to remember and what a child remembers is impacted by many complex factors. While children's reports may be accurate, they may also be inaccurate. Attention, prior knowledge and stress will impact memory development. The strength of memories will be affected by repeated exposure and memory maturation. While children's reports and memory will be based on their direct experience, these can also be based on what children have overheard or what they think they have overheard. Further, memories can be influenced by suggestions of adults (including loved ones and interviewers), selective reinforcement, exposure to negative stereotypes, creating an atmosphere of accusations, and exploitation of power differential. Summarizing the research, Crossman and her colleagues reported that children have been found to lie to avoid punishment, in the context of a game, when coached by a family member, to obtain material rewards and to avoid personal embarrassment and when they are asked to do so, even those as young as three years old.

Of particular interest is that in addition to memories being influenced by direct and implied suggestion, research has demonstrated that children can make false and distorted reports simply on the basis of being repeatedly asked yes/no questions as to whether an event that did not actually occur, did occur (Ceci & Bruck, 1995; Crossman, Powell, Principe & Ceci, 2002). This is particularly relevant in our work since children are often interviewed multiple times by different interviewers, especially in cases where allegations of abuse have been made. Children may incorrectly conclude that if a question is repeated, their first answer was incorrect and thus change that answer. Children may also incorrectly conclude that the interviewer is privy to the information the child provided previously to another interviewer.

An abundance of research demonstrates that poor interviewing can lead to invalid statements and incorrect opinions and conclusions by assessors (Ceci & Bruck, 1995; Ceci & Hembrooke, 1998; Crossman, Powell, Principe & Ceci, 2002; Kuehnle, Greenberg & Gottlieb, 2004; Underwager & Wakefield, 1998). Resources for valid methods of interviewing have been previously noted (see endnotes 10 and 11). Interviews with each child will include inquiries into their lives and relationships with both parents and the parenting they receive. Additional information may be obtained from psychological testing of the child as well as from third parties who have directly observed parent and child. It is common for these reports to differ from the child's account and stated preferences.

As previously noted, a child's stated wishes are not all equally valid across the board. Moreover, a child's preferences are not necessarily equivalent to what is in his/her best interests and furthermore may not reflect the child's real feelings. Accordingly, the child's rationale needs to be scrutinized. For example, it is not uncommon for adolescents to make poor and/or risky decisions and to have an illogical basis for making them. Both younger and older children, for different reasons, may prefer the parent who gives them what they want (e.g., candy, freedom, few limits, no chores) to the parent who gives them what they need (e.g., good diet, structure, expectations, limits). The child may want to spend more time with the parent who has more money or a larger home, or who buys them more electronics, toys, or clothing. Children's attitudes and feelings change frequently, sometimes within minutes depending on the time, day, place, and they may also change under different circumstances and with maturity.

Writers have indicated that a child's wishes should be given more weight when they are consistent over time (Wallerstein, 1995; Wallerstein & Tanke, 1996). In contrast, Warshak (2003) noted that by definition, an unduly influenced child's views are consistently expressed with conviction over time. What's more, it is not uncommon for a child's stated wishes to escalate during an assessment precisely because of the potential impact the process may have on outcome (Lee & Olesen, 2001). The child can "up the ante" with more and more concerns and complaints about the non-preferred parent, each one more bizarre than the previous. Moreover, these opinions become deeply entrenched and highly resistant to change. It is uncommon for a child who has been vehemently refusing contact with one parent to all of a sudden reverse his or her opinion and agree to resume contact. This escalation, while caused by a combination of factors and influences, is consistent with research that indicates that a person may alter contradictory beliefs to avoid dissonance, in turn making their beliefs consistent (i.e., theory of cognitive dissonance, Festinger, 1957).[14] In addition, once a person forms a negative opinion, they tend to behave in a manner that reinforces that very opinion, this being especially true when the opinion is expressed publicly (Warshak, 2003).

Those who spend any time with children know full well that their words do not always express how they genuinely feel. A child may refuse or be reluctant to see a parent for many reasons. A child may align with a needy parent and/or the one they perceive is not responsible for the divorce. In an effort to appease a parent, obtain their approval and avoid the parent's anger and disappointment, a child may say and do what he/she perceives that parent needs to hear. Accordingly, a child's stated wishes and preferences should not only be heard but also assessed for undue influence, whether it is conscious or unconscious on the part of the parent. The assessor must attempt to differentiate a realistic and understandable fear, refusal and/or reluctance to see one parent (i.e., a realistic estrangement) from an age-appropriate alignment or affinity, or from a pathological alienation.[15]

In addition, the more weight given to the child's preferences, the greater the risk that the child will be manipulated or pressured by parents (Warshak, 2003). Knowing that the child will be interviewed, parents, whether intentionally or not, often put direct or indirect pressure on the child. Influence can occur through the questions the parents ask or don't ask, and through what they say or don't say. Specific processes, conscious or unconscious, may include selective attention, repetition, intimidation, reward, punishment, overindulgence, and suggestion (Clawar & Rivlin, 1991; Waldron & Joanis, 1996; Warshak, 2003).

Warshak (2003) suggests that the more eager the child is to participate in choosing one parent over the other, the more caution should be taken in accepting these views than in a situation where the child is more reluctant to voice opinions. He advises that the less conflict there is between parents, the easier it is to listen to a child's input in a manner that eases rather than exacerbates anxiety. Furthermore, obtaining a child's preference in the context of a non-adversarial process like mediation or collaborative law poses less risk to the child because any expressed preferences cannot be used in any subsequent litigation. Kelly (2006) points out that most children know the difference between being given the opportunity to provide input into decisions that impact their lives, and being burdened with the responsibility for making adult decisions they are not prepared to make and which only add emotional stress.

Citing other research, Warshak (2003) notes that child development research (e.g., Baumrind, 1971) indicates that children are better adjusted when they are parented with an "authoritative" as opposed to an "authoritarian" or "permissive" style or approach. Authoritative parenting combines warmth and control. Warshak indicates that giving children too much control and authority even if they want it—which most do—can create excessive anxiety, a narcissistic sense of entitlement, and impaired relationships with adults. In addition, children raised in a non-authoritative environment are more likely to become impulsive, aggressive and irresponsible (Warshak, 2003).

Given that what children say may not always be what they truly want and/or is best for them, and the risks associated with empowering children to the point that their adjustment suffers, Warshak suggests that the "collective voice of children" be relied upon. This collective voice is reflected in the vast literature, both empirical and clinical, on children's long-term adjustment and on their preferences, attitudes and feelings about divorce (Ahrons, 2003; Baker, 2005a; 2005b, 2006; Fabricus & Hall, 2000; Hetherington & Kelly, 2002; Hetherington, Cox & Cox, 1985; Kelly & Emery, 2003; Laumann-Billings & Emery, 2000; Parkinson and Smythe, 2004; Pruett, Ebling & Insabella, 2004; Pruett, Williams, Insabella & Little, 2003; Wallerstein & Kelly, 1980). We explore this further in Chapter 5.

Considerable debate surrounds the degree to which children should be involved in custody decisions and the weight afforded to their input. With increasing age, a child's views and preferences, genuine or not, unduly influenced or not, tend to be given more weight by assessors and ultimately the court, which may conclude that children "vote with their feet" and that we are helpless to do anything if that is what the child chooses to do. It is important for children to be involved and to feel heard, with careful consideration given as to how this can be done without subjecting them to undue emotional burdens. Their input may assist the parents in their own views about what would be best for their children.

Still, a child's views and preferences alone are *not* determinative. The weight given to their feelings and wishes will need to take into account their age, competence, maturity, coping skills, family dynamics and parent-child relationships as well as many other factors. Treating them as hypotheses, once the child's views and preferences have been heard, weighed, and interpreted, they must be considered along with all of the other information obtained in combination with the literature, in the final analysis, of the risks and benefits of the various options for custody and access. The child's views and preferences are but one of many factors that require consideration in determining a best interest or least detrimental recommendation. Their wishes, even when they reach adolescence, do not and should not always prevail.[16]

DISCLOSURE AND REPORTING OF FINDINGS AND RECOMMENDATIONS

Disclosure

Assessors vary in their procedures for providing findings and recommendations. Some provide a comprehensive written report, including their recommendations, directly to the lawyers, who then communicate these to the parents. Others provide the written report to both the lawyers and the parties involved. Still others believe there is an ethical obligation to provide feedback (including the psychological testing results) directly to the parents. Some provide verbal feedback and written recommendations initially, followed by a comprehensive report should the parties not reach settlement.

Turning first to verbal feedback, the format for the disclosure meeting will depend on several factors, including whether there are one or two lawyers, the nature of the findings and recommendations, and potential reactions and risks based on the recommendations. Verbal feedback may be done in a joint meeting with both parents and their lawyers, or with each parent and their respective lawyers. The latter format may be unacceptable to some lawyers who maintain that *ex parte* feedback is improper. The ideal circumstance would be to provide feedback in a meeting with parents and counsel, during which an overview of the findings and recommendations and the reasons for them are summarized. Sometimes, though, this is not possible and the parents need to be seen separately.

Irrespective of the format, at least two important documents—the Sources of Information and the recommendations in the form of a Parenting Plan—accompany the verbal feedback. Additional documents may include a reference and resource list, seminal articles, and/or a prototype

Parenting Coordination Agreement if applicable.[17] If recommendations are made for further intervention or treatment, it is important that the reasons and objectives for the recommendations are provided, as well as at least two referral sources. A specific recommendation for the assessor to be able to provide relevant information to the therapist and/or for the assessment report and recommendations to be made available to subsequent professionals involved with the family is advised.

At the outset of the verbal disclosure meeting, certain rules need to be established and undertakings documented. One such rule pertains to whether or not the disclosure will be taped. Another pertains to counsel's agreement to refrain from summarizing or paraphrasing the assessor in subsequent letters or affidavits. Experience has taught us that allowing counsel to speak (in writing) for the assessor is never a good idea as they may slant what we have said to support their client's position. Invariably, we are misquoted and/or statements are taken out of context. Furthermore, while we may have said what counsel subsequently writes in a letter or affidavit, there may be many other relevant statements that are not included. In our practice, before we launch into our disclosure, we require the lawyer's undertaking to show to us anything that he/she writes about what we have said or have not said before it is released. We prefer, though, to speak for ourselves, and counsel are free to request a report or a sworn statement from us should they require any further submissions. From our experience, counsel usually agrees that this is good practice and they usually comply.

To date, guidelines, model standards and authoritative texts provide little direction with respect to delivering feedback and the recommendations to both the parents and the children. This shortcoming raises important questions: When are the children told? Are the children told the recommendations only to later be told that in fact one or both parents have not accepted them? What are the children told? Who tells them? Does each parent tell them the same thing at the same time? We believe the assessor should address these questions during the disclosure phase of the work in an effort to ensure a coordinated approach that is consistent with the children's best interests.

Some practitioners may add a caveat on the first page of the Parenting Plan Recommendations and any subsequent report, for example: "This report has been prepared for the parents, their lawyers, and the court. Under *no* circumstances should its content be revealed to the children except under the supervision of a trained professional." In addition, at the outset of the feedback meeting there is a requirement that the parents agree not to speak to the children (or let any other relative or friend do so) until after they have had a chance to assimilate the Parenting Plan recommendations and determine, with the assistance of their lawyers, whether or not a settlement can be achieved. A plan for what the children will be told about the recommendations, as well as for when and where they will be told, needs to be developed. A therapist currently involved or one who will be involved may assist the family in this regard. Alternatively, the assessor may facilitate these discussions with the children alone and/or accompanied by their parent(s).

The Report

Considerable variability exists in the type, style and substance of child custody reports. Regardless of whether it is a summary or comprehensive, the report tells the story of the assessment. Writing a good report involves training, skill and experience. There is also an art to writing a good report. A report should be easy to read and understandable. Jargon should be avoided. Recognizing there will be some variability in the style, organization and extent of substance, there are key features that differentiate a well prepared report from others. What follows is an overview of the organization and substance of the report, much of the latter available in the appendices. We pay particular attention to pitfalls and inadequacies we have come across during our consultation with peers and supervision, and based on our training and critiques of other assessments.

Organization

Careful consideration needs to be given to the organization of the report. Managing the voluminous and complex information obtained during the assessment and then writing the report can be a daunting task. Keeping a report outline in mind as the assessment progresses will assist in the management of the extensive information. A logical sequence is imperative. Specific content is more accessible and easier for the reader to locate when the report is organized with headings and subheadings. The information contained within the headings and subheadings need to accurately reflect those headings. Moreover, similar to the format of a research article, clear distinctions must be made between the four levels of inference cited by Tippins and Whittman (2005) discussed in Chapter 2. In other words, much like the results section of a research article, the reporting of statements and behaviour and test results (the data) by the children, parents and collateral sources in a custody case need to be distinguished from the assessor's inferences (clinical impressions and opinions) about psychological and custody-specific variables that are based on these data. These must then be distinguished from the assessor's parenting plan recommendations. Table 5 outlines typical headings and subheadings of the report.

Table 5

Report Headings and Subheadings[18]

I. Identifying Data

II. Referral Information and Current Situation

III. Sources of Information (may be a separate document):

(a) Interviews and Observations

(b) Professional Collateral Sources

(c) Court Documentation, Letters, Email and Reports Reviewed

(d) Collateral Sources

(e) Interpretation of Psychological Tests, Inventories & Checklist Results:

i. Completed by parents and step-parents

ii. Completed by teachers

iii. Brief summary of psychological tests and checklists used

IV. Parents' Proposals & Concerns (Section for each parent)

V. Relevant Background Summary

VI. Parents' Individual, Social, Employment Histories

VII. Summary of Reports and Behavioural Observations:

(a) Individual Parent Interviews and Self-Report Data (separate section for each parent):

i. General Observations and Approach to Assessment

ii. Response to Parenting Protocol Questions

(b) Joint Parent Interviews

(c) Individual Interviews with Children (separate section for each child)

(d) Observations:

i. Parent and Child (office and home visit)

ii. Other Observations (transition, school, daycare)

VIII. Interpretation of Psychological Test and Inventory Results

(a) Parents

(b) Children

IX. Collateral Source Reports

X.	Clinical Impressions, Opinions, Conclusions and Discussion	
XI.	Parenting Plan Recommendations (available in separate document)	

Substance

Allowing for some variability in terms of what and how much is contained within each section, a useful report should include certain information that you will find in Appendix 11. Any evaluation of an assessment occurs on the basis of the report, and subsequently on examinations and cross-examinations. While many more things are said and done during an assessment and that run through the mind of the assessor than can be included, a good report must contain enough information so that the court can be properly advised as to what exactly was done (the methodology), and in turn can evaluate the reliability and validity of the subsequent opinions, conclusions and recommendations. If best practice guidelines are not adhered to, the report needs to explain the rationale for why not.

As previously noted, the synthesis and formulation, followed by the assessor's conclusions and recommendations, must stand separate from the reporting of the obtained data (i.e., information obtained during the interviews, observations, from collateral information, psychological testing, reports, etc.). New data should not be provided in the section detailing the conclusions and recommendations. The synthesis involves hypothesis testing, in effect looking for confirming and disconfirming information within and between sources and types of information. The report should include a clearly stated rationale for how the recommendations follow logically from the data (the results), taking into account the relevant social science literature. Both the risks and benefits of the recommendations, as well as the risks and benefits of alternative options, should be included in the report. This exposition then provides the rationale for why one option was selected over another.

In addition, attention needs to be paid not only to the ultimate recommendations regarding parenting time and decision-making, but also to addressing the specific referral questions, concerns and allegations. If opinions and conclusions about the various allegations are not possible because the data are ambiguous or unavailable, this needs to be stated in the report. Clinical experience is one important component in making recommendations. Still, distinctions need to be made in the report between those conclusions that are based on the social science literature and those based on clinical experience.

A summary of *all* the data obtained from all sources—parent and child interviews, self-report questionnaires and inventories, observations, psychological testing and measures, interviews with significant others, collateral source interviews, and reports, etc.—needs to be included. Careful attention needs to be paid to avoid different types of biases that are commonly seen in assessment reports. For example, a "primacy bias" is the tendency to rely on the first pieces of the information the assessor hears, while a "recency bias" is relying on the last pieces of information the assessor hears (Martindale, 2005).

In addition, the report must include not only information that supports the conclusions and recommendations, but also that which does not. To not do this amounts to a confirmatory bias or confirmatory distortion (Martindale, 2005). In fact, noting that which does not support the conclusions, and why, often preempts this very criticism from arising in the future. In attempting to discredit the assessment (and assessor), it is common to allege that the assessor did not consider one parent's concerns and allegations sufficiently, or even at all. Anticipating the reactions and criticisms in advance and addressing these head-on in the report is likely to go some distance towards refuting this allegation (and may prevent it), and demonstrates that the assessor did in fact consider the parents' concerns and perspectives. In other words, if it is in the report, the assessor must have obtained the information.

Considerable debate continues about whether or not literature citations ought to be included in reports, which vary widely in this regard. Some maintain that for every citation supporting one perspective, another can be found refuting it, and therefore it is futile to provide any citations. While this may be the case, in our view, the report provides an opportunity to educate the professional community and the parties involved. Competing citations should also be included in the report. Keeping in mind that we are not operating from presumptions but rather on a case-by-case analysis, one vantage point may be more applicable than the other based on specific family circumstances. Ultimately, the assessor may choose to provide citations in the body of the report, at the end of the report in a reference list, or not at all. Irrespective of this decision, the assessor needs to know and be able to point specifically to the relevant literature (empirical and otherwise) that both supports and does not support the conclusions and recommendations provided.

Given the potential impact of the recommendations and the fact that we have little empirical data supporting one custody (parenting) arrangement over another (residential schedule, sole and joint legal custody), opinions and conclusions must be made cautiously, acknowledging the inherent limitations.

Reports are necessarily inflammatory; this cannot be avoided entirely. Still, while the assessor needs to "tell it like it is" and avoid being equivocal, opinions and conclusions need to be communicated in a fair and balanced manner, noting both the strengths and challenges of each parent, the latter written in as respectful a manner as possible. Parallel information needs to be provided. For example, if the report includes information on one parent's method of discipline, it should include the same type of information regarding the other parent. The assessor should avoid over-pathologizing. Positive connotation and reframing can be useful (Madanes, 1984; Watzlawick, Weakland & Fisch, 1974). Advocacy for one parent needs to be avoided; instead, the focus should be on what is in the child's best interests.

The assessor cannot be expected to be omniscient. Sometimes, the more we know, the more we don't know. Life is extremely complicated and the assessment, albeit thorough and representative of a best practice methodology, is still only a tool. It amounts to a compilation of one very large piece of evidence. There may, however, be additional information the assessor cannot reasonably be expected to ascertain. In addition, relevant events may occur after the assessment and before the trial. Acknowledging the limitations of the assessment and what we don't know is extremely important, as it demonstrates the assessor's recognition of the complexity of the task and the fact that we simply do not have empirical support for all of our recommendations.

In this chapter, we discussed the clinical assessment of parents and children during interviews and observations. Interviewing children and consideration of their views and preferences were addressed. Frameworks for assessing each parent's adjustment, parenting strengths and challenges, the quality of the parent–child relationships, the children's adjustment, and the co-parenting relationship were provided, along with detailed appendices to assist the assessor. We concluded with a discussion of the disclosure of the conclusions, recommendations and frameworks for writing reports.

Notes

1. [1986, adapted from the movie, 1994, Forest Gump].
2. For further elaboration see Ainsworth, 1979; Ainsworth, Blehar, Waters & Wall, 1978; Bowlby, 1969; 1980).
3. Two examples are the Strange Situation (Ainsworth et al., 1978) and adaptations for preschool and early-school-age children (Cassidy, Marvin & The MacArthur Working Group on Attachment, 1992).
4. The Adult Attachment Interview (AAI) is a semi-structured interview process developed by George, Kaplan & Main (1996) to assess attachment. During this interview the parents provide reports of their own childhood experiences of separation, rejection, loss, and past and current attachment experiences. Research has identified four types of adult attachments: Secure and Insecure: (a) Dismissing; (b) Preoccupied; and (c) Unresolved (Main & Goldwyn, 1998).
5. A good practice is to include the semi-structured protocol in the file, indicating with check marks, for example, which questions were asked.

6. This sample protocol is a compilation of questions obtained from the literature over 25 years of practice by the second author (see e.g., Gardner, 1999; Adult Attachment Inventory (AAI) George, Kaplan & Main, 1996; Working Model of the Child Interview (WMCI) Zeanah & Benoit, 1995; Schutz et al. 1989; Stahl, 1994).

7. Additional joint interviews may also occur later in the assessment, for example, to review the parents' proposals, agreements and impasses related to the Special and Holiday Schedules.

8. This sample protocol is a compilation of questions obtained from the literature over 25 years of practice by the second author. The cooperative, problem-solving and teaching tasks are adapted from Schutz et al., 1989.

9. The second author, by coincidence, had the opportunity to observe a father with his daughter at the local grocery store. The child had been asserting fear of her father and a strong reluctance to see him. During this observation (the parent and child did not see the assessor), the child seemed happy, laughing and engaged positively with her father, who appeared to be responsive and appropriate. This observation was reported in the assessment report.

10. This child interview protocol has been informed by general guidelines for interviewing children as well as a compilation of questions obtained from the literature over 25 years of practice by the second author, from the following sources: Bourg et al., 1999; Ceci & Bruck, 1995; Ceci & Hembrooke, 1998; Gardner, 1999; Hoorwitz, 1992; Hynan, 1998; Poole & Lamb, 1998; Schutz et al., 1989; Stahl, 1994; Zaragonza et al., 1995.

11. For further elaboration on children's competence to remember and testify and on interviewing children generally and specific to child custody assessments, the reader is referred to: Bourg, Broderick, Flagor, Kelly, Ervin & Butler, 1999; Ceci & Bruck, 1995; Bruck, Ceci & Hembrooke, 1998: Crossman, Powell, Principe, & Ceci, 2002; Gardner, 1992b; 1999b; Hoorwitz, 1992; Hynan, 1998; Kuehnle, Greenberg & Gottlieb, 2004; Poole & Lamb, 1998; Schutz et al., 1989; Underwager & Wakefield, 1989; Wakefield, 2006; Warshak, 2003; Wilson & Powell, 2001; Zaragoza, Graham, Hall, Hirschman & Ben-Porath, 1995.

12. For example, any drawing the child likes, or a drawing of the child's family doing something together.

13. Specifically, with respect to separation and/or divorce, the *United Nations Convention on the Rights of the Child* (Articles 12 and 13 in particular) provides a framework for involving children and youth in judicial and administrative proceedings, either directly or indirectly.

14. The reader may wish to explore these areas more fully in our companion book, *Special Topics in Child Custody Assessments*.

15. The literature elucidating these vehemently debated constructs and models for understanding the etiology of parent–child contact problems as well as relevant considerations for assessment follow in our companion book, *Special Topics in Child Custody Assessments*.

16. See for example, *Parks v. Barnes* (2002), [2002] O.J. No. 890, 2002 CarswellOnt 776, 24 R.F.L. (5th) 81, 157 O.A.C. 112 (Ont. C.A.); *Boukema v. Boukema* (1997), [1997] O.J. No. 5313, 1997 CarswellOnt 5151 (Ont. Gen. Div.); *Bailey v. Bailey* (June 12, 1996), Doc. Welland D13709/94, [1996] O.J. No. 4891 (Ont. Gen. Div.); *Roda v. Roda* (2000), [2000] O.J. No. 3786, 2000 CarswellOnt 3558 (Ont. S.C.J.); *Forte v. Forte*, [2004] O.J. No. 1738, 2004 CarswellOnt 1461, [2004] O.T.C. 321 (Ont. S.C.J.); *Reeves v. Reeves* (2001), [2001] O.J. No. 308, 2001 CarswellOnt 277 (Ont. S.C.J.).

17. Coates, Deutsch, Starnes, Sullivan, and Sydlik (2004) define parenting coordination as an intervention for high-conflict families whereby the parenting coordinator assists the parents in implementing their parenting plan, most typically one that has already been determined. Parenting coordinating is a hybrid role combining education, coaching, facilitation, negotiating and, where necessary, decision-making. In many jurisdictions,

some governed by legislation and some not (as in Ontario), the parenting coordinator has final decision-making authority for matters unrelated to legal custody decisions (i.e., health/welfare, education and religion), permanent changes to the residential schedule, and jurisdictional moves. In sole legal custody situations, one parent may have final decision-making authority, while in joint legal custody, the parenting coordinator may be authorized to make final decisions if the parents cannot agree. See AFCC Task Force on Parenting Coordination, (2003) and Parenting Coordination: Implementation Issues, *Family Court Review* (2003), 41, 533-564. Also, see *Guidelines for Parenting Coordination* developed by the AFCC Task Force on Parenting Coordination, May, 2005, which can be found at: http://www.afccnet.org.

[18.]   More recently, we have noted the practice of providing an "executive summary" on the first page of the report.

References

Achenbach, T.M. & Edelbrock, C. *Manual for the Child Behavior Checklist 4-18* (Burlington, VT: Queen City Printers, 1991).

Ackerman, M.J. "Transfusion maybe, laid to rest, no: A response to the Mary Connell review of the Ackerman-Schoendorf Scales for Parent Evaluation of Custody (ASPECT)" Journal of Child Custody 2:1/2 (2005b), 211-214.

Ackerman, M.J. *Clinician's Guide to Child Custody Evaluations, Third Edition* (New Jersey: John Wiley and Sons, Inc., 2006).

AFCC Model Standards of Practice for Child Custody Evaluation (Task Force for Model Standards of Practice for Child Custody Evaluation 2004, revised 2007).

Ahrons, C.R. & Tanner, J.L. "Adult children and their fathers: Relationship changes 20 years after parental divorce" Family Relations 52 (2003), 340–351.

Ainsworth, M. D.S. "Infant-mother attachment" American Psychologist 34 (1979), 932–937.

Ainsworth, M. D. S., Blehar, M., Waters, E. & Wall, S. *Patterns of Attachment: A Psychological Study of the Strange Situation* (Hillsdale, NJ: Lawrence Erlbaum, 1978).

Austin, W. & Kirkpatrick, H.D. "The investigation component in forensic mental health evaluations: Considerations for parenting time assessments" Journal of Child Custody 1:2 (2004), 23–46.

Baker, A.J.L. "Parent alienation strategies: A qualitative study of adults who experienced parental alienation as a child" Journal of Forensic Psychology 23:4 (2005a), 41–64.

Baker, A.J.L. "The long-term effects of parental alienation on adult children: A qualitative research study" The American Journal of Family Therapy 33 (2005b), 289–302.

Baker, A.J.L. "Patterns of parental alienation syndrome: A qualitative study of adults who were alienated from a parent as a child" The American Journal of Family Therapy 34 (2006), 63–78.

Bala, N. "Alienation of children: Conflict reduction strategies & Ontario legal responses" Presented at the National Family Law Program of the Federation of Law Societies of Canada (La Malbaie, PQ, 2004).

Baumrind, D. "Current patterns of parental authority" Developmental Psychology Monograph 4:1, Part 2 (1971), 1–103.

Ben-Porath, Y.S., Graham, J.R., Hall, G.C.N., Hirschman, R.D. & Zaragoza, M.S. (Eds.). *Forensic Application of the MMPI-2* (Thousand Oaks, CA: Sage, 1995).

Bourg, W., Broderick, R., Flagor, R., Kelly, D. M., Ervin, D. L. & Butler, J. *A Child Interviewer's Guidebook* (Thousand Oaks, CA: Sage Publications, 1999).

Bruch, C. "Parental alienation syndrome and parental alienation: Getting it wrong in child custody cases" Family Law Quarterly 35 (2001a), 527–552.

Bruch, C. "Parental alienation syndrome: Junk science in child custody determinations" European Journal of Law Reform (2001b), 383–404.

Bruck, M., Ceci, S.J. & Hembrooke, H. "Reliability and credibility of young children's reports: From research to policy and practice" American Psychologist 53:2 (1998), 136–151.

Budd, K.S. "Assessing parenting competence in child protection cases: A clinic practice model" Clinical Child and Family Psychology Review 4 (2001), 1–18.

Butler, I., Scanlon, L., Robinson, M., Douglas, G. & Murch, M. "Children's involvement in their parents' divorce: Implications for practice" Children and Society 16:2 (2002), 89–102.

Byrne, J.G., O'Conner, T.G., Marvin, R.S. & Whelan, W.F. "Practitioner review: The contribution of attachment theory to child custody assessments" Journal of Child Psychology and Psychiatry 46:2 (2005), 115–127.

Calloway, G.C., Grace, N. & Lee, S.M. "How Attachment Relationships Inform Custody Evaluators" Workshop presented at the 43rd Annual Conference, Association of Family and Conciliation Courts (Tampa Bay, FLA: June 1, 2006).

Cashmore, J. (2003a). Linking research, policy and practice: Including children's input. *Childrenz Issues, 7(2)*, 12-17.

Cashmore, J. (2003b). Children's participation in family law matters. In C. Hallett & A. Prout (Eds.), *Hearing the voices of children: Social policy for a new century* (pp. 158-176). London: The Falmer Press.

Cassidy J. & Shaver, P.R. (Eds.) *Handbook of Attachment: Theory, Research and Clinical Applications* (New York: Guildford Press, 1999).

Ceci, S. & Bruck, M. "Jeopardy in the courtroom: A scientific analysis of children's testimony" Washington, D.C. American Psychological Association (1995).

Clawar, S. & Rivlin, B. *"Children Held Hostage: Dealing with Programmed and Brainwashed Children"* (American Bar Association Section of Family Law, 1991).

Crossman, A., Powell, M.B., Principe, G.F. & Ceci, S. "Child testimony in custody cases: A review" Journal of Forensic Psychology Practice 2 (2002), 1-31.

Davies, C.D. "Access to justice for children: The voice of the child in custody and access disputes" Canadian Family Law Quarterly 22:2 (2004), 153–175.

Emery, R.E. "Children's voices: Listening – and deciding – is an adult responsibility" Arizona Law Review 45 (2003), 621–627.

Fabricus, W. & Hall, J. "'Young adults' perspectives on divorce: Living arrangements" Family and Conciliation Courts Review 38 (2000), 446–461.

Festinger, L. *A Theory of Cognitive Dissonance* (Stanford, CA: Stanford University Press, 1957).

Fidler, B.J. & Birnbaum, R. "Child custody disputes: Private and public assessments" Canadian Family Law Quarterly 25:2 (2006), 137–167.

Gardner, R. *The Parental Alienation Syndrome: A Guide for Mental Health and Legal Professionals* (Cresskill, New Jersey: Creative Therapeutics, Inc., 1992a, with updated addenda in 1994 and 1996).

Gardner, R. *True and False Allegations of Child Sex Abuse* (Cresskill, New Jersey: Creative Therapeutics, Inc. 1992b).

Gardner, R.A. "Guidelines for assessing parental preference in child custody disputes" Journal of Divorce and Remarriage 30:1/2 (1999a), 1–9.

Gardner, R. "Differentiating between the parental alienation syndrome and bona fide abuse/neglect" The American Journal of Family Therapy 27 (1999b), 97–107.

George, C., Kaplan, N. & Main, M. *Adult Attachment Interview (3rd Ed.)* (Berkeley, CA: University of California at Berkeley, Department of Psychology, 1985).

Gould, J.W. *Conducting Scientifically Crafted Child Custody Evaluations* (Thousand Oaks, CA: Sage Publications, 1998).

Gould, J.W. "Scientifically crafted child custody evaluations: Part One: A model for interdisciplinary collaboration in the development of psycho-legal questions guiding court-ordered child custody evaluations" *Family and Conciliation Courts Review* 37:1 (1999), 64–73.

Gould, J.W. *Conducting Scientifically Crafted Child Custody Evaluations*, 2nd Ed. (Sarasota, Florida: Professional Resource Exchange, Inc., 2006).

Greenberg, M. T. "Attachment and psychopathology in childhood" in *Clinical Implications of Attachment* (Eds.) Cassidy, J. and Shaver, P.R. (New York: Guilford Press, 1999), 469–496.

Greenberg, L.R., Gould-Saltman, D.J. & Schnider, R. "The problem with presumptions – A review and commentary" Journal of Child Custody 3:3/4 (2006), 139–172.

Hetherington, E.M., Cox, M. & Cox, R. "The long-term effects of divorce and remarriage on the adjustment of children" Journal of the American Academy of Child Psychiatry 24 (1985), 518–530.

Hetherington, E. M. & Kelly, J.B. *For Better or for Worse: Divorce Reconsidered* (New York: Norton & Company, 2002).

Hesse, E. "The Adult Attachment Interview: Historical and current perspectives" in J. Cassidy & P.R. Save (Eds.) *Handbook of Attachment: Theory, Research and Clinical Applications* (New York: Guildford Press, 1999), 395–433.

Hoorwitz, N.A. *The Clinical Detective: Techniques in the Evaluation of Sexual Abuse* (New York: W.W. Norton & Company, 1992).

Hynan, D.J. "Interviewing children in custody evaluations" Family and Conciliation Courts Review 36:4 (1998), 466–478.

Johnston, J.R., Lee, S., Olesen, N.W. & Walters, M.G. "Allegations and Substantiations of Abuse in Custody Disputing Families" Family Court Review 43:2 (2005), 283-294.

Kelly, J.B. "Children's living arrangements following separation and divorce: Insights from empirical and clinical research" Family Process 46:1 (2006), 35–52.

Kelly, J.B. & Emery, R. "Children's adjustment following divorce: Risk and resilience perspectives" Family Relations 52 (2003), 352–362.

Kirkpatrick, H.D. "A floor, not a ceiling: beyond guidelines – an argument for minimum standards of practice in conducting child custody and visitation evaluations" Journal of Child Custody 1:1 (2004), 61–75.

Kuehnle, K. Coulter, M. & Firestone, G. "Child Protection evaluations: The forensic stepchild" Family and Conciliation Courts Review 38 (2000), 368–391.

Kuehnle, K., Greenberg, L.R. & Gottlieb, M.C. "Incorporating the principles of scientifically based child interviews into family law cases" Journal of Child Custody 1:1 (2004), 97–114.

Laumann-Billings, L. & Emery, R.E. "Distress among young adults in divorced families" Journal of Family Psychology 14 (2000), 671–687.

Lee, S. M. & Olesen, N.W. "Assessing for alienation in child custody and access evaluations" Family Court Review 39:3 (2001), 282–298.

Madanes, C. Behind the One-Way Mirror: Advances in the Practice of Strategic Therapy (San Francisco: Jossey Bass, 1984).

Main, M. & Goldwyn, R. "Adult Attachment Scoring and Classification System" Unpublished manuscript, Department of Psychology, University of California at Berkeley (1998).

Main, M. & Hesse, E. "Parent's unresolved traumatic experiences are related to infant disorganization attachment status: Is frightened and/or frightening parental behavior the linking mechanism?" in M.T. Greenberg, D. Ciocchetti & E.M. Cummings (Eds.) Attachment in the Preschool Years: Theory Research and Intervention (Chicago: University of Chicago Press, 1990), 161–182.

Martindale, D.A. "Confirmatory bias and confirmatory distortion" Journal of Child Custody 2:1/2 (2005), 31–48.

Martindale, D. A. "Play therapy doesn't play in court" Journal of Child Custody 3:1 (2006), 77–86.

Marvin, Robert, Cooper, Glen, Hoffman, Kent and Powell, Bert. "The circle of security project: Attachment-based intervention with caregiver-preschool dyads" (2002).

Moloney, L. "Children in family law: Moving beyond the 'best interests' rhetoric" Journal of Family Studies 10:2 (2004), 160–169.

Moloney, L. "Children voices: Reflections on the telling and the listening" Journal of Family Studies 11:2 (2005), 216–226.

Poole, D. & Lamb, M. *Investigative Interviews of Children: A Guide for Helping Professionals* (Washington, D.C.: American Psychological Association, 1998).

Pruett, M., Ebling, R. & Insabella, G. "Critical aspects of parenting plans for young children: Interjecting data into the debate about overnights" Family Court Review 42:1 (2004), 39–59.

Pruett, M., Williams, T., Insabella, G. & Little, T. "Family and legal indicators of child adjustment to divorce among families with young children" Journal of Family Psychology 17:2 (2003), 169–180.

Schmidt, F., Cuttress, L.J., Lang. J., Lewandowski, M. & Rawana, J.S. "Assessing the parent-child relationship in parenting capacity evaluations: Clinical applications of attachment research" Family Court Review 45:2 (2007), 247–259.

Schutz, B., Dixon, E., Lindenberger, J. & Rutter, N. *Solomon's Sword: A Practice Guide to Conducting Child Custody Evaluations* (San Francisco: Jossey Bass, 1989).

Smart, C. "From children's shoes to children's voices" Family Court Review 40 (2002), 307–319.

Smart, C. "Introduction: New perspectives on childhood and divorce" Childhood 10:2 (2003), 123–129.

Smith, A.B., Taylor, N.J. & Tapp, P. "Rethinking children's involvement in decision-making after parental separation" Childhood 10:2 (2003), 201–216.

Stahl, P. *Conducting Child Custody Evaluations* (CA: Sage Publications, 1994).

Steinhauer, P.D. "Assessing for parenting capacity" Journal of Orthopsychiatry 53 (1983), 468–481.

Tapp, P. & Henaghan, M. "Family Law: Conceptions of childhood and children's voices – The implications of Article 12 of the United Nations Convention on the Rights of the Child" in A. Smith, N.J. Taylor & M. Gollop (Eds.) *Children's voices: Research, policy and practice* (Auckland, NZ: Pearson Education, 2000), 91–109.

Thomas, N. & O'Kane, C. "When children's wishes and feelings clash with their 'best interests'" International Journal of Children's Rights 6 (1998), 137–154.

Tippins, T.M. & Wittmann, J.P. "Empirical and ethical problems with custody recommendations: A call for clinical humility and judicial vigilance" Family Court Review 43:2 (2005), 193–222.

Underwager, R. & Wakefield, H. "Evaluating the child witness in sexual abuse cases: interview or inquisition?" American Journal of Forensic Psychology 7:3 (1989), 43–69.

van IJzendoorn, M.H. "Adult attachment representations, parental responsiveness, and infant attachment. A meta-analysis on the predictive validity of the Adult Attachment Interview" Psychological Bulletin 117 (1995), 387–403.

Wakefield, H. "Guidelines on investigatory interviewing of children: What is the consensus in the scientific community?" American Journal of Forensic Psychology 24:3 (2006), 57–74.

Waldron, K.H. & Joanes, D.E. "Understanding and collaboratively treating parental alienation syndrome" American Journal of Family Law 10:3 (1996), 121–133.

Walker, L., Brantley, K. & Rigsbee, J. "A critical analysis of parental alienation syndrome and its admissibility in the family court" Journal of Child Custody 1:2 (2004), 47–74.

Wallerstein, J.S. "Amica Curiae Brief of Dr. Judith S. Wallerstein, Ph.D. filed in Cause No. SO46116" In re Marriage of Burgess (Supreme Court of the State of California, December 7, 1995).

Wallerstein, J.S. & Kelly, J.B. *Surviving the Breakup: How Children and Parents Cope with Divorce* (New York: Basic Books, 1980).

Wallerstein, J.S., Lewis, J. & Blakeslee, S. *The Unexpected Legacy of Divorce: A 25-Year Landmark Study* (New York: Hyperion, 2000).

Wallerstein, J.S & Tanke, T. "To move or not to move" Family Law Quarterly 30:5 (1996), 1–18.

Warshak, R.A. "Payoffs and pitfalls of listening to children" Family Relations 52:4 (2003), 373–384.

Waltzlawick, P., Weakland, Ch.E. & Fisch, R. *Change: Principles of Problem Formation and Problem Resolution* (New York: W.W. Norton & Company, 1974).

Wilson, J.C., & Powell, M.B. *A guide to interviewing children.* (Sydney, Austrailia: Allen & Unwin, 2001).

Zaragoza, M. S., Graham, J. R., Hall, G. C. N., Hirschman, R. & Ben-Porath, Y. S. (Eds.) *Memory and Testimony in the Child Witness* (Thousand Oaks, CA: Sage Publications, 1995).

Zeanah, C.H. & Benoit, D. "Clinical applications of parent perception interview in infant mental health" Child and Adolescent Psychiatric Clinics of North America 4 (1995), 439–554.

Appendix 6

Standard Parent Semi-Structured Interview Protocol[1]

JOINT INTERVIEWS WITH PARENTS

1. **Orientation** (1–1.5 hours; done individually if joint meeting inappropriate)

    *   Review Parenting Plan Assessment Retainer Agreement.

    *   Clarify what children have been told about assessment. There may not be enough time to review that information, but at the very least the assessor should gain an agreement that the children not to be told anything until further discussions take place.

2. **Standard Marital History** (1–1.5 hours; may be done jointly or individually)

    *   Courtship: how the parents met, what they liked about the other person when they first met and then later after getting to know them.

    *   Were their families in favour of the union?

    *   Whether yes or no, how did their families impact on their marriage?

    *   If there were "in-law problems," elaborate; how did the spouse deal with this?

    *   How did the marriage go. . . good and not so good.

    *   When did problems begin? Were they always there or was there a specific precipitant, or two or three?

    *   What were the problems about? What were the hot spots, or areas of conflict (e.g., children, money, in-laws, sex, division of labour, work, etc.).

    *   How did the conflict manifest; assess the nature/dimensions of conflict *and* level/intensity (the assessor may wish to use screening tools).

    *   What was the marriage like before problems began? Before children?

- What efforts were made to resolve difficulties (i.e., talking, therapy); elaborate on what was tried and why it didn't work.

- Nature and extent of conflict-resolution, problem-solving

- Explore physical, sexual and emotional abuse.

- If yes to abuse, obtain details (see abuse screening tools).

- Explore their thoughts if they haven't spoken of this: "Most marriages take two to work and usually in most cases both parents contribute to the breakdown. What would you say your part in the breakdown of the marriage was?"

- Who initiated the separation?

- Assess with various questions where each parent is on the separation process continuum.

3. **Additional Joint Interviews**

- To review holiday and special day schedule.

INDIVIDUAL INTERVIEWS WITH PARENTS (at least three or four interviews, sometimes more; sequence may vary)

1. **First Meeting:**

- Why are we here? What do you think is most important for me to know? (It is important for each parent to feel you have heard his/her story, and that you understand what they have been through. This could take all of first interview time.)

- Obtain proposals for decision-making (legal custody: sole, joint, shared, etc.).

- Obtain proposals, if any, for residential usual schedule.

- Why are the above proposals best for the children?

- Are they open to the assessor's recommendations about what might be best for the children after a thorough assessment is completed, or are they clear what they want and think children need and hoping for validation of this from the assessment process?

- Canvass and explore concerns about the other parent vis-à-vis children's best interests.

- What can the other parent do to satisfy these concerns?

- What do you like about the other parent?

- Get marital history, if not obtained in joint session, or follow up in individual session on some points raised in the joint meeting. (You may not get to this in first meeting.)

2. **Subsequent Individual Interviews**

Separation History (review from time of physical separation until the present; first or second meeting):

- Obtain a detailed account of what happened since the physical separation, or if in same house the date of separation in terms of each parent's time with the children

- What are the current parenting arrangements: what works, what doesn't, and why?

- Examine how roles, functions, responsibilities are shared before and since separation.

- Review parents' communication: nature and level of conflict, conflict-resolution and problem solving skills.

- Look at "a day in the life".

- Obtain information about children's behaviour, activities, reactions.

- Ascertain what, where, how, when have the children been told about the separation.

Individual History (second or third meeting):

- Tell me about your childhood upbringing: where you were born, siblings, parents?

- What was life like growing up in your family?

- Were there any moves?

- Did your parents work outside the home? What type, hours, etc.?

- Siblings: what are they doing now, where are they living, their families, the quality and quantity of relationship with each?

- Grandparents' roles, and those of other extended family members.

- Were others living in the home?

- What kind of marriage did your parents have?

- Did they argue much? How (i.e., out loud or silent and distant)?

- How did they resolve conflict?

- Were alcohol or drugs a problem for either of your parents?

- Was there a family history of mental illness?

- If they divorced, probe the circumstances, custody, etc.

- Describe your relationship with each parent as a young child.

- Describe your relationship with each parent now.

- Provide three to five adjectives that reflect your relationship with your mother/father as a young person; explain the memories/experiences that led you to choose each one.

- What are the good and bad qualities of each parent?

- Which parent did you feel closest to? Why? Why not with the other?

- How were you alike and unalike each parent?

- Upsets as a child (e.g., hurt physically, ill, hurt feelings)? Who did you go to? What did your mother, your father do?

- Separations (including first) from parents? Impact?

- Did you ever feel rejected, abandoned, betrayed? Of course, looking back you may realize it was not really rejection, but as a child you felt that; why did your parent do that? Did your parent realize he/she was acting in a way that caused you to feel rejected?

- How were you disciplined (spanked, isolated)? What would you have to do for that to happen? What was the impact on you then and now?

- Were your parents ever threatening, maybe while disciplining, or perhaps as a joke? Did you ever feel threatened or afraid when your parents disciplined you? What was the impact of that on you then and now?

- How have these experiences with your own parents affected your personality, how you relate to others at work, or to your spouse and as a parent?

- What are the lessons you learned from how you were parented—positive or negative?

- Were you ever physically, sexually, or emotionally abused by parents or anyone else? Expand on this. What was the impact on you then and now?

- Have you suffered any other traumas (car accident, rape, mugging, etc.)? Explain the impact on you then and now.

- Have you had significant losses? Who, when, how; what were the circumstances? Describe the impact on you then and now.

- If these losses occurred when you were a child, how did it affect your parents, your family?

- Were there any other adults you were close to, who made a difference in your life and to who you are today?

- Impact question: Looking back through your entire life is there a person or event, positive or negative, that made a significant impact on you and who you are today? What would that be?

- What have you learned from your own childhood experiences?

- Mental-health history: list all therapists, counsellors, etc., as child, adolescent and adult to date, psychiatric hospitalizations, psychotropic medications, reasons for ending, changing therapy, etc.

- Review current medical health, problems.

- Review educational and academic history.

- Discuss peer relationships during school years.

- Examine friendships now, how many close friends, etc.

- Discuss criminal history, trouble with the law as child, adolescent, adult to date.

- History of alcohol and drug use: current quantity and frequency use.

- How do you spend your leisure time, hobbies, interests, activities?

- Previous significant relationships, common-law, previous marriages? How did they end? Why?

- Do you have other children? Explore that marriage, separation, role in children's lives.

- Work history: review Parent Intake and ask about moves from job to job and why.

- What would happen if your scheduled work hours conflicted with a special event at school? Or if child is ill?

- What are the work-related skills that you do well?

- As a person, what is your biggest strength? Your biggest challenge/limitation?

- What is the other parent's biggest strength? His/her biggest challenge, biggest limitation?

- Discuss current new relationships, dating, how serious, children part of that, etc.?

3. **Parenting Assessment Protocol** (third or fourth meeting; some of this information may be obtained from Child Questionnaire which can be used as spring board)

Pregnancy, Delivery/Labour, Developmental History:

- Consider previous questions asked about the parent's relationship with own parents.

- Pregnancy: planned, wish for children, number, gender preference.

- Nature of labour and delivery.

- Post-partum depression.

- Type of baby in terms of temperament: easy; slow to warm up; fussy; colicky.

- How did routines go: breast-fed, bottle-fed, sleeping, bathing?

- Developmental milestones: smiling; laughing; sitting up; crawling; walking, first single word, three words, sentences, toileting night and day.

- How did baby and, later, young child respond to separations?

- Do you have pictures of your child with you?

- Who took the child to the doctor, dentist?

- Describe a typical weekday/weekend day from morning until bedtime and each parent's involvement (see task list).

Perceptions of Child and Parents' Relationship with Child:

- What are your child's favourite activities and interests?

- What makes your child feel happy, excited, sad, scared, worried?

- Describe the strengths and challenges of your child.

- What parts of child would you like to change?

- How would you describe your child's personality? Choose three to five adjectives and give examples from experience that makes you think this.

- How is your child like you? Different?

- How is your child like other parent? Different?

- How would you describe your relationship with your child?

- How would you describe your child's relationship with other parent?

- What do you think should change about your relationship with your child?

- What do you think should change about your child's relationship with other parent?

- How have you affected your child's personality?

- How has other parent affected your child's personality?

- What would you say has been a setback for your child?

- Tell me a favourite story you have about your child.

- What is unique about your child?

- How would you describe your relationship with the child? Choose three to five adjectives.

- As you look ahead, what do you think might be difficult for your child?

- As you look ahead, what do you think your child might find easy?

Parenting Practices, Strengths, Challenges:

- What do you see as your parenting strengths? Challenges?

- What do you see as the other parent's parenting strengths? Challenges?

- What do you think the other parent will say about your parenting strengths? Challenges?

- Do you have any regrets? What would you do differently as a parent?

- Name three wishes for your child, 20 years from now.

- What do you hope child might have learned from his/her experiences of being parented by you?

- What is your experience with caring for children prior to having had children?

- What do children need most?

- What are your aspirations for your child?

- Most parents have challenges. What are you really good at and what could you do better or do you need to learn more about?

- Have you read anything on parenting (or taken courses or seminars)? If so, what? If not, why? What have you found most helpful about your reading?

- What is the best thing you ever did for your child?

- What is the worst thing you ever did as a parent?

- What do you find easiest about parenting? Hardest?

- What do you like most about parenting? Like Least?

- What does your spouse think about your parenting? Your assets and your limitations?

- What do you think about your spouse's parenting? Assets and limitations?

- What is your approach to discipline?

- What do you discipline for?

- Do you spank? For what deed? How often? With what? When, where, and how?

- Tell me about the last time you got too angry at your child?

- What might you do if your child (pick several that seem age-appropriate for now and in the future):

  - refuses to eat, refuses a simple request when you are busy (e.g., to answer the door), is rude, hides from you/does not respond to calls when you are rushing/late, interrupts, has temper tantrums, whines, demands an item/argues in a store, lies, uses profanity, climbs on the table when you have said no, wanders off when you have told him/her to stay nearby, won't share with other children his/her age, accidentally breaks something and does not tell you, refuses to do homework, argues about bedtime, refuses to go to bed, is rude to elders or grandparents, fights with siblings, engages in sex play with another child, refuses to eat, breaks your favourite item and then lies, becomes pregnant at 15, masturbates, uses drugs?

- Follow-up questions: What if he/she does the same thing again the next day? What would you do then? What would you probably do if he/she did it again?

- Does your child have chores?

- Does your child get an allowance? What is the system for the allowance?

- Does your child have friends in, go out to see friends, get invited to birthday parties?

- How does Hallowe'en happen? Who makes the costume?

- How involved are you at your child's school? Specifics?

- What are the child's teachers' names?

- Does your child do activities outside of school?

- Do you want your child to go to college or university? Why?

- Prior to the separation, which parent took the children to the doctor and dentist, or took time off work when they were ill?

- Explore various tasks and what percent each parent did:

   - getting child up, dressed, getting breakfast, bathing, preparing meals, food shopping, clothes shopping, homework, getting up in middle of night, registering and taking to activities, taking to and picking up from school

- What have you told and/or taught your child about sex and sex education?

- Questions asked of parents who have school-age children in order to understand the parent's ability to deal with age-appropriate issues:

   How does your child like school (and teachers)?
   How does your child get along with peers?
   How does your child express himself if he is angry?
   Is she/he afraid to be alone for short time?
   Does your child have nightmares or other signs of emotional distress?
   Has your child started to sleep over at friends' houses?
   Does your child show frequency following rules, dealing with authority?

- Questions asked of parents who have adolescents in order to understand the parent's ability to deal with age-appropriate issues:

   How does your child deal with authority?
   Does your child get excited, afraid to get more independent?

Does your child push your rules and limits very much?
Is your child open to talking with you about sex, drugs, peers, school, etc.?
Is your child responsible for his/her age?
Does your child have ideas about what he/she wants to do when finished high school?
Does your child have a job after school or on weekends?

Approach to Separation/Divorce, Other Parent, Future Parenting:

- What have you told the children about the separation, about the reasons why etc.? What was the child's reaction?

- What have you told the children about this assessment?

- How important do you think the child's preferences are in making decisions about legal custody and residential schedule?

- What do you think are the obstacles in the way of your improving your relationship with the other parent? What suggestions do you have for improving this?

- Are you aware of the impact that the way you relate to the other parent has on your child? How could you improve this? To what extent can you compromise?

- What have you told (or do you tell) the child about other parent?

- What questions has the child asked about the other parent, about the separation?

- How does your arguing with the other parent affect your child?

- How do you suppose your feelings about the other parent affects your child?

- What do you sometimes do to contribute to the problems between you and the other parent?

- How did you make decisions about school, doctors, vacations, religion, etc. when you were married?

- How do you make these decisions now?

- How are the rules different in each home?

- When you try to talk to the other parent about the children, what happens?

- When you have school and other information, how does that get to the other parent?

- How does the child treat you in front of the other parent?

- Who attends the child's events and how does the child deal with it when both parents are present?

- What can you do to help disengage from the other parent to help your children?

- What can you do to share in the parenting with the other parent more cooperatively?

4. Investigating and Addressing Concerns of the Other Parent

Final Interview:

We've talked about a lot of things. Is there anything else you want me to know or is there anything you would like me to ask?

- To ensure parents feel heard and process was fair.

- Overly critical parents tend to criticize one last time.

- Child-focused parents tend to express feelings, thoughts, and concerns about children and their needs.

[1.] A compilation of questions obtained from the literature over 25 years of practice by the second author (see e.g., Gardner, 1999; Adult Attachment Inventory (AAI) George, Kaplan & Main, 1996; Working Model of the Child Interview (WMCI) Zeanah & Benoit, 1995; Schutz, et al. 1980, Stahl, 1994).

Appendix 7[1]

Family Interview

1. Meet with parents and children to introduce them to the assessment process, to assess family processes one-half to one hour required; usually done in assessor's office, but may be in the home if parents are living in the same home).

    *   Child's age, birthday, school, grade.

    *   Knowledge of separation or not (determines what can be covered).

    *   Socializing stage.

    *   Acknowledge that the process may be uncomfortable; determine who may be most uncomfortable (ask kids).

    *   Ask the child/ren: Do you know why your mom and dad have brought you here today?

    *   What has your mom and dad told you? (Also ask this again in individual interview). Ask parents to explain *or* explain and elaborate thus: I am helping parents to come up with plans for children, how to share job of parenting.

    *   Assure the child/ren that children do not make these decisions, and that we do care about how they think and feel.

    *   Parent to each give each child permission to be honest, to not worry about parent's feelings, to tell parents whatever they want, and assure child that parent will not ask child what we talked about.

    *   Review limits of confidentiality (may do this alone with child).

HOME VISITS

1. Spontaneous observations (e.g., eating meal, whatever activity parent/child chooses).

2. Structured activity: play game; family activity; drawing (e.g., "draw a picture of your family doing something together").

PARENT–CHILD OFFICE OBSERVATIONS

1. Observation of each child with each parent doing structured tasks (choose age-appropriate task; takes up to one hour).

Cooperative Task:

Examples: plan a vacation, build best possible house in Lego, replicate sample, draw a picture together, observe clean-up

The assessor could also choose a real-life topic the parent and child are dealing with and/or in conflict about.

Problem-Solving Task:

Examples:

Ages 3–5: "What are the things a mother could do about a little girl who always leaves her toys all over the floor?"

Ages 6–11: "What possible things could a parent do about a child who keeps hitting other kids, and what are some of the reasons a child would do this?"

Age 12 and over: "What are the things that could be done to help a kid who kept getting bad grades, and which things would be the best?

Again, the assessor could also choose a real-life topic that parent and child are dealing with and/or in conflict about.

Teaching Task:

Examples: shape ball, card game, tie a shoelace, write a cheque, sew a button.

[1.] Based on an idea taken originally from Schutz et al. (1989).

Appendix 8

Child Interview Protocol[1]

1. HOW TO ANSWER:

    - I don't know.

    - I don't want to say.

    - I don't understand question.

    - I'm afraid to answer.

2. CONFIDENTIALITY:

    - Explain that there is no confidentiality when it comes to safety.

    - Explain that you can hold back on specific words (in report and to parents), but may have to share in general terms what the child has said.

    - Explain that you can use discretion.

    - At the end of *each* interview, ask the child if there is anything they do not want their parents to know.

    - If so, why? What are the concerns? What is the worst thing they worry will happen if their parents know?

    - Do they want or is it okay if the assessor tells their mother/father this?

    - Do they want the assessor to help them to speak to their parents about that?

3. SIMPLE DATA QUESTIONS:

    - Name, age, birthday, grade, school, teachers' names, pets.

    - Likes, dislikes regarding subjects in school.

    - What they are really good at in school, and not so good at.

    - Strengths outside school.

    - What he/she likes to do outside of school: activities; games; television shows.

    - Sports, lessons, activities. Parents' involvement in these.

    - Who is in your family?

4. PEERS:

- Ask neutral and easy questions about friends: how many; names; what you like to do with friends, etc.

- What about your best friend? Problems making friends?

- What do you like to do when you are with your friends?

- Do your friends come over to play? Do you go to their house? Where (how far away) do they live?

- Do you have any problems, worries about friends, keeping friends, being teased?

- Are you lonely?

5. SCHOOL:

- About school: likes; dislikes; teachers; what is easiest; most fun; hardest; what are you best in; not so good at; most challenged by?

- What's your favourite subject? Least favourite?

- Do you have other problems at school? Are there things that are really hard for you?

- How well do you do at school?

6. HETEROSEXUAL INTERESTS:

- Probe: Boyfriend, girlfriend; how long, how many.

7. GENDER IDENTITY:

- What are your favourite toys?

- Who do you want to be like?

8. HOBBIES:

- Probe games, activities, lessons they like.

- Activities at school, out of school: who takes you to these activities; how does it feel with both parents there? Does the child want that if that doesn't occur, or prefer as is?

9. FUTURE:

- What do you want to be when you grow up?

10. AFFECT/MOOD:

- Using the terms happy, sad, worried, scared, upset, nervous, angry:

- What makes you feel _____?

- What do you do when you feel _____?

- Who do you tell when you feel _____?

- Most kids _____ (worry) at a time like this. What do you worry about?

- What makes you nervous?

- Are you a happy kid, a sad kid?

- One boy said he worried about _____. Do you ever worry about that?

11. SELF-ESTEEM:

- Do you wish you were someone else?

- What do you like about yourself?

- Do you ever hate yourself?

- If there was one thing you could change about yourself, what would it be?

12. EMPATHY/CONSCIENCE:

- Do you feel badly when you hurt someone? Why?

13. PERCEPTUAL DISTORTIONS:

- Do you ever: hear voices; feel things crawling on you; see things others don't?

14. THOUGHT DISORDER:

- Do you ever think someone is out to get you?

- Do you ever think you are really someone else?

- Does something make you do things?

15. ANXIETY:

- Do you ever feel afraid that you can't get enough air, and think you'll die?

16. TYPICAL DAY:

- Tell me about an ordinary weekday/weekend day from the time you get up (with each parent) to when you go to sleep. (Begin in an open-ended way, then go on to specifics about waking up, getting ready, having breakfast, getting to school, getting picked up from school, homework, dinner, bedtime, reading stories, bathing, lunch, etc.)

- What does your mom/dad do to help with homework? Do you like that method/approach/involvement?

- Describe your day pre- and post-separation.

- Who takes care of you when you are with your mom/dad, or when they have to go out? Explore feelings about the place/person.

- Who takes you to the doctor, dentist?

- Who helps you with homework?

- Who comes to your school events?

- Tell me about your homes. Describe them.

- Tell me about some things you like and dislike about your homes.

- (*If preference expressed*):
  If your other parent had that, would you want to live there?
  What would you do if your father moved into the house where you are now and you moved into father's house?

17. DISCUSSION RE. ASSESSMENT/DIVORCE:

- Do you know why you are here? Do you know who I am? Do you know what I do? If the answer is no, ask if they want to know. Probe further.

- What did your mom/dad tell you about coming here/about me?

- How do you feel about being here?

- Possible explanation: I'm involved to make things easier for you and to make things as good as they can be. When parents don't agree or are having difficulty deciding about how things are going to be, I help parents make plans so children can see both parents, etc.

- What's going on in your family, to your mom and dad, to you?

- Discussion about separation/divorce if appropriate.

- Do you know why they are separating/divorcing?

- What did your mom/dad tell you about the separation/divorce?

- What do you really think happened?

- Was it one parent's idea to leave/separate or did they both decide?

- Is one parent more to blame?

- What did your parents argue about?

- How do you feel about the separation/divorce?

- What are the good parts and not-so-good parts?

- How are things different now from before? Is it better or worse, and how?

- How was it when your parents lived together?

- How did they get along?

- Many kids tell me _____ Do you feel that way?

- One boy told me the divorce made him think he was a bad boy, that he caused it. Do you feel that way?

18. PARENT–CHILD RELATIONSHP & PARENTING:

- Depending on age: Family Crest Task.

- Describe your mom/dad.

- What fun things do you do with your mom/dad?

- What kind of other things do you do with your mom/dad? Do you like them? Do you wish you could do other things?

- How do you get along with your mom/dad?

- Most kids tell me things they really like about their moms and dads and things that kind of bug them about their moms and dads. What things do you really like about your mom/dad? What really bugs you about your mom/dad?

- What is the best/worst part of your mom/dad?

- If there was one thing you could change about your mom/dad, what would it be?

- When something _____ happens to you, who do you tell?
  Insert each of these into the above question:
  really good
  scary
  upset, unhappy, sad
  When you _____, who do you talk to?
  Insert each of these into the above question:

have nightmares/bad dreams
do something good/nice at school
need help with school work
fight with a friend
have a problem you want to talk about

- Who usually helps you best with problems and worries?

- With whom can you talk best about things that are important to you?

- Do you feel closer with one parent? What does that parent do that makes you feel that way?

- What are the rules in your home with your mom/dad?

- What do your parents do when you misbehave or don't follow the rules?

- Probe: what happens if you do the same thing a second and third time?

- What do you have to do to get punished or grounded?

- What do you do that makes your mom/dad angry?

- What happens when you get mad at your mom/dad?

- How do you know when your mom/dad is mad? Sad? Worried? Happy?

- Probe parents' attitudes regarding friends, birthday parties, play dates, sleepovers.

- Do you have chores? Do you get an allowance?

- What would it be like to live with mom/dad?

19. SIBLINGS:

- How do you all get along with _____?

- How does each sibling get along with each parent?

- Who takes care of the baby?

- Probe each sibling's relationship with each parent, preferences.

- If a preference is expressed: what do you think about that preference?

20 TIME WITH PARENTS:

- If not seeing one parent: explore reasons, feelings, fears, etc.

- If supervised time, explore reasons, feelings, fears, etc.
- Who is there during your time?
- Probe reasons for wanting to go.
- Probe punctuality, reliability.
- Probe how child feels if plans change.
- Probe quality, quantity of time, overindulgence, neglect.
- Probe satisfaction with time: enough, too little, too much, just right.
- Probe how child feels about the other parent in terms of missing him/her, wanting to see him/her.
- Does your mom/dad ask questions about the other parent?
- Does your mom/dad ever say bad things about the other parent?
- How does that make you feel?
- How do your parents treat/feel about each other?
- If child living in one place primarily: how is it where you are living now?
- What do you like/dislike about it?

21. GRANDPARENTS:

- Identify the extended family.
- Probe contact, activities, etc.
- Tell me about _____.
- Probe feelings, relationships, likes, dislikes.

22. FANTASY:

- Drawings:
  - Family doing something together,
  - House–Tree–Person.
- Desert Island question.
- Three Wishes (Further question: If you had all the money you wanted to buy all the stuff you want, what would you buy?)
- If you had magic powers what would you do?
- Tell me about your dreams.

- Do you have nightmares? Can you recall any?
- Do you have imaginary friends? Explain.
- Do you have fears?
- Tell me about your fears.
- What animal do you remind yourself of? Why?
- What animal does your mother remind you of? Why?
- What animal does your father remind you of? Why?

23. DRUGS/ALCOHOL:

- What alcohol/drugs do you use, and how often?
- How much do you have to drink before you get drunk?
- Do you do things you then feel badly about?

24. SUICIDE:

- Have you ever thought of hurting yourself? Why?
- Have you ever hurt yourself? How?
- What would you do to hurt yourself?
- Why do you feel this way?

25. ANTISOCIAL BEHAVIOUR:

- Have you ever been in trouble for fighting, stealing?
- Have you ever done these things and not been caught?

26. PREFERENCES:

- Assess carefully whether or not to ask direct questions
- If the child volunteers a preference, then explore it carefully and in an age-appropriate manner.
- Probe the extent to which the preference,
  - is related to being indulged, having no limits set, getting lots of goodies;
  - reflects negative feelings for the parent perceived to be at blame for separation, to have abandoned family, kicked the other parent out;
  - is a caretaking effort vis-à-vis the parent the child perceives as being at disadvantage, hurt, sad, ill;

- is part of an identification with the aggressor;

- is coached and part of an alienation process;

- is related or not to the parent with whom they feel safer to be angry;

- I know you have been very clear that you want to live with _____. What would you do if the judge disagreed and thought it was best for you to live with _____?

- If the child persists in expressing a preference and giving a litany of complaints against one parent, allow this to continue for a while and then say: I know you feel this way and I understand completely. Now that you have told me and I know what you are saying, let's move on to other things.

27. MAKING THINGS BETTER, FUTURE-ORIENTED QUESTIONS:

- What could your mom/dad do to make things easier for you?

- What needs to happen to make things better, easier for you?

- What would happen if your parents knew you felt this way?

- Are you worried about hurting their feelings, getting into trouble?

- Is there anything you want me to tell your parents?

- What do you not want me to tell your parents? Why?

- Is it okay for me to tell your parents what we talked about?

- I'd like to make things easier for you. What can I do to help with that?

- Did your mom/dad ask you to tell me anything today? (This could be asked at any time during the interview when it seems appropriate. Don't overuse.

- What did you mom/dad want you to tell me today?

[1.] The following have informed general guidelines for interviewing children as well as the following compilation of questions obtained from the literature over 25 years of practice by the second author: Bourg et al., 1999; Ceci & Bruck, 1995; Ceci & Hembrooke, 1998; Gardner, 1999; Hoorwitz, 1992; Hynan, 1998; Poole & Lamb, 1998; Schutz, et al. 1989; Stahl, 1994; Zaragonza et al., 1995.

Appendix 9

How Children Think

5–7 YEAR OLDS:

- Thinking is egocentric; can't take points of view of others; child assumes you know what they know.

- Thinking is prelogical; can't explain own thinking vs. reporting events; may attribute causation inaccurately.

- Time sense is poorly developed (don't understand day after tomorrow, how long an hour or week is).

6–11 YEAR OLDS:

- Concrete, literal (in comprehension of questions and response); be specific.

- Communication may appear confused—inconsistencies, omissions, may provide different information at different times.

- Only answer questions you ask.

- Difficulty with future-oriented, hypothetical: "what-ifs" (e.g., "What would it be like to have five with. . ..?"); are likely to guess.

- Never ask the child to guess.

- Avoid "Do you remember. . .?"

- Don't ask "why" questions: the child will perceive blame, responsibility (egocentric).

- Ask other "wh" questions (What do you and your mom/dad do together that you like?) are preferable to questions requiring a Yes/No response (Do you and your mom/dad have fun together?).

12 AND OLDER:

- Developing abstract reasoning skills.

- Better conception/sense of time.

- Often seek fairness and justice.

- May focus on own needs.

Appendix 10

Question Types And Examples

CONTINUUM OF SUGGESTIVENESS IN QUESTIONS

- Open-ended or free narrative
- Focusing or specific
- Leading or suggestive (avoid these)

Open-Ended Questions

- "Tell me what happened."
- "Can you tell me more about that?"
- "Do you know who I am?"
- "Do you know why you have come here today?"
- "What did your mom/dad tell you?"
- "Do you know why your mom/dad live in two different homes?"
- "What did mom/dad tell you?"
- "Tell me what you do for fun with mom/dad."
- "Tell me more about . . . .."
- "And then what happened?"
- "What happened next?"
- "Sorry, I don't understand what you mean. Can you try again?"
- "Before you said. . .. Can you tell me more about that?"
- "What do you think might be important for me to know?"
- "Is there anything you want me to tell your parents?"
- "What advice do you have for your parents?"
- "Pretend I am the magic genie from *Aladdin*. What are your three wishes?"
- "If you had a magic wand and could change something about mom/dad/brother/sister/yourself, what would it be?"
- At the end of the session: "Is there anything else you want to tell me?" "Do you have any questions?"

Focusing Questions

- "Wh" questions
- Direct attention to specific topics (and details):
    - New partner
    - Rules and routines
    - Parental conflict
    - What happens when parent gets mad?
    - Schedule, transitions
    - Activities (type and parents' presence)
    - Risk/harm (punishment, domestic violence, alcohol), elaborating on child's input
        - Multiple choice questions: limit to three
        - Explore whether routine or exception
        - Avoid bias: Give all options, not just the ones you think support your hypothesis (two choices, feel he/she must pick one)
    - Yes/no question: Use on limited basis, followed by "Tell me more about that."

Leading and Coercive Questions

Avoid asking questions such as:

- "You're telling the truth, aren't you?"
- "You're not making that up, are you?"
- "Don't you want to live with your mother more?"
- "Doesn't your father make you feel sorry for her?"

Appendix 11

Substance Of The Assessment Report By Heading

I. IDENTIFYING INFORMATION

(a) Names, ages, birth dates of parents, step-parents, children, and siblings.

(b) Date of marriage, separation/divorce.

(c) Lawyers' names and telephone numbers.

II. REFERRAL INFORMATION AND CURRENT SITUATION

(d) Date, source and type of referral (i.e., on consent, court-ordered, Section 30, Section 112).

(e) Date assessment began.

(f) Referral questions and issues.

(g) Current parenting time schedule, status regarding legal custody, decision-making, court orders.

(h) Parents' occupations and location of residences relative to one another.

III. SOURCES OF INFORMATION[1]

(i) *Interviews and Observations*: a detailed list of *all* interviews, observations, telephone contacts with parents, stepparents, children, and significant others, including the date and length of each contact.

(j) *Professional Collateral Sources*: a list of all third parties interviewed by the assessor in person or by telephone.

(k) *Court Documentation, Letters, Emails, Records, and Professional Reports Reviewed*: a list of all documentation reviewed, organized by category (i.e., who provided it—court, lawyers, parents, collateral source), indicating the date and in the case of letters or emails the sender and the receiver.

(l) *Psychological Tests, Inventories, Checklists and Questionnaires* (list tests with citations):

a. Completed by parents and step-parents.

b.   Completed by children.

c.   Completed by teachers, daycare providers.

(m) *Brief Summary of Psychological Tests and Checklists Used*: include brief statement as to why the test was used, how it was scored (by hand with templates, by computer), if a computer-generated report was relied upon, caveats with respect to weight of testing[2] and group data and individual differences.[3]

IV. PARENTS' PROPOSALS AND CONCERNS[4]

(n) *Mother/Father*: summary of each parent's concerns, allegations, and proposals for the parenting arrangements (i.e., Parenting Plan, child's time with each parent, including before/after school care or daycare arrangements, how major decisions will be made, legal custody).

V. RELEVANT BACKGROUND

(o) *Mother/Father*: a summary from each parent's perspective of the relationship/marriage (courtship, relationship before/after children, strengths and challenges, communication and conflict, relationship with extended families, reasons for separation and events since history, with a focus on that which is relevant to the referral questions.

VI. INDIVIDUAL HISTORIES

(p) *Mother/Father*: a summary of each parent's individual history (identifying data pertaining to their parents, ages, occupations, health, siblings) perceptions of their family, parents, relationships with parents and siblings (previous and current), upbringing, discipline and how they were parented; moves, childhood social, educational and employment histories, previous relationships/marriages; mental health history, including all contacts with mental health professionals and use of medications; significant events and influences (positive and negative), traumas and losses; alcohol and drug history, problems with the law.

VII. SUMMARY OF REPORTS AND BEHAVIOURAL OBSERVATIONS

Individual Parent Interviews and Self-Report Data: summary of parents' and assessor's reports, and behavioural observations of the parents and step-parents (with a subheading for each parent and step-parent)[5] regarding: their perceptions of their children's developmental history and academic, social and emotional adjustment generally and specific to the separation/divorce; what they have told the children regarding the separation; how they understand the children's views and preferences if any; perceptions of the quality of the sibling relationships, the quality of:

(q) The parent–child relationship, the nature of the relationship with the other parent (i.e., communication, problem-solving and conflict-resolution skills, level and type of conflict, willingness to share child-related information); responses to the other parent's concerns and allegations; responses to the parenting protocol (e.g., description of their parenting approach/philosophy, aspirations for their children, rearing/discipline, sensitivity to child's emotional needs, needs to be protected from parental conflict, etc., perceptions of their and the other parent's parenting obtained;

(r) The strengths and challenges of each parent; where obtained got their ideas about parenting, etc.; extent to which they support the child's relationship with the other parent; if not, why not; manner and degree to which they involve the child in the parental conflict (e.g., using children as messengers, disparaging the other parent, asking child to keep secrets, taking no interest in child's life with the other parent, being intrusive into child's life with the other parent, over-reliance on child to meet parent's needs);

(s) *Joint parent interviews*: behavioural observations and summary of reports with focus on the nature of the parents' relationship, level and quality of conflict and cooperation, power and control struggles, abuse, etc.;

(t) *Individual interviews with children*: behavioural observations of child's presentation and summary of the children's reports during individual interviews, where these interviews occurred, who brought the children, summary of any other self-report information provided by child via questionnaires, checklists, etc.;

(u) *Observations*: summary of reports and behavioural observations of parents and children during office, home visits and/or transitions, and of children during any other observed settings (i.e., school, daycare, etc.).

VIII. INTERPRETATION OF PSYCHOLOGICAL TEST AND INVENTORY RESULTS

(v) Summary of interpretation of psychological test and inventory results for parents and children, with reference to the caveats previously noted in Sources of Information.

IX. COLLATERAL SOURCE REPORTS

(w) Summary of the personal and professional collateral source reports.[6][7]

X. OPINIONS, CONCLUSIONS AND DISCUSSION

(x) Clinical impressions of the parents' approaches during and attitudes towards the assessment.

(z) An analysis and integration of *all* the obtained data to explain (formulate) individual and family functioning.[8]

(aa) A statement and discussion of the assessor's opinions and conclusions, relying on the relevant social science literature, with specific reference to key issues, relevant allegations and cross-allegations and referral questions, including results and data that may *not* support the conclusions reached.

(bb) Explicitly stated rationale for the recommendations, including any limitations of the assessment; discussion regarding: how the conclusions about the various areas of investigation lead logically to the recommendations; why alternative recommendations were not made; and the advantages and disadvantages of the recommendations (weighing of risks and benefits to the children).

(cc) Parenting Plan Recommendations.[9]

Notes

[1] If the assessor chooses to provide verbal feedback and written recommendations prior to releasing a comprehensive report, the Sources of Information will stand as a separate document. If not, the Sources of Information will be contained in the body of the report.

[2] The testing is conducted within the context of a comprehensive Parenting Plan Assessment, and consequently the test results must be interpreted with caution and treated as hypotheses to be tested further and integrated with all the obtained data. No inferences should be drawn *from the test results alone* as to what would be in the child's best interests with respect to the parenting plan arrangements.

[3] For example, the MMPI-2 and MCMI-III are objective measures that have been standardized on known clinical populations, "normal" samples. Data on custody/access disputing litigants are available for both of these measures. The personality descriptions that derive from the profile are thus reflective of an identified group of individuals. As such, an individual displaying a specific profile in response to the scale would have some, but not necessarily all of the characteristics of the group described. In addition, caution must be exercised in inferring the validity of results as they may relate to an individual's true personality characteristics and functioning. In this regard, the reliability and validity of these measures increase when integrated with relevant background, information and other diagnostic instruments, including additional psychological tests, diagnostic interviewing impressions, third-party collateral source reports, etc.

[4] Caveats with respect to Section IV, V, and VI would note that the information contained in these sections represents the reports provided by each parent during interviews and

any written material they provided (email, intake questionnaires, etc.) and is not meant to be necessarily factual or supported by other data.

5. This section of the report would contain summarized responses to the standardized semi-structured interview protocols as well as those to the standardized questionnaires (see Appendices 3 and 3A).

6. Although ultimately there is no confidentiality (and the collateral sources need to be advised of this in advance of their reports provided), careful consideration needs to be given to what is written in the report about what the collateral sources, both personal and professional, have reported to the assessor, given that the parents and children may need to maintain relationships with these individuals.

7. Information obtained from professional collateral sources may be obtained in writing or during telephone or in-person interviews. More recently, in response to the occurrence of subsequent conflicts and ethical dilemmas and in the interest of a truly transparent process (not to mention being a defensive practice), some collateral sources and assessors insist on providing written as opposed to verbal reports from third parties. In the case of the former, the assessor may choose to append the collateral report to the assessor's report to avoid misstating the collateral's report and/or subsequent conflicts regarding what was said or not said. Alternatively, for ease of review, the assessor may choose to summarize the information in the body of his/her report while also appending the collateral report, in turn providing validation of the summary report. If a written report is not provided by the collateral source, the assessor will need to summarize the obtained information in the assessment report. This may prove problematic, however, if at a later time the third party does not confirm the assessor's report of the information (which could be due to the assessor getting it wrong, to a reluctance on the part of the third party to admit to what they said, or to their changing their mind).

8. In developing their explanation or formulation, assessors may choose to consider combining both a family systems and a medical model approach by identifying the predisposing, precipitating, perpetuation and protective factors while also providing a discussion of the dynamic between the parents, children and other significant family members and mutually reinforcing negative and positive feedback loops. For example, the father's need to wait, distance himself and avoid only reinforces the mother's need to approach and resolve without delay. The more she approaches, the more he avoids, etc.

9. Whether or not verbal feedback precedes the delivery of a comprehensive report, the recommendations stand as a separate document entitled Parenting Plan Recommendations. Parenting Plans are elaborated upon and discussed in Chapter 5.

Chapter 4

Post-Assessment Activities:

Critiques, Second Opinions And Testifying

The most powerful person in the process is not the judge, it is not the other parent, not one of the lawyers, not even the child. No, the most powerful person in determining who gets custody, and on what terms, is frequently a court-appointed forensic evaluator. . . and the judges usually go along with it.
New York Times.[1]

Over the years, a growing chorus of concerns and criticisms has been expressed by mental health clinicians and researchers about the quality of child custody and access assessments (Bowermaster, 2002; Emery, Otto & O'Donohue, 2005; Melton, Petrila, Poythress & Slobogin, 1987; O'Donahue & Bradley, 1999), the lack of empirically validated methodology and outcomes for children (Birnbaum & Radovanovic, 1999; Fidler & Birnbaum, 2006; Kelly & Johnston, 2005; Lee, Beauregard & Hunsley, 1998), and the use of psychological testing in child custody and access assessments (Bow & Quinnell, 2002; Brodzinsky, 1993; Erickson, Lilienfeld & Vitacco, 2007; Erard, 2007). Yet, the *New York Times* article quoted above appears to suggest that custody assessors are the final arbiters in child custody and access disputes.

Assessors' recommendations carry significant weight in the legal system, especially where the conclusions reached by the assessor coincide with the facts as found at trial.[2] The prevailing judicial view is that an assessment report is only one, albeit important, piece of evidence to be weighed with all of the other evidence. However, if the findings of fact of the trial judge are similar to the findings of the assessor, the assessment will be given significant weight. Bala & Miklas (1993) suggested long ago that assessors are viewed as having a quasi-judicial function in resolving these disputes before the court. Tippins and Wittmann (2005) argue that once a recommendation is made, the dissatisfied attorney will tell the client "the judge is highly likely to go with the recommendation."[3] Given the weight that the child custody and access assessment *may* carry, despite the concerns raised and the limitations set out, it would seem that the assessment process and the assessor should be accountable not only to the court but to the consumer of the product. As noted in Chapter 2, child custody-related complaints to the various regulatory colleges have steadily increased over the years.

In the two previous chapters, we provided a theoretical and empirically based approach to conducting child custody and access assessments. That is, the assessment must follow the acceptable standards and guidelines of the profession in the assessor's jurisdiction, be empirically based, and utilize the most current social science literature and clinical knowledge in reaching recommendations. Conducting such assessments is demanding work, and some assessors may not have a full appreciation of their role or the expectations of the court and the parties when providing these professional services. The question, then, is what can parents do if they believe there are problems with the assessment because the assessor did not follow the acceptable methodological guidelines, or if the recommendations are seriously flawed?

The social science literature identifies several options parents can choose if they have concerns about an assessment. For example, they can retain another assessor to provide a critique of the report, and/or they can request that a different assessor complete another assessment. A trend that has been occurring in the United States is to obtain direction from the court to provide an order for a specific expert to provide the critique and/or review of the first assessment (Day, Kuehnle & Starnes, 2005; Stahl, 1996). While this approach has been used in Canada infrequently, it does provide the parties and the court with transparency in the process. Justice Starnes[1] in Florida, for instance, has brought the expert who provided the critique and/or review into his chambers with the initial assessor to help facilitate settlement. No similar type of settlement or negotiation process is available in Canada.

Some mental health professionals have suggested that providing a critique and/or a second opinion prolongs litigation, placing a focus on the adversarial process and further, that assessors should not even be challenging their colleagues' work in this arena (Ackerman, 2006; Stahl, 1996). Others have suggested that parents who complain are likely disgruntled individuals who want to discredit the mental health assessor and reverse an unfavourable recommendation (Greenberg, Martindale, Gould & Gould-Saltman, 2004). On the other hand, lawyers and their clients may have reasonable and possibly genuine concerns about the assessor's competency and the recommendations made (Ackerman, 2006). Herman (1999) and Heilbrun (2001) suggest that a thorough and competent critique allows the court to be a more sophisticated consumer of child custody and access assessments. At the very least, the court is informed about the robustness and reliability of the assessment, which in turn informs the judge's determination of the weight the assessment should be given in combination with all of the other evidence before the court.

Child custody and access disputes reveal the most difficult issues a court will hear, as they involve complex human emotions intersecting with the law. Issues such as overnights for young children, assisted reproductive technology, child alienation, religious differences, domestic violence, child physical and sexual abuse, and cases where one parent wishes to move away can challenge even the most seasoned assessor. Rarely in child custody and access disputes is the potential for a clash of personal values—or biases, misunderstandings, and harm—as great as when mental health professionals conduct these assessments. In the final analysis, given the significant impact the recommendations may have on the lives of children after separation and/or divorce, every assessor must be held accountable for the opinions he or she provides in a case.

In this chapter, we explore: (1) the role of critiques and second opinions as a means to educate the court and help the mental health professional gain greater skill and knowledge in conducting child custody and access assessments; (2) how the courts view these two post-assessment activities; (3) some common problems and pitfalls arising from critiques; and (4) the role of the assessor testifying about their recommendations.

STANDARDS OF PRACTICE, PRACTICE GUIDELINES AND BEST PRACTICES

In the previous chapters, we listed the standards of practice and ethical codes relating to social work, psychology and psychiatry work in general, as well as the existing guidelines specific to forensic work, including custody assessments. Guidelines and standards uniformly caution against assuming dual roles (e.g., mediator and assessor, therapist and assessor), be they simultaneous or sequential. With the exception of the Ontario Psychological Association (January 1998), none specifically addresses critiques and/or second opinions. However, embedded within the guidelines and/or standards one can find a number of acceptable protocols for providing a critique.

The Ethical Guidelines for Psychological Practice Related to Child Custody and Access (Ontario Psychological Association, 1998) identifies the various roles a professional can assume, namely: consultant; counsellor/therapist; mediator; child development expert; expert advisor; assessor; and arbitrator. Critiques and reviews would be included in the roles of the "child development expert" and the "expert advisor."[5] See Table 6 for a summary of the various roles.[6]

Table 6		
Various Roles for Mental Health Professionals		
Role	**Retained by/Duties**	**Type of Witness**
Consultant	• contracted by one or both parents • general information required based on theory, literature, research (e.g., child development, impact of divorce and/or various kinds of custody and access arrangements, etc. • no formal assessment • no recommendations re: custody	Fact Witness[7]
Counsellor Therapist	• contracted by one or both parents, children, and/or family • provides counselling, advice • usually private/confidential • assessment may be conducted, however, no recommendations re custody are made	If called, fact witness; not expert witness re custody

Role	Retained by/Duties	Type of Witness
Mediator (open)	• assist with development of parenting plan • advice, etc. may be given • not conducting assessment • may report to court • should not be making recommendations re custody/access arrangements	Fact Witness
Mediator (closed)	• as above, but confidential	Witness rarely, but possible (e.g., court proceeding)
Child Development Expert	• contacted by one or both parents, lawyers, court to provide impartial evidence on research, best practices about matter related to court decision-making re custody/access arrangements • assists court • *no* direct involvement with any family member • not referring to specific case • academic, may be on fact situation presented • called Expert Witness in Alberta	Expert Witness

Role	Retained by/Duties	Type of Witness
Expert Adviser	• contracted by one or both parents, a lawyer, or court to critique a formal assessment report prepared by assessor for court • Alberta refers to this role as advisor • offers critique of another assessor, also called reviews in some states in the U.S. • no direct involvement with family members • no recommendations re custody • may contact first assessor, and/or send report to first assessor	Expert Witness
Assessor (first or second)	• contracted by parents, lawyer, and/or court • neutral, impartial, assess entire family • makes recommendations providing all relevant members are assessed • one piece of evidence court considers	Expert Witness

Role	Retained by/Duties	Type of Witness
Arbitrator	• parties must consent, obtain independent legal advice • makes binding decisions regarding custody and access • awards subject to rights of appeal and judicial review • governed by relevant legislation	Does not testify
Parenting Coordinator	• post parenting plan service • assist with implementation and monitoring of parenting plan • hybrid role: educate, facilitate/mediate, assess, case management, monitor, arbitrate • parties must consent, obtain independent legal advice • makes binding decisions within limited scope (excluded are decisions relating to custody, permanent parenting time schedule (access) and relocation • awards subject to rights of appeal and judicial review • arbitration component governed by relevant legislation	May testify as Fact or Expert Witness

CRITIQUES

What are they and how are they done?

There is no Canadian literature about providing critiques and/or reviews of child custody assessments. However, a number of practising psychologists in the United States have provided thoughtful frameworks and protocols that can be used to guide the mental health professional (Gould, Kirkpatrick, Austin & Martindale, 2004; Greenberg, Martindale, Gould & Gould-Saltman, 2004; Stahl, 1996; Martindale, 2005, 2006; Pickar, 2007). For example, Gould et al. (2004) identify six major tenets for providing critiques. The critique, they suggest, should,

(1) be ethically grounded and factually based;

(2) provide a clear, cogent, and current review of the social science literature;

(3) provide for alternative or rival hypotheses to the ones made in the assessment;

(4) provide a bias-free and objective report;

(5) provide a thorough analysis of not only the limitations of the assessment but also of the limitations of the critique; and

(6) be written in a respectful, open and honest tone.

Heilbrun (2001) identifies seven principles, framed by the following questions, which should be utilized in conducting both assessments and critiques:

(1) Has the role and purpose of the assessor been clearly defined?

(2) Has the data gathered been consistent with current social science literature and professional practice?

(3) Has information been obtained from collateral sources?

(4) Has the data gathered been subject to current scientific analysis?

(5) Has the information gathered been useful to a court of law?

(6) Have the limitations of the information gathered been noted?

(7) Have the recommendations been provided with current empirical support?

The role of a critique is to provide the court with information that describes the strengths and limitations of the assessment methodology and of the recommendations made based on the obtained information and the observations of the child/ren and family. The critique focuses on: (1) information missing in the assessment that the assessor did not collect; (2) information that should have been included in the assessment and that the assessor did not address; and (3) the strengths and limitations of the assessment (Gould et al., 2004; Stahl, 1996). In addition to analyzing the assessment methodology, the critique examines the extent to which the recommendations follow logically from the reported data, observations, and conclusions, and the extent to which these are commensurate with the social science literature. While infrequently done, the professional providing the critique may also—with the written permission of both parties—speak to the assessor.

A critique must always be accompanied by disclosure of the limitations inherent in examining the assessor's report only and, in the absence of meeting family members and reviewing the other documentation. Surprisingly, it is not uncommon for the expert providing the critique to mistakenly interview only one of the parents, and sometimes even the child/ren without the consent and/or knowledge of the other parent, and moreover, to follow with recommendations regarding best interest parenting arrangements. Such practice is troublesome in two respects. Firstly, it is contrary to all standards of practice and ethical guidelines that warn against assuming dual roles—in this case providing a critique and a second opinion. Secondly, the second opinion as described is based on a one-sided and incomplete assessment, since the entire family and the other critical components of a proper assessment (obtaining information from collateral sources, etc.) are not included. It is not permissible to include opinions and recommendations about parenting arrangements believed to be in the children's best interests, when all parties and/ or their child/ren have not been assessed and when the other essential components of the assessment process have not been included.

Process and Role Clarification

It is essential that experts be clear about the specific role they assume and about who has retained them. If only one parent retains the expert, the process often unfolds by way of a two-stage process (Gould et al., 2004). In the first stage, the practitioner conducts a preliminary critique/ review followed by a consultation with the referring lawyer. From a legal perspective, the expert is the agent of the lawyer and the information shared is anchored to solicitor–client confidentiality. At this stage, no formal report is written and no expert testimony is given in court. The purpose of this type of critique may be twofold: First, to provide information to the referring lawyer as to the facts so that the lawyer may give the client further background; and second, to assist the lawyer in formulating questions for cross-examination of the assessor. In the second stage, and once properly retained by the lawyer, the expert writes a report and testifies if permitted by the court. This may well occur, as presumably the parent believes the critique will assist them in court. There is no solicitor–client confidentiality once a report is written and submitted.

If both parents retain the expert, privilege is no longer at issue. In some cases, the expert so retained may contact the first assessor, with the permission of both parties, to discuss the first report. While we found no case law in North America that legally provides for this, the authors believe that this approach would provide neutrality and reduce the incidence of pitting experts against one another. It would also discourage using what is often referred to as a "hired gun" (Ackerman, 2006) to clear up what turned out to be misunderstandings. For example, the expert may ask the assessor why personal and/or professional collateral sources were not obtained and, in doing so, learn that in fact these were requested from both parties but not documented in the report, or that the requests were made but the collateral sources did not reply.

The expert must also negotiate with the lawyers as to the nature and limitations of the retainer; all terms should be clarified and put in writing *before* any work commences. In addition, the expert needs to negotiate the parameters of the contract: whether they are being retained as an expert for trial only; offering coaching to the lawyer on questions to ask at trial based on the assessment; providing a critique and/or review of the child custody and access assessment; or any other clinical opinion/consultation. Table 7 summarizes the two-stage process that the expert undertakes.

Table 7

Two-Stage Process in Critiquing/Reviewing a Child Custody Assessment

Stage 1:

1. Expert conducts a preliminary critique/review of the methodology and conclusions reached in the original assessment.

2. Expert provides privileged consultation with lawyer.

3. No formal report is written and no expert testimony is given in court.

4. Decision is made to further retain the expert for report and providing testimony.

Stage 2:

1. Once the critique/review is completed, the mental health professional may want to speak to the author of the original report.

2. Consent from both parents is required before the reviewer can proceed.

3. Solicitor–client privilege is waived between the expert reviewer and the lawyer retained.

4. Expert writes report and may testify in court.

It is incumbent upon experts to be clear about their role and when that role changes. Once their opinions and/or written reports are used for court purposes, solicitor–client privilege no longer exists. These issues must be thoroughly canvassed with the lawyer who retains the expert. The expert also needs to be aware that all notes, collected data, and fees for the critique and/or review may be subject to the same rules of evidence applied to the child custody and access assessment.

Issues and Questions to Examine in Critiques

The following tables highlight some of the questions that an expert might ask while critiquing another professional's assessment. These compilations are not exhaustive, but rather represent current, albeit sparse, literature in this area to date (Gould et al., 2004; Day; Pickar, 2007). In addition, the guidelines and/or standards discussed in the previous chapters provide a background as to what may be critiqued if the assessor did not follow the appropriate guidelines and/or standards.

Table 8

Questions to Consider in Reviewing an Assessment[8]

1. Did the evaluator clearly define the main problems or issues to be resolved?

2. Did the evaluator clearly identify the legal questions relevant to the behavioural data to be collected?

3. Did the evaluator identify the factors to be measured?

4. Did the evaluator articulate testable hypotheses for the evaluation?

5. Did the evaluator consider rival and/or plausible alternative hypotheses?

6. Have the criteria defining the best interests of the child been clearly outlined?

7. Did the evaluator identify developmental outcomes and the data upon which the specific predictions are based?

Table 9

Questions to Consider in Reviewing the Interviews of Litigants

1. Did the evaluator explain how credibility of interview data was assessed?

2. Did the evaluator obtain interview data from each parent about the specific areas of functioning that are the focus of the court's concern?

Table 10

Questions to Consider in Reviewing Behavioural Observations

1. Did the evaluator explain how credibility of self-report data was assessed?

2. Did the evaluator obtain self-report data from each parent about specific areas of functioning that are the foci of the court's concern?

3. Was the choice of each self-report measure clearly related to the psycho-legal questions that are the focus of the evaluation?

4. If not, was the relationship between choice of self-report measure and the psycho-legal questions clearly explained to the trier of fact?

5. Did each self-report measure possess the characteristics of a test that are suggested when using psychological tests in a forensic context? If not, why not?

6. Did the evaluator explain the basis for the selection of each test administered and how its results would be used?

7. Did the evaluator clearly identify the hypotheses drawn from the self-report measures?

8. Did the evaluator compare discrete sources of data drawn from the self-report measures and then compare them to information obtained from collateral sources?

9. Did the evaluator discuss how information from self-report measures was analyzed for the degree of convergent validity in the data?

Table 11

Questions to Consider in Reviewing Collateral Records and Interviews

1. Did each parent provide a list of collateral interview sources knowledgeable about each parent's relationship with the minor child?

2. Were the collateral interview sources interviewed in a consistent manner, using a common set of questions to form the basis of the interview focus from which the evaluator could compare responses across information sources?

3. Were the questions asked of the collateral interviewees focused on specific questions of concern in this specific evaluation, along with more general questions about parenting skills? If not, why not?

4. If yes, what hypotheses were generated based upon the collateral information?

5. Did the evaluator examine similarities and differences across interview data (convergent validity)?

6. How did the evaluator assess the credibility of collateral interviewees?

7. Did the evaluator obtain the names of other people to interview from the collateral sources? Were these people interviewed?

8. Were the choices of collateral interview sources representative of people involved in the child's life across a wide range of activities as opposed to limited interviews of family and friends?

9. If not, were the limitations of the obtained collateral data discussed?

Table 12

Questions to Consider in Reviewing the Use of Psychological Tests

1. Was the psychological testing administered in a competent manner in accordance with ethical standards and professional practice guidelines?

2. Were tests administered as outlined in the test manuals?

3. Did the evaluator explain how test response style/bias was interpreted?

4. Did the evaluator seek external support from collateral sources to confirm response style interpretations?

5. Did the evaluator obtain test data from each parent about the specific areas of functioning that are the focus of the court's concern?

6. Was the choice of each objective test clearly related to the psycho-legal questions that are the focus of the evaluation?

7. If not, what rationale is offered for the instruments selected?

8. Was the relationship between choice of objective tests and the psycho-legal questions clearly explained to the trier of fact?

9. Did each objective test possess the characteristics of a test that are suggested when using psychological tests in a forensic context? If not, why not?

10. Did the evaluator explain the basis for the selection of each test administered and how results would be used?

11. Did the evaluator clearly identify the hypotheses drawn from the objective tests data?

12. Did the evaluator compare discrete sources of data drawn from the objective test data and compare them to information obtained from collateral sources?

13. Did the evaluator discuss how information from objective tests data was analyzed for the degree of convergent validity in the data?

While the above tables provide a framework the expert can use to critique and/or review the child custody and access assessment, this does not necessarily mean that: (1) the court will accept the critique and/or review; or (2) the expert's opinion will carry greater or equal weight than that of the initial assessor. The critique and/or review may be no different from what was already gathered and offered, and at the end of the day, the expert's view is just another *opinion* based on his or her version of the information critiqued and/or reviewed.

SECOND OPINIONS

Second opinions are much more comprehensive than critiques, as they provide for a new child custody and access assessment. While they are rare because of the financial and emotional expense involved and the necessary protraction of the dispute, they do provide the court with another interpretation of the information/allegations and of what may or may not have been covered in the first assessment. Second opinions may also be helpful if a lengthy period of time has passed since the completion of the first assessment and the court requires an update that takes into account new and relevant events and circumstances that have occurred during the intervening period. Moreover, second opinions may help facilitate resolution when a first assessment has not done so (Stahl, 1996).

A report prepared by an expert conducting an assessment, critique or second opinion assessment may indeed be influential, but ultimately, the trier of fact is always the final arbiter. In the Ontario decision of *More v. Primeau*,[9] Justice Blair articulated the accepted judicial view that "expert opinion is of great value in these cases, but the decision must be made by the court. It is a responsibility that cannot be delegated."[10]

EXPERTS IN FAMILY LAW

The general rule in litigation is that the presiding judge is the trier of fact. The judge will reach a decision on the issues in dispute based on the evidence that is presented at the trial and the inferences that he or she draws from that evidence. The court will often rely on the opinion evidence given by expert witnesses for assistance in reaching its decision.

Expert witnesses are not bound by the same evidentiary restrictions as ordinary witnesses. Generally, a witness is able to provide a recitation of facts, but not inferences and/or conclusions drawn from those facts. The sole exception to this rule is expert testimony.[11] The use of expert evidence in the courtroom operates as an exception to the common law "opinion rule," which requires a witness to testify only to facts within their personal knowledge. An expert is one who, by education and practical experience in an area, is qualified to form an accurate, professional opinion and arrive at valid conclusions, unlike persons without such special training and knowledge. In matters calling for special knowledge, an expert in the field may draw inferences and state an opinion.[12] To be of assistance to the court, expert evidence must remain objective and impartial. It should not be perceived as the views of an advocate.

In family law, the "best interests" principle has resulted in frequent use of custody expert opinions in the courts. Mental health professionals have knowledge and expertise that are useful to the court, as this will assist the trier of fact in making informed custody decisions. This information can find its way before the court in any number of ways. The court can order a custody assessment (as stated previously, every province has legislative provisions that enable a court to order an assessment); the parties can jointly agree to an assessment; and/or one of the parties to the dispute can retain an expert to provide evidence to the court.

In a court-ordered custody and access assessment, a clinician with known credentials is chosen by the parties or by the court, and so for the most part is over the initial hurdle of being accepted by the court as an expert witness. In all cases, however, the professional must be qualified by the court as an expert in a specific area or areas of practice prior to providing opinion evidence. The court will consider the education, training, and experience of the individual in determining whether this person ought to be qualified as an expert in his or her field in relation to the matters at hand. Once qualified, the assessor can include hearsay in his or her evidence, and draw inferences based on facts, research, and other relevant sources for arriving at an opinion; an expert is also allowed to state opinions based on hypothetical questions. A well-qualified expert can make a tremendous difference in the evidence presented to a court and the ultimate decision of the judge in a custody case.

Although the court is the final arbiter of the dispute, the assessment report is given significant weight where the assessor has appropriate training and experience and the information contained in the report coincides with the findings of fact as found by the trial judge. Little weight is given to assessments, however, when the assessor:

(a) shows bias or partiality for or against one party;

(b) shows a preconceived bias;

(c) does not follow accepted guidelines and methodology;

(d) makes observations or recommendations outside his or her area of expertise;

(e) applies incorrect assumptions;

(f) applies incorrect legal principles;

(g) relies on limited or incorrect facts;

(h) submits an assessment that is incomplete; and/or

(i) submits an assessment that is out of date.

The trial judge is obligated to weigh the evidence prior to reaching a decision. This process becomes even more apparent when more than one expert report is obtained and admitted into evidence. The court will consider all reports and decide on the weight and credibility to be assigned to each, depending on several factors. It may consider:

(a) the assessor's qualifications;

(b) the depth of the assessment interviews and the time devoted to the assessment;

(c) the choice of people interviewed;

(d) the collateral information gathered, and the breadth of information;

(e) the psychological tests conducted;

(f) adherence to appropriate guidelines and methodology; and

(g) issues relating to culture and values.

Although these lists are not exhaustive for determining the weight assigned to expert reports, they are considerations that all mental health professionals should keep in mind when undertaking custody assessments.

Mental health professionals have an important role to play in family disputes. It is a humbling responsibility, and one that must be taken seriously. The court process itself creates a tremendous burden of accountability for custody/access assessors, placing upon them an obligation and responsibility to be fair, thorough, professional and of assistance to the court. This is not meant to be a "how to" guide for testifying, as several books available on the market outline the court process, the rules of evidence, and the specifics of testifying (Barsky & Gould, 2002; Vogl & Bala, 2001).

Assessors have a significant role to play in child custody disputes, and can be important witnesses in a trial. They are one of the few professionals involved with the family who has had the benefit of speaking with the parties, the children, other family members, and relevant collateral sources of information. They have knowledge of the issues, the needs of the child and those of the family, and have the ability to educate the parties and the court on these matters. They have the ability to make recommendations to the court based on the best interests of the child, and the ability to influence the outcome of a trial, if their assessment is conducted in a proper, fair, and thorough manner. The purpose of the assessment is to provide expert assistance to the trial judge in making his or her determination of the best interests of the child. Assessors should ensure that they do so professionally and ethically.

Child custody assessments are fraught with conflict and highly charged emotions. Knowledge, training, experience and clear standards and guidelines for practice are critical in this field of practice, given the limits of our knowledge, the lack of uniformly accepted standards of practice and the limited number of well controlled, empirically validated studies on which parenting arrangements are best for which children. While it is fine to have pride in one's work, this pride should also be tempered with an equal dose of humility.

HOW THE COURT VIEWS POST-ASSESSMENT ACTIVITIES

To date, there has been little, if any, discussion in the social science literature regarding the use, function, and process of providing post-assessment assistance to the court when it comes to child custody and access cases. There appears to be more debate and controversy surrounding this issue in judicial decisions.

For example, in Ontario there are conflicting legal decisions on the admissibility of critiques or second opinions, and the weight given to them if they are admitted. As we noted in Chapter 1, Madam Justice Wein, in *Mayfield v. Mayfield*,[13] has suggested that the evidence of an expert retained to comment on an initial assessment will rarely be admissible. In that case, the judge would not allow the author of the critique (although she was eminently qualified in her field) to testify at the trial saying that the report did not meet the four-pronged test that would allow for its admissibility. Relying heavily on the Supreme Court of Canada decision in *R. v. Mohan*,[14] Justice Wein stated:

> Prior to the decision in *Mohan*, the general standard of admissibility of expert evidence was the relatively low threshold of "helpfulness." However, even then a judge still had to be satisfied that the trier of fact might not have sufficient knowledge of, or experience in human behaviour to draw an appropriate inference from the facts without the benefit of the expert evidence. Subsequent to *Mohan*, the Court in effect had been asked to function as a "gatekeeper," keeping out novel scientific evidence. The standard of helpfulness was explicitly rejected as being too low a threshold for admission; the issue of

admissibility was to be determined against four specific criteria, which had the effect of raising the threshold of admissibility for all kinds of expert evidence.[15]

In this case, the judge, while finding that there was not an issue with respect to the first three criteria, held that the critique was not admissible, as it did not satisfy the standard of being "necessary."

Justice Quinn, on the other hand, in *Greenough v. Greenough*,[16] allowed the author of the critique to testify, positing that critiques are helpful to the court as they can highlight lapses in accepted methodology and, more importantly, the significance of such lapses.[17]

While these two cases may seem to be polar opposites with respect to the reception and view of critiques in the courts, an examination of the sparse case law in this area confirms that there is no consensus on the issue amongst the judiciary in Canada. As with much else in family law, many of the decisions that deal with the admissibility of critiques are fact-driven, and the admission into evidence of a "critique" is generally decided on a case-by-case basis.

Parties and/or Children not Interviewed

While there may not be consensus amongst the judiciary with respect to the admissibility of critiques, there is, as mentioned earlier, consensus on the weight assigned to reports when the expert has not met with all the requisite players. Courts have been reluctant to place much, if any, weight on reports that make recommendations on custody and access without having met with both parents and all children at issue. Difficulties also arise, and perhaps are more likely, when the author of the second report only meets with the party who has retained them. In that instance, courts are reticent to place any weight on the recommendations contained in the report.

In *M. (C.) v. M. (G.)*,[18] the parties selected Dr. W., a psychologist, to conduct a formal assessment to assist in determining custody of the children. The expectation of the parties was that the report would be presented to the court as expert evidence. Mr. M. objected to the assessment, alleging that Dr. W. was biased against him. He in turn consulted with Dr. S., who had impressive credentials and extensive experience in the field of assessments, to obtain a second opinion. Dr. S. reviewed the assessment report and material provided by both Mr. M. and his counsel and identified various deficiencies. She arrived at a different conclusion than Dr. W.; however, she did not meet with the children or the parties. On cross-examination, Dr. S. admitted that in arriving at her conclusions she had assumed that the various complaints set out to her by Mr. M. and his counsel were accurate. Justice Wallace found that her evaluation of the assessment had such an incomplete and faulty base that it was of little assistance to the court.

Similarly, in *Huxtable v. Huxtable*,[19] Justice Mossip found the critique report by L.P. to be "singularly unhelpful and of no assistance to the court."[20] In this case, Dr. A. completed the custody assessment pursuant to an order of the court. The mother, unhappy with the findings of Dr. A., retained L.P. to review the report. L.P. provided an expert report that formed part of the material filed on behalf of the mother and read by Justice Mossip.

The Justice, in referring to L.P.'s, report, stated,

> [H]er 'critique' of Dr. A.'s assessment when she had not seen any of the parties or the child is to be given as much weight as those assessments that only see one party and that child - little or none. I am sure that L.P. had no ill will when she prepared her report, but at least from this Judge's perspective, these issues are complex and difficult enough, without having professionals "wade in" and critique assessments done by professionals who have in fact seen all the parties and the child, when they have not seen, or talked to anyone.[21]

The result was that Justice Mossip accepted Dr. A.'s assessment of the family dynamics.

In *Bjorge v. Bjorge*,[22] with the consent of both parents, the assessor prepared a report on custody and access of the child. After the receipt of the report, the mother, Ms. B. raised allegations of bias against the assessor, claiming that she was a friend of Mr. Bjorge's counsel. Ms Bjorge retained Dr. B. to comment on the original assessment. Dr. B. interviewed the mother and her partner, but no other persons were consulted. Justice Owen-Flood, in rejecting the findings of Dr. B., stated, "I afforded Dr. B's written critique less weight as a result and in particular the doubts he raises about parental alienation in this case."[23]

In *Moody v. Moody*,[24] Mr. G. conducted an assessment into the issues of custody and access of the parties' son. In addition to meeting with the parents and the child, Mr. G. interviewed relatives of the parents and others who were able to provide him with relevant information. The interview process began in May 1993 and concluded in December 1993. Mr. G. filed an extensive report outlining his contacts and the information gathered, which Justice Forestell considered.[25] Mr. Moody subsequently retained Mr. H. to review Mr. G.'s assessment report. Although Mr. H.'s academic credentials were similar to those of Mr. G., he had only conducted one custody assessment, whereas Mr. G. had been involved in custody and access assessments since 1969. Much to the trial judge's amazement, the report filed with the court by Mr. H. comprised only one full page and part of another. He had never spoken with the mother or her partner and, further "shocking" the judge, stated his belief that he could come to a conclusion in a custody and access assessment without talking to one parent or to one parent with the child. Little weight was placed on his opinion; however, the judge gave serious weight to Mr. G.'s report, varying the existing status quo by granting primary residence of the child to the mother.

The above-noted cases clearly show that courts will put little or no weight on the evidence of an expert who makes custody recommendations without having first interviewed all of the relevant parties and children involved. Any mental health professional considering providing a court with comments on another assessment through a report or oral evidence, while also making alternate recommendations in a custody or access case, is well advised to keep this in mind.

Flawed Methodology and Reports

As stated by Justice Quinn in *Greenough v. Greenough, supra*, critiques can be helpful in highlighting lapses in methodology and their significance. Though battles between experts do little to assist in family disputes, the best interests of children are ill served when flawed reports go unchallenged and they become the basis upon which the judge rests his or her decision.

In *Sidhu v. Sidhu*,[26] the Office of the Children's Lawyer, at the request of the court, conducted an investigation and made recommendations with respect to the issue of access. The clinical investigator assigned by the office completed her investigation and provided her recommendations in a written report filed with the court. The clinical investigator also included alternative recommendations that called for the father to consider amending his application for custody; if he did so, she stated, her recommendation would be that custody be granted to him. As twelve months had passed since the formulation of the original report, the report of the Children's Lawyer was updated prior to trial. In the updated report, the clinical investigator stated that many of the concerns about the mother in the original report were being addressed, and that the mother and child were making great progress. Notwithstanding these observations, the clinical investigator continued to recommend a change of custody from the mother to the father. The mother then retained B.C. to critique the report of the Children's Lawyer.

B.C. testified that the report of the Children's Lawyer was "fatally flawed." The primary issue was that the clinical investigator's report failed to take into account the potentially negative impact upon the child of a change of custody when there appeared to be no cogent reason for uprooting the child from her mother's home. B.C. maintained that the report lacked the professionalism expected of an experienced assessor and that it appeared to have been prepared by someone of limited experience. Justice Wolder accepted the evidence of B.C., and rejected the recommendations of the Children's Lawyer, finding that they could not be supported in view of the overwhelming evidence to the contrary. Custody was granted to the mother.

Similarly, in *T. (M.) v. T. (J.)*,[27] the court placed little weight on the assessment of Dr. G. because of its shortcomings. In this case, both parties sought custody of their five-year-old daughter, as well as orders prohibiting the other parent from removing the child from the province. There were also allegations of sexual abuse against the father. In June of 1992, the parties agreed to an order for an assessment regarding the issues of custody and access to be conducted by Dr. G., who met with the parents and arranged for psychological testing of both. Although he also met with the child on one occasion in what was primarily an observation session, Dr. G. deliberately did not see the child again—despite the fact that she disclosed to him that her father had done something bad to her—stating that in his view the child was over-investigated. Dr. G. believed he could gather sufficient information about the case by focusing on the relationship between the child's parents and by obtaining information from other sources regarding the progress of the supervised access. He concluded that the father had not been involved in any sexual abuse of his daughter, and recommended that the parents be involved in filial therapy to address issues with their daughter and minimize her exposure to parental conflict. He further recommended unsupervised access between the father and child following these sessions.

The mother retained two experts to review Dr. G.'s assessment. Dr. H. was of the opinion that the assessment conducted by Dr. G. was neither a valid assessment of the child nor an investigation of the sexual abuse allegations. In his opinion, Dr. G. assessed the parents only, with limited contact with the child, and did not have sufficient involvement with the child to reach conclusions about the allegations of sexual abuse. Dr. H. also criticized the lack of foundation for Dr. G.'s conclusion that the father did not sexually abuse his daughter. He found that Dr. G. had not pursued relevant areas identified in the psychological assessment of the father and had minimized the disclosures made by the child.

The second expert retained by the mother testified that the investigation of sexual abuse allegations required specialized, post-graduate training, familiarity with the developing theoretical and clinical research, ongoing training by experts in the area, and intensive clinical experience. An assessment of sexual abuse allegations, the expert testified, would include several interviews with a child over a considerable period and should include observations with both parents. Dr. H. similarly found that Dr. G. had conducted a custody and access assessment, but had not followed the accepted protocol to determine whether the child had been sexually abused.

Justice Hatton concurred with the critiques of both doctors with respect to the shortcomings in Dr. G.'s assessment. The judge found it difficult to determine on what basis Dr. G. had reached his conclusions about the child's sexual abuse allegations, as his findings were not consistent with the psychological testing that he had arranged through Dr. C. It appeared that Dr. G. had accepted the father's contention that the mother was encouraging and coaching the child. The court was satisfied that the father had inappropriately touched the child in a sexual manner, and ordered supervised access for three hours on alternate Sundays.

In another case, A.L. was retained by the father, in *Redden v. Rhyno*,[28] to review the report and recommendations made by the assessor, S.N., of the Family Court Clinic. In this case, on May 1, 1989, the Nova Scotia Family Court had granted custody of the then three-year-old child to his father. The child had been in the care and control of his father since December of 1988. The new proceeding was an application by the mother to vary that order. S.N. recommended that the child's interests on a long-term basis would be better served if custody were awarded to the mother. The assessor's reasons included the father's lifestyle and addiction to drugs and alcohol, as well as his defensiveness concerning these issues and his failure to grasp the seriousness of his behaviour as it related to the child.

The critique provided by A.L. concluded that the assessment report was generally unbalanced in favour of the mother and that several areas were not adequately addressed and explored. Additionally, there seemed to be an imbalance in how the information about the parents was presented, with a tendency for information about the mother to be framed positively and information about the father to be framed negatively. The assessor's recommendations did not discuss the potential effect that a change of residence would have on the child, or how the transfer was to take place. A.L. concluded that there was a definite bias in the report in favour of the mother.

Justice Main held that the cross-examination of S.N. and the critique conducted by A.L. demonstrated that the assessment was flawed and that the recommendations should be accorded less weight than would otherwise have been the case.[29]

In *Apesland v. Apesland*, [30] H.G., a counsellor/therapist, prepared a custody/access report that was filed on behalf of the mother in a Saskatchewan court. H.G. testified that she had interviewed both parents and the three children involved. In addition, she had made home visits to both residences when the children were present. She had also obtained additional information from personal and professional third parties supplied by the parents. H.G. made seven recommendations, including a suggestion that the 14-year-old live with her mother, despite her expressed wish to the contrary.

Dr. R., a registered clinical psychologist, was retained by the father to give expert evidence on H.G.'s report and the general standards of home studies in the province. Dr. R. reviewed a number of criteria required in the development of a report and outlined the shortcomings of H.G.'s report. Additionally, Dr. R. concluded that the assessor had used inappropriate techniques. The trial judge held that the purpose of the custody/access report was to assist the court in determining the custody of the children and to provide an objective opinion for the placement of the children of the family. The evidence of Dr. R. concerning the custody and access report prepared in this case is very important.[31] Given the expert evidence of Dr. R. on the shortcomings of the report, the trial judge was not prepared to accept the recommendations of H.G.

Critiques Having Little Impact on the Court

In a number of other cases, "critiques" were admitted into evidence and the authors of these reports were allowed to testify at trial, even though their reports did not call into question the assessor's recommendations. In *Boomhour v. Boomhour*, [32] Dr. M. prepared a critique of A.N.'s assessment report and it was filed with the court with the consent of the parties. In reviewing the critique, the court found that Dr. M. had some valid criticisms in terms of the assessor's methodology and the way the report was written, but overall nothing that would dispute the assessor's recommendations. Similarly, in the case of *Children's Aid Society of Simcoe (County) v. D. (D.)*,[33] the court admitted the critique conducted by Dr. B. The critique was restricted to a review of Dr. M.'s methodology and the foundation of his conclusions. The court found that the critique did not seriously challenge the conclusions reached by Dr. M. in his parenting capacity assessment.

In many of the cases reviewed above, the court admitted the critique into evidence and heard oral evidence. This is not to suggest, however, that the court will readily admit this type of report or evidence. There has been an increase in judicial scrutiny of experts over the past several years, and recent case law suggests that the courts are considering the role of the expert witness more closely.

Given the various interpretations by the court regarding critiques and second opinions, expert assessors who provide these services should be cautious, and above all transparent and ethical, when acting in either roles. Table 13 offers a list of do's and don'ts that the assessor should consider.

Table 13

Do's and Don'ts of Critiques, Reviews and Second Opinions

1. Given the lack of standards and guidelines for conducting these practices, at the very least do no harm.

2. Do not be the cheerleader for either side.

3. Avoid dual roles, both simultaneous and sequential:

    • Do not conduct a critique and second opinion on the same case.

    • Do not go beyond the information given—if you conduct a critique, do not provide recommendations about parenting arrangements.

4. Provide your expert opinion based on your knowledge and do not go beyond that expertise.

5. Be ethical, balanced, and transparent by including both the limitations and strengths of the critique itself (avoid confirmatory bias).

6. If you provide a second opinion, avoid one-sided assessments (being a "hired gun"); conduct a proper assessment including the entire family using the multi-source, multi-method approach.

7. Be humble—the court has the final say.

ETHICAL DILEMMAS AND PRACTICE ISSUES

Child custody disputes are all about conflict, and mental health professionals practising in this area need to understand the distinction between the limits of their expertise and providing the court with assistance rather than an ultimate solution. As previously noted, part of the difficulty has been the confusion and merging of roles, both simultaneously and sequentially (Greenberg & Shuman, 1997; Greenberg & Gould, 2001; Greenberg et al., 2004; Herman, 1999; Martindale, 2006; Pickar, 2007). For example, the role of an assessor is very different from that of a therapist, parenting coordinator, mediator or mediator/arbitrator. An example of a simultaneous dual role occurs when a therapist of a child or one parent provides recommendations to the court regarding parenting arrangements. In most cases, a change in roles (dual sequential roles) is improper. For example, a mediator or therapist should not become an assessor or parenting coordinator. A parenting coordinator should not become a therapist, mediator, or assessor. Moving from being an assessor to a parenting coordinator, while frequently requested by parents for what in many cases are good reasons, should be done cautiously, if at all. Any changes in roles that may be perceived improper must be transparent, understood, and agreed to by all parties.

Greenberg and Shuman (1997) articulate 10 differences between therapeutic and forensic relationships, and clearly identify these different roles as having irreconcilable conflicts. Greenberg and Gould (2001) address the hybrid roles that have been emerging in the field while considering firm boundaries between being a therapist and being an assessor. Martindale (2005) delineates the differences between clinical and forensic assessments. Amundson, Lux and Hindmarch (2005) compare and contrast the various tasks, processes, methods employed, and evidentiary issues, along with the function of the assessor in relation to the court, as a means to distinguish the various roles that mental health professionals play. The common theme that resonates throughout the work of all of these authors is the importance of knowing, and being clear about, your role throughout the process.

The courts in Canada have had little opportunity to address the issue of the merging and dual roles of mental health professionals in custody disputes. Although some assessors attempt to assist the parties to reach a settlement on the basis of the recommendations, there is some legal authority to suggest that they should not attempt to do so. In *Delisle v. Delisle*,[34] the court-appointed assessor had unsuccessfully attempted to mediate a settlement of the outstanding parenting issues between the parties prior to the completion of the assessment. The mother refused to return to the assessor and the father, consequently, brought a motion to compel her to complete the assessment. The mother cross-motioned to have the original s. 30 order set aside and sought a new order with a newly appointed assessor. The court, in ordering a new assessment, stated:

> There is an important distinction between the role of an assessor and that of a mediator. The assessor, as a personally uninvolved expert witness, is required to provide observations, opinions and potentially make recommendations to the court that could be detrimental to one side or the other. By contrast, a mediator becomes personally involved and takes an active role in helping the parties find a solution to issues in dispute. Presumably, in this case, when the assessor made recommendations to the parties on how to resolve the problem in question, he did so with the needs of the children foremost in his

mind. How could the mother (or the father for that matter) then reject his suggestions when he was also the person appointed to assess each parent's willingness to satisfy the needs of the children? Normally, a mediator makes certain that power imbalances between the parties are kept in check so that a fair settlement can be freely negotiated by them. It goes without saying that the mediator, himself, should not be in a position of power over the parties. Otherwise there would be no guarantee that a settlement has been achieved through fair negotiation rather than coercion. Normally when attempts at mediation fail, the parties are able to terminate the services of the mediator without the perception that a rejection of the mediator's proposal could prejudice their case.[35]

Justice Glenn further stated,

> An assessor climbs out on a very long limb when she or he attempts also to mediate issues which are also the subject of their own assessment. It is recognized that people who are qualified to assess custody and access disputes are, by training, often eager to resolve such disputes. But, not only is their role as a mediator hampered when they are also the assessor, but also, their role as an assessor also becomes compromised.[36]

In addition to issues of partiality and credibility, assessors run the risk of increased exposure to liability if they undertake multiple roles during the assessment process. While it is clear from the case law that, generally, an expert witness is immune from suit by any person with whom his or her only relationship derives from a judicial proceeding,[37] this immunity may not extend to an expert who undertakes multiple roles. The protection extends to the actions of an expert witness in collecting, considering, and evaluating material upon which the expert may be called later to give evidence. The policy behind the immunity is primarily the protection of the integrity of the judicial process by ensuring that expert witnesses are free from the fear of reprisals and litigation by those against whom they give evidence. What happens, though, when the practitioner's role as an assessor merges with other roles he/she has undertaken? Does the expert witness immunity apply to professionals who undertake several and/or differing roles in a family law dispute?[38] Does expert witness immunity extend to court-appointed experts who have exceeded their jurisdiction by taking on additional roles, such as mediator? These questions, and many more, have yet to be addressed by the family courts.

In a similar vein, the courts have held that expert witness immunity is not available to a party who acts as an assessor or mediator in an entirely private capacity. Perhaps this is reason enough for assessors to insist that a request for an assessment on the agreement of both parties be incorporated into a court order. Immunity is also unavailable to an expert engaged to provide a report in a non-litigious situation. If an expert is engaged privately by parties, without any intention that the expert would be available as an expert witness in any legal proceedings involving the parties, that individual may be subject to actions in negligence or breach of contract in respect of the performance of his or her retainer.[39] Assessors, who undertake mediation, parenting coordination, counselling, and the like, need to be aware of their potential for liability in carrying out these different roles, simultaneously or sequentially.

Although much of the discussion thus far has focused on post-assessment activities, many of these same issues often arise during the initial assessment process. Pickar (2007) suggests that the assessor needs to be mindful of his/her role as assessor distinct from that of a therapist, and to be self-inspecting of one's own biases/personal values and countertransference issues. On the other hand, having biases does not necessarily mean that one is biased in the case at hand or that the bias is negative (Ackerman, 2006). Being aware of one's own biases and values is the key.

Williams (1992) and Martindale (2005) review issues of bias and distortion that the assessor needs to be aware of when conducting assessments. They argue that looking for evidence to support your own hypothesis while ignoring others (confirmatory bias) can easily occur. Martindale and Gould (2004) identify the following issues that the assessor needs to be clear about at the outset to avoid later criticisms:

(1) identifying who the client is;

(2) addressing the court's referral questions, and providing expertise on no more and no less; and

(3) being aware of the virtues of not being helpful.

Table 6 identifies the various roles mental health professionals play.

In the next section, we review three distinct areas of confusion that often arise for the mental health professional, and provide case examples. Our goal is to highlight how mental health professionals can confuse their roles and diminish the good work they are providing. These areas are: (1) the differences between the therapeutic role and the role of the assessor; (2) issues of confidentiality; and (3) limits of competency in expressing opinions.

The Therapeutic Role Versus the Assessor's Role

The main distinction between these two roles is one of intervention. The purpose of the child custody assessment is to:

(1) gather information about the strengths and limitations of each parent's parenting abilities;

(2) assess the child–parent relationship;

(3) assess the developmental needs of each child, along with each parent's ability to meet those needs;

(4) assess the alignment and influence of the extended family; and

(5) obtain information from significant professional and personal sources and review significant records and reports about each parent and the child in order to assist the court in answering the question of which parenting arrangements are in the best interest of the child.

In a custody assessment, the focus is determined solely by the court. The expectation is that the court will consider the assessor's recommendations in the decision-making process, but the assessor answers to the court. In contrast, the purpose of therapy with a client is to help the client define his or her personal goals. The client chooses whether to use the therapist's services; the therapist answers to the client. The implicit assumption in therapy is that the client is motivated to provide accurate information to the therapist, in order to mitigate their difficulties. The therapist uncritically accepts the statements made by the client with whom he or she is engaged in a supportive atmosphere. In contrast, the parties and personal collateral sources in child custody assessments provide information that often presents one parent or the other in a more favourable light with respect to their parenting abilities and relationships. The role of the assessor is to properly challenge and question the individuals involved, and to gather collateral information to support or refute the statements and observations made by the parents and/or collaterals. The assessor evaluates everyone, while the therapist provides support to his or her own individual client.

Difficulties can arise for therapists in a variety of different situations in child custody disputes. For example, sometimes a parent brings a child for treatment and neglects, unintentionally or intentionally, to mention that he/she is separated from the other parent. Alternatively, the parent may acknowledge a separation but fail to mention they are also involved in litigation regarding child custody and access, and then later request a report for court confirming their parenting strengths and the child's adjustment or maladjustment, depending on what suits their claim in court. It is very easy to be seduced by a parent when you hear a very convincing story without the benefit of hearing from the other parent. As a therapist, you want to be helpful; your role is to offer support and encouragement to your client. You may unwittingly reinforce and even amplify (by tone and behaviour) what your client is saying about the other parent. However, life always has three sides to every story: each parent's version, and reality. It is important to understand the different roles and expectations of therapists and assessors, and not compromise the good work that often goes on; and also to avoid complaints.

Confidentiality

Different types of mental health services have different expectations regarding limits of confidentiality. Services that provide counselling and treatment typically provide clients with *some* degree of confidentiality, but not necessarily complete confidentiality, especially when faced with a summons to court. Most mental health professionals have an ethical duty to maintain a confidential relationship with their clients. At times, there is a conflict between privilege and confidentiality, in that professional communications may not be privileged even though the professional has promised to keep the information private. Unless the court makes an order otherwise, a mental health (or other) professional can be compelled to testify in court, and any information provided to the professional by the client or patient may consequently be admitted as evidence.

Child custody assessments completed for the court are explicitly *not* confidential, and all information gathered is expected to be brought before the court. It is incumbent upon assessors to make explicit for the parties the limits of confidentiality—in effect, the lack of confidentiality—in child custody assessments. Additionally, each parent should be fully informed of the specific service being provided, as well as the scope and nature of the therapist's potential to become involved in the litigation process, and any limits of confidentiality with respect to the child's treatment information.

For example, when a parent going through a difficult separation or divorce attends for counselling, he/she must be made fully aware—if they also happen to be involved in a custody and access dispute before the court—that any information disclosed through their confidential, therapist/client relationship *may* also become subject to disclosure by an assessor (with written consent) or by way of a court order.

Similarly, children involved in any type of counselling should also be provided with the knowledge and understanding of the limits of confidentiality if their parents are involved in custody and access litigation before the court. That is, the child should be made aware that whatever he/she may say to their therapist might not always be kept confidential if litigation is undertaken. This rule also applies to the assessor who interviews children involved in a child custody and access assessment.

One or both parents may be legally required to give consent for a child to receive treatment from a health care practitioner. Complaints are common when a mental health professional with no knowledge of the separation or understanding of the legal custodial arrangements (consent issues) treats a child without the consent of the other parent. Although only one parent may be legally required to give consent, such as in sole or *some*[40] joint custody arrangements, obtaining information from both parents is likely to be best practice from a clinical perspective and furthermore, avoids the child feeling they must keep a secret from one parent.

Limits of Competency in Expressing Opinions

Assessors must be knowledgeable about the social science literature, specifically related to separation and/or divorce. This includes, but is not limited to:

(1) child development;

(2) parent–child relationships;

(3) domestic violence;

(4) alienation from one parent;

(5) child maltreatment;

(6) substance abuse; and

(7) mental health issues.

Competence in child custody assessments involves a combination of education, continuing education, training, experience, knowledge of current research, child, and family psychopathology, the impact of separation and/or divorce on children and parents, extended families, knowledge of high-conflict dynamics, issues of diversity, domestic violence, child and adult suggestibility, as well as judicial decision-making. Additionally, child custody assessors and therapists should be aware of their own personal and societal biases, histories, and beliefs—their attitudes, for instance, about one type of custodial arrangement over another, overnight access with young children, and/or gender issues with respect to domestic violence—and limit their conclusions based on what they know rather than crystal ball gazing.

For example, as previously noted, sometimes a parent may attend or bring his/her child in for counselling; the parent and/or the parent's lawyer may subsequently request a letter from the therapist on behalf of his/her client and/or child client. Usually, these well-meaning letters are attached to the parent's affidavit to support their position vis-à-vis one custodial or access arrangement over another, or to limit the other parent's access. Wanting to be helpful and supportive, the therapist may compromise good work by framing such support in the form of a letter directed to "to whom it may concern"—in other words, the judge in the case. Therapists have an ethical obligation to limit their opinions to what they know and to report the limits of their expertise, knowledge and role with the parent and/or child. Providing information related to a therapeutic context (often after seeing one person only) is not synonymous with a full and thorough psychosocial assessment of the entire family for the purposes of a legal proceeding.

It is important for any child custody assessor to understand what it is that they are doing on behalf of the court, and what their ethical obligations are: that is, who is the client? Consideration of these issues will prove helpful to the therapist who becomes part of the litigation process, whether or not they choose to do so.

Other Common Pitfalls

Johnston (2007), Kelly & Ramsey (2007), Gelles (2007) and Pruett (2007) have eloquently identified various common pitfalls for the mental health professional. We would agree with Johnston (2007) that many of the problems in child custody assessments quite often lie in translating a social science question about parenting abilities and children's development into a legal question of the child's best interest. Some child custody assessors fall into traps, but because they are considered experts, they can mislead parents and the courts. Johnston (2007) refers to these traps as:

(1) the straw man (inaccurately restating or oversimplifying original research data, or misrepresenting the data altogether);

(2) cherry-picking (using social science or theoretical literature that only supports your conclusions, while providing some of the limitations of the research to look more balanced, or dismissing valid and important research as it did not conform to your conclusions);

(3) leading authority declarations (using the work of well known researchers or influential leaders in the field to back up your own conclusions); and

(4) scholarly rumours (misquoting research continually without having consulted the original source).

In this chapter, we discussed post-assessment activities, including critiques, second opinions and testifying. We differentiated various roles that mental health professionsals can assume in child custody-related work, stressing the importance of role clarification in conducting critiques and second opinions. Questions the assessor can ask when reviewing another colleague's assessments were provided. We provided an overview of the court's perspective on these post-assessment activities. We concluded the chapter with a discussion of several ethical dilemmas and common pitfalls that arise when assessors do not clearly differentiate their roles.

Notes

[1] May 23, 2004.

[2] See *Tolstoy v. Tolstoy* (2004), 2004 CarswellOnt 876 (Ont. S.C.J.); *Inglis v. Inglis* (1993), [1993] O.J. No. 2498, 1993 CarswellOnt 1652 (Ont. Gen. Div.); *Tock v. Tock* (2006), [2006] O.J. No. 5324, 2006 CarswellOnt 8553 (Ont. S.C.J.).

[3] Tippins, T.P & Wittmann, J. P. (2005). Empirical and ethical problems with custody recommendations: A call for clinical humility and judicial vigilance. *Family Court Review* Vol. 43:2, p. 217.

[4] Workshop in Seattle, Washington, Association of Family and Conciliation Courts, 2005.

[5] These guidelines define an expert advisor as a practitioner contracted by one or both parents and their lawyers, or the court, to critique a formal assessment report prepared by an assessor for submission to the court. If called to present an opinion to the court, the practitioner acts as an expert witness. An expert witness is someone who, by reason of education or specialized experience, is considered by the court to be qualified to give an opinion to the court about a specific question that is not within the knowledge of an average person.

[6] The role of parenting coordinator is not listed in the OPA 1998 Guidelines. Those are under review and may incorporate this role.

[7] A fact witness is someone who attests or swears to facts (i.e., a meeting that occurred, the results of an assessment, the focus and outcome of therapy, or statements made in therapy, or any other incident, event or occurrence). If providing interpretations or opinions to the court, a fact witness limits them to the factual nature of interpretations and opinion formulated and commented at the time of the event being attested to.

[8] Tables 8, 9, 10, 11, and 12 are reproduced with permission from Haworth Press, Inc. (Gould et al., 2004). The term evaluator is used in the U.S., while assessor is used in Canada.

[9] (1977), 2 R.F.L. (2d) 254, [1977] O.J. No. 913, 1977 CarswellOnt 141 (Ont. C.A.).

[10] *Ibid.* at p.269.

[11] *Scott v. Crerar* (1886), 11 O.R. 541 (Ont. C.P.), reversed (1887), 14 O.A.R. 152.

[12] *R. v. Abbey* (1982), [1983] 1 W.W.R. 251, 138 D.L.R. (3d) 202, [1982] 2 S.C.R. 24, 43 N.R. 30, 39 B.C.L.R. 201, 29 C.R. (3d) 193, 68 C.C.C. (2d) 394, 1982 CarswellBC 230, 1982 CarswellBC 740 (S.C.C.) at p.217 [D.L.R.].

[13] 18 R.F.L. (5th) 328, [2001] O.J. No. 2212, [2001] O.T.C. 429, 2001 CarswellOnt 2036 (Ont. S.C.J.).

[14] [1994] 2 S.C.R. 9, 18 O.R. (3d) 160 (note), EYB 1994-67655, 29 C.R. (4th) 243, 71 O.A.C. 241, 166 N.R. 245, 89 C.C.C. (3d) 402, 114 D.L.R. (4th) 419, 1994 CarswellOnt 1155, 1994 CarswellOnt 66, [1994] S.C.J. No. 36 (S.C.C.).

[15] *Supra*, note 12 at pp. 337-338.

[16] (2003), 46 R.F.L. (5th) 414, 2003 CarswellOnt 4320 (Ont. S.C.J.).

[17] *Ibid.* at para. 16

[18] (1992), 40 R.F.L. (3d) 1, [1992] O.J. No. 1164, 1992 CarswellOnt 252 (Ont. U.F.C.).

[19] (2001), [2001] O.J. No. 533, 2001 CarswellOnt 469, 17 R.F.L. (5th) 82 (Ont. S.C.J.).

20. *Ibid*. at para. 6.
21. *Ibid*. at para. 6.
22. [2004] B.C.J. No. 927, 2004 CarswellBC 1046, 2004 BCSC 596 (B.C. S.C.).
23. *Ibid*. at para. 25.
24. (1995), 1995 CarswellOnt 1959, [1995] O.J. No. 1137 (Ont. Gen. Div.).
25. *Ibid*. at para. 7.
26. (1999), 1999 CarswellOnt 4850 (Ont. C.J.), additional reasons at (2000), 2000 CarswellOnt 3764 (Ont. C.J.).
27. (1993), [1993] O.J. No. 3379, 1993 CarswellOnt 3941 (Ont. Prov. Div.), additional reasons at (1994), 1994 CarswellOnt 4454 (Ont. Prov. Div.), affirmed (1997), 1997 CarswellOnt 4774, 33 R.F.L. (4th) 430 (Ont. Gen. Div.)
28. (February 12, 1992), Doc. Toronto D2677/90, [1992] O.J. No. 259 (Ont. Gen. Div.).
29. *Ibid*. p. 6.
30. (1999), [1999] S.J. No. 416, 1999 CarswellSask 436 (Sask. Q.B.).
31. *Ibid*. at para. 56.
32. (2002), [2002] O.J. No. 3124, 2002 CarswellOnt 2626, 31 R.F.L. (5th) 48 (Ont. S.C.J.).
33. (1998), [1998] O.J. No. 4808, 1998 CarswellOnt 4486 (Ont. Gen. Div.).
34. (1998), 43 R.F.L. (4th) 186, 1998 CarswellOnt 5283, [1998] O.J. No. 6539 (Ont. Prov. Div.).
35. *Ibid*., at para. 8.
36. *Ibid*., at para. 9.
37. See *Fabian v. Margulies* (1985), 53 O.R. (2d) 380, [1985] O.J. No. 2729, 1985 CarswellOnt 1632 (Ont. C.A.), leave to appeal refused (1986), 55 O.R. 576n, 73 N.R. 398n, 21 O.A.C. 78n, [1986] S.C.C.A. No. 290 (S.C.C.); *Carnahan v. Coates* (1990), 71 D.L.R. (4th) 464, 47 B.C.L.R. (2d) 127, 27 R.F.L. (3d) 366, [1990] B.C.J. No. 1421, 1990 CarswellBC 145 (B.C. S.C.); *M. (N.) (Guardian ad litem of) v. M. (I.A.S.)*, 69 B.C.L.R. (2d) 99, 41 R.F.L. (3d) 164, 93 D.L.R. (4th) 659, [1992] 5 W.W.R. 585, (sub nom. *M-A v. M-A*) 14 B.C.A.C. 269, 26 W.A.C. 269, [1992] B.C.J. No. 1351, 1992 CarswellBC 193 (B.C. C.A.).
38. See *Varghese v. Landau*, 3 R.F.L. (6th) 204, 2004 CarswellOnt 347, [2004] O.J. No. 370, [2004] O.T.C. 97 (Ont. S.C.J.) for a discussion on expert witness immunity.
39. *Zittrer c. Sport Maska Inc.*, [1988] 1 S.C.R. 564, 38 B.L.R. 221, EYB 1988-67850, 83 N.R. 322, 13 Q.A.C. 241, 1988 CarswellQue 27, 1988 CarswellQue 134, [1988] S.C.J. No. 19 (S.C.C.).
40. While the law in Ontario indicates, for example, that in situations where there is no custody determination, one parent may consent to a child receiving treatment, it is more typical for parenting plans with joint custody to spell out a decision-making process that requires the parents to consult with one another and the relevant professionals, and for the parents to come to a mutual decision.

References

Ackerman, M.J. *Clinician's Guide to Child Custody Evaluations* (Hoboken, NJ: John Wiley & Sons, Inc., 2006).

Amundson, J.K., Lux, G. & Hindmarch, B. "Investigative vs clinical emphasis in child custody evaluation: A reflection on Austin and Kirkpatrick (2004)" Journal of Child Custody 2:4 (2005), 69–83.

Bala, N. & Miklas, S. *Rethinking Decisions about Children: Is the "Best Interests of the Child" Approach Really in the Best Interests of Children?* (Ottawa: The Policy Research Centre on Children, Youth and Families, 1993).

Barsky, A.E. & Gould, J.W. *Clinicians in Court: A Guide to Subpoenas, Depositions, Testifying, and Everything Else You Need to Know* (New York, NY: The Guilford Press, 2002).

Birnbaum, R. & Radovanovic, H. "Brief intervention model for access-based post-separation disputes: Family and court outcomes" Family and Conciliation Courts Review 37:4 (1999), 504–513.

Bow, J.N. & Quinnell, F.A. "A critical review of child custody evaluation reports" Family Court Review 40:2 (2002), 164–176.

Bowermaster, J.M. "Legal presumptions and the role of mental health professionals in child custody proceedings" Duquesne Law Review 40 (2002), 265.

Brodzinsky, D.M. "On the use and misuse of psychological testing in child custody evaluations" Professional Psychology: Research and Practice 24:2 (1993), 213–219.

Day, D., Kuehnle, K. & Starnes, H. "Child custody critiques" Presentation at 42nd Annual Conference of Association of Family and Conciliation Courts, Workshop #13, Seattle, Washington, May 18–21, 2005.

Emery, R.E., Otto, R.K. & O'Donohue, W.T. "A critical assessment of child custody evaluations" American Psychological Society 6:1 (2005), 1–29.

Erard, R.E. "Picking cherries with blinders on: A comment on Erickson et al. (2007) regarding the use of tests in family court" Family Court Review 45:2 (2007), 175–184.

Erickson, S.K., Lilienfield, S.O. & Vitacco, M.J. "A critical examination of the suitability and limitations of psychological tests in family court" Family Court Review 45:2 (2007), 157–174.

Fidler, B.J. & Birnbaum, R. "Child custody disputes: Public and private assessments" Canadian Family Law Quarterly 25:2 (2006), 137–167.

Gelles, R.J. "The politics of research: The use, abuse, misuse of social science data—The cases of intimate partner violence" Family Court Review 45:1 (2007), 42–51.

Gould, J.W., Kirkpatrick, H.D., Austin, W. & Martindale, D.A. "Critiquing a colleague's forensic advisory report: A suggested protocol for application to child custody evaluations" Journal of Child Custody 1:3 (2004), 37–62.

Greenberg, L.R. & Gould, J.W. "The treating expert: A hybrid role with firm boundaries" Professional Psychology: Research and Practice 32:5 (2001), 469–478.

Greenberg, L.R., Martindale, D.A., Gould, J.W. & Gould-Saltman, D.J. "Ethical issues in child custody and dependency cases: Enduring principles and emerging challenges" Journal of Child Custody 1:1 (2004), 7–30.

Greenberg, L.R. & Shuman, D. W. "Irreconcilable conflict between therapeutic and forensic roles" Professional Psychology: Research and Practice 28:1 (1997), 50–57.

Heilbrun, K. *Principles of Forensic Mental Health Assessment* (New York: Kluwer Academic, 2001).

Herman, S.P. "Child custody evaluations and the need for standards of care and peer review" Journal of the Center for Children and the Courts 1 (1999), 139–150.

Johnston, J.R. "Introducing perspectives in family law and social science research" Family Court Review 45:1 (2007), 15–21.

Kelly, J.B. & Johnston, J.R. "Commentary on Tippins and Wittmann's 'Empirical and ethical problems with custody recommendations: A call for clinical humility and judicial vigilance'" Family Court Review 43:2 (2005), 233–241.

Kelly, R.F. & Ramsey, S.H. "Assessing and communicating social science information in family and child judicial settings: Standards for judges and allied professionals" Family Court Review 45:1 (2007), 22–41.

Lee, C.M., Beauregard, C.P.M. & Hunsley, J. "Attorneys' opinions regarding child custody mediation and assessment services: The influence of gender, years of experience, and mediation practice" Family Court Review 36 (1998), 216–226.

Martindale, D.A. "Psychological assessment: Evaluating the evaluations" The Matrimonial Strategist 22:12 (2005), 3–5.

Martindale, D.A. "Consultants and role delineation" The Matrimonial Strategist 24:4 (2006), 4–7.

Martindale, D.A. & Gould, J.W. "The forensic model: Ethics and scientific methodology applied to child custody evaluations" Journal of Child Custody 1:2 (2004), 1–22.

Melton, G.B., Petrila, J., Poythress, N.G. & Slobogin, C. *Psychological Evaluations for the Courts* (New York: Guilford Press, 1987).

O'Donohue, W. & Bradley, A.R. "Commentary. Conceptual and empirical issues in child custody evaluations" Clinical Psychology: Science and Practice 6:3 (1999), 310–322.

Pickar, D.B. "On being a child custody evaluator: Professional and personal challenges, risks, and rewards" Family Court Clinic 45:1 (2007), 103–115.

Pruett, K.D. "Social science research and social policy: Bridging the gap" Family Court Clinic 45:1 (2007), 52–57.

Roseby, V. "Use of psychological testing in a child-focused approach to child custody evaluations" Family Law Quarterly 29:1 (1995), 97–110.

Stahl, P. "Second opinions: An ethical and professional process for reviewing child custody evaluations" Family and Conciliation Courts Review 34:3 (1996), 386–395.

Tippins, T.M. & Wittmann, J.P. "Empirical and ethical problems with custody recommendations: A call for clinical humility and judicial vigilance" Family Court Review 43:2 (2005), 193–222.

Vogl, R. & Bala, N. *Testifying on Behalf of Children: A Handbook for Canadian Professionals* (Toronto, ON: Thompson Educational Publishing, Inc., 2001).

Williams, A.D. "Bias and debiasing techniques in forensic psychology" American Journal of Forensic Psychology 10 (1992), 19–26.

Chapter 5

Formulating Parenting Plans: Overview Of The Literature And Practical Considerations

Like Humpty Dumpty, a family broken by divorce cannot be put back together in precisely the same way. [Tropea v. Tropea][1]

INTRODUCTION

The assessor faces a challenging task when attempting to organize and assimilate the information collected in preparation for making recommendations that are in children's best interests. These recommendations are typically contained in a parenting plan. Kisthardt and Fines (2005) define parenting plans as detailed descriptions of how parents intend to continue caring for their children after separation and divorce. More specifically, a parenting plan delineates the incidents of custody and access, namely, how major (legal custody) decisions will be made and the schedules for regular and holiday parenting time ("access," residential schedule). In addition, parenting plans typically address parenting principles and guidelines, parent communication, information exchange, transitions, transportation, extracurricular activities, clothing and belongings, day-to-day decisions (e.g., routine medical and dental matters, attendance at parent–teacher meetings and school events, etc.), travel, residential and jurisdictional moves, change of name and future dispute resolution.

By definition, parents referred for custody and access assessments are engaged in moderate to high levels of conflict. When finalizing parenting plans, legal and mental health practitioners need to carefully consider and assess not only the frequency of parental conflict, but also, more importantly, the nature of the conflict and how children are involved in this conflict by their parents (Buchanan, Maccoby & Dornbusch, 1991; Garrity & Baris, 1994, Johnston, 1994, 1999; Kelly, 2000). To protect children from parental conflict, parenting plans require considerable detail and specificity (Johnston, 1995; Kelly, 2002). The greater the parental conflict, the more structure and detail required in the parenting plan, which provides a blueprint for the parents to disengage; this will minimize their conflict while allowing them to parent independently (also known as parallel parenting) and focus on their children's developmental and psychological needs.

Developing and evaluating parenting plans requires considerable knowledge and experience. This chapter is divided into two parts. In Part I, we provide an overview of the social science literature relevant to parenting plans, including the effects of separation and divorce on children, adolescents, and adults whose parents separated when they were children, father absence and involvement, parental conflict, and other important risk and resilience factors. We then discuss attachment, overnights for young children, the approximation rule, and the primary parent presumption as these are key to the determination of parenting time schedules. In Part II, we discuss practical considerations for developing these schedules, with an emphasis on young children and families with moderate to high levels of conflict. Specific parenting time options are provided.

PART I: IMPACT OF SEPARATION AND DIVORCE

Types of Studies and Methodological Limitations

A large body of literature can be found on the effects of separation and divorce on children and adolescents and, to a lesser extent, on adults whose parents separated when they were children. While most studies are cross-sectional in design, we have the benefit of several national surveys (see for example, Aquilino, 2006; Carlson, 2006[2]; Furstenberg & Cherlin, 1991; King, 2006; King & Sobolewski, 2006[3]; Menning, 2006; Stewart, 2003[4]) and longitudinal studies.[5]

Research reviews and meta-analyses are especially useful in our assimilation of the voluminous and oftentimes contradictory data (see Bauserman, 2002; Amato, 2000; 2001; Amato & Cheadle, 2005; Amato & Gilbreth, 1999; Amato & Keith, 1991; Kelly, 1993, 1997, Kelly & Lamb, 2003; Lamb, Sternberg & Thompson, 1999). In some respects there is what appears to be a *War of the Roses* evident in the separation and divorce literature; some report devastating effects (Wallerstein, Lewis & Blakeslee, 2000), while others report risk but considerable resiliency and mostly positive outcomes (Ahrons & Tanner, 2003; Fabricius, 2003; Hetherington & Kelly, 2002; Kelly & Emery, 2003).

Generally, different results and conclusions can be accounted for by the diverse paradigms and research methodologies used (Ahrons, 2007; Amato, 2003; Emery, 2004). Specifically, studies rely on different samples (clinical vs. community), different cohorts (families in the 1970s compared with families in the 1990s), different and/or uncontrolled variables, different designs (random, non-randomly assigned; cross-sectional vs. longitudinal), and different measurements (subjective, standardized), making comparisons difficult and oftentimes unreliable. Given the significant legal reforms and accompanying changes in practice, we cannot be sure that the findings reporting on data gathered during the 1970s and 1980s can be generalized to children who have experienced their parents' divorce more recently. Family income is an important predictor of adjustment; however, it is not routinely controlled. Many studies do not include the large group of children whose parents separated but never married. Frequently, studies include the mother's report of child adjustment, neglecting to include the father's perspectives when these have been shown to differ significantly (Block, Block & Gjerde, 1988; Emery, 1982; Lee, 1997). In addition, important variables, such as remarriage and the presence of a step-parent, and the child's age at the time of separation and at the time of measurement are frequently not studied or, if they are examined, the findings are not comparable across studies.

Summary of Findings

Notwithstanding these considerations and limitations, empirical studies and meta-analyses indicate that separation and divorce increases the risk for adjustment difficulties in children and adolescents compared with their continuously married counterparts (Amato, 2000, 2001; Amato & Gilbreth, 1999; Clarke-Stewart, Vandell, McCartney, Owen & Booth, 2000; Hetherington, Bridges & Insabella, 1998; Kelly & Emery, 2003; Leon, 2003; McLanahan, 1999; Wallerstein & Kelly, 1980). Further, the adjustment of children from divorced and remarried families is similar (Amato & Keith, 1991; Cherlin & Furstenberg, 1994). Summarizing the literature in broad strokes, children from separated, divorced and remarried families are more likely to exhibit cognitive limitations, poorer academic achievement, and psychological maladjustment, including both externalizing problems (acting out, conduct problems, aggression) and internalizing problems (depression, anxieties and phobias). Social difficulties with siblings, peers and parents, along with poor self-concepts and self-esteem, are evident. Unlike findings relating to the negative effects on older children, those relating to younger children are less consistent, with some reporting greater risk (Zill, Morrison & Coiro, 1993) and others reporting less risk (Amato & Keith, 1991).

Adolescents from separated and divorced families have also been found more likely to exhibit difficulties, including delinquent behaviour, substance abuse, and higher school-dropout rates. They are also more likely than those from two-parent families to become sexually active at an earlier age and have children while unmarried (Carlson, 2006; Menning, 2006; Stewart, 2003).

Retrospective and longitudinal studies of adults who experienced their parents' divorce during childhood, compared to those from continuously married families, showed that the former also scored lower on various indices relating to educational attainment, psychological adjustment, and interpersonal functioning (Amato & Cheadle, 2005; Hetherington, Bridges & Insabella, 1998; Wallerstein, Lewis & Blakeslee, 2000). In addition, studies of adult children of separation and divorce indicate less satisfaction with life, lower socio-economic attainment, a greater likelihood to be on welfare, less marital stability and higher divorce rates—as high as 70 per cent—in the first five years of marriage for adult women from divorced families (Bumpass, Martin & Sweet, 1991). Remarkably, marital discord and divorce may be transmitted not only to the second but also to the third generation (Amato & Cheadle, 2005).

The literature consistently indicates that about 20 to 25 per cent of children and adolescents from separated and divorced families have significant social and emotional problems compared with about 10 per cent of those from non-divorced families, the former being twice as likely to be at risk for psychosocial difficulties (Amato & Cheadle, 2005; Hetherington & Kelly, 2002; Leon, 2003). This leaves the majority (about 80 per cent) functioning well and without significant adjustment difficulties.

Notwithstanding the increased risk unanimously noted, disagreements are evident regarding the extent and severity (i.e., the effect size) of these adjustment difficulties (Amato, 2003). Overall, differences between divorced and non-divorced groups remain small. In addition, considerable overlap exists between the two groups, indicating notable diversity in children's responses (Amato & Keith, 1991; Hetherington, Bridges & Insabella, 1998). In other words, many children from divorced families do well, while many of those in non-divorced families have adjustment difficulties.

Making sense of these studies is difficult because the impact of separation and divorce is complex. Few, if any studies, have simultaneously considered all of the variables accounting for this complexity. More specifically, outcome is influenced by the various concomitant changes (stressors) that accompany separation and divorce, such as economic hardship—especially for mothers—relocation, and changes in schools, neighbourhoods, and friends (Amato & Cheadle, 2005; Kelly & Emery, 2003; Kelly, 1994; Leon, 2003). In addition, changes in the custodial parent's psychological adjustment, emotional stability, and parenting effectiveness influence adjustment (Hetherington, Cox & Cox, 1985; Pruett, Williams, Insabella & Little, 2003). Remarriage and repartnering are also important factors related to post-divorce adjustment, with reports indicating that as many as two-thirds of the children involved will have a step-parent in their lives at some time (Ahrons, 2006; King, 2006). Individual child-specific factors impacting adjustment to varying degrees include the child's gender, age at separation (and measurement), temperament, and adaptability. Children with easy temperaments are likely to cope better with stress, including separation and divorce (Hetherington & Kelly, 2002; Rutter, 1987).

Of note is that data from longitudinal studies indicate that many of the children's and adolescents' adjustment difficulties existed before the parents' separation, and adjustment to divorce may be due to factors other than the separation or divorce per se (Amato & Booth, 1996; Cherlin et. al. 1991; Hetherington, Bridges & Insabella 1998; Kelly & Emery, 2003). Prior to their parents' separation, children may have been exposed, for example, to their parents' stress and conflict, parenting deficiencies, and/or mental health problems. Alternatively, children's pre-existing emotional and behavioural problems may contribute, in part, to their parents' marital problems and subsequent separation.

Factors Mediating Divorce Adjustment

Parental Conflict

The short- and long-term negative effects of parental conflict on child, adolescent and adult adjustment in divorced and continuously married families is well documented (Amato, 2000; Amato & Afifi, 2006; Amato & Booth, 1996; Ayoub, Deutsch & Maraganore, 1999; Buchanan, Maccoby & Dornbusch, 1991; Cummings & Davis, 1994; Emery, 1999; Grych, 2005; Hetherington & Kelly, 2002; Johnston & Roseby, 1997; Kline, Johnston & Tschann, 1991). Troxel and Matthews (2004) note that parental conflict and divorce affect children's long-term physical health. Children raised in high-conflict divorced and non-divorced families are at increased risk for psycho-social adjustment problems compared with their counterparts in low-conflict divorced and non-divorced families, indicating that it is the interparental relationship and not the marital status or structure of the family (mother-headed, father-headed, joint-custody) that is more predictive of outcome (Amato & Keith, 1991).

Conflict alone, however, is not necessarily harmful to children. Some conflict may be destructive, while other conflict, in particular that which is outside the children's knowledge and/or accompanied by resolution, may have no effect or even have positive effects (Grych, 2007). What is critical then, is how parents manage and express the conflict. Studies have found that the quantity and frequency of parental conflict is not as predictive of outcome as the quality (intensity and focus) of the conflict and further *how* children are involved in their parents' disputes (Cummings & Davies, 1994; Grych, 2007; Johnston, 1994; Kelly & Emery, 2003). However, given that there is little empirical research differentiating levels of conflict or their corresponding impacts on children, it is difficult, if not impossible, to know the extent to which conflict is harmful to children (Kelly, 2000). In other words, we cannot say what the tipping point or threshold is for conflict to move from being helpful or having no negative impact to being harmful.

More specifically, witnessing parental aggression and hostility (in particular that related to children) without resolution is a risk factor for children in both divorced and non-divorced families (Grych, 2007). Conflict can be overt or covert. When children and adolescents are exposed to bad-mouthing, used as messengers to give and obtain information, or pressured to take sides—effectively caught in the middle and experiencing loyalty conflicts—they are more likely to be maladjusted than those who are not actively involved in their parents' conflict (Buchanan, Maccoby & Dorbush, 1991; Grych, 2007; Johnston, 1993; Maccoby and Mnookin, 1992). Similar results have been found relating to adults whose parents separated when they were children (Amato & Affifi, 2006).

Of further interest are findings that children exposed to higher levels of marital conflict may do better after separation than those exposed to lower levels of conflict (Amato & Cheadle, 2005; Amato, Loomis & Booth, 1995). These findings suggest that remaining together in a low-conflict, unhappy marriage may be better for children than divorcing, providing that children are protected from parental conflict.

Changes in Parent–Child Relationships

Examining the impact of the previously mentioned family-process variables (e.g., parenting competency, quality of parent–child relationship, degree, and type of interparental conflict, etc.), Pruett et al. (2003) reported that neither parental conflict nor parent adjustment directly predicts child behaviour problems. Using sophisticated data analyses, they found that it was the impact of parental conflict and parent adjustment on the parent–child relationship that more directly predicted negative outcomes in children.

Losses and changes in the quality of children's relationships with *both* their mothers and their fathers are typical during times of separation or divorce, and these changes affect adjustment (Amato & Cheadle, 2005; Amato & Gilbreth, 1999; Kelly & Emery, 2003; Leon, 2003). Mothers, for example, may either return to work outside the home or work more, thus spending less time with their children and having less opportunity than previously to provide them with guidance and supervision (Hetherington & Kelly, 2002). Maternal adjustment and symptomatology were found to be the best predictors of negative changes in the post-separation mother–child relationship (Hetherington & Kelly, 2002; Pruett, et al., 2003).

Children in both divorced and non-divorced families are better off psychologically and developmentally when they have warm and positive relationships with two involved parents (Amato, 2000; Amato & Gilbreth, 1999; Amato Loomis & Booth, 1995; Emery, 1988; Hetherington, Bridges & Insabella, 1998; Hetherington & Stanley-Hagan, 1977, 1999; Lamb, 1999, 2002; Lamb, Sternberg & Thompson, 1997; Selzer, 1994). Having good relationships with two involved parents mitigates the negative effects of divorce (Kelly & Emery, 2003; Maccoby & Mnookin, 1992).

Father Absence and Involvement

The frequency and quality of contact with non-custodial parents, usually fathers, is another important change that affects outcomes for some children (Amato & Gilbreth, 1999; O'Connor & Bridges, 2004). The effects of father loss due to separation and divorce are greater than the effects of father absence due to parental death (Amato & Keith, 1991). It is not uncommon for children to have less regular and/or frequent contact with their fathers, who often become less involved in their day-to-day care (Kelly & Emery, 2003). Studies have found that the level of parental conflict predicts father involvement, with lower levels associated with greater father involvement (Kelly, 2000; Pruett, et al., 2003; Whiteside & Becker, 2000).

The importance of father involvement in child and adolescent post-divorce adjustment, though, has been questioned, given that frequency of contact alone has not been found to be a good predictor of adjustment or father–child closeness (Amato & Gilbreth, 1999; Furstenberg, Morgan & Allison, 1987; Buchanan, Maccoby & Dornbusch, 1996; King, 1994; King & Heard, 1999; Whiteside & Becker, 2000). These findings have been relied upon by some to support claims for a presumption in favour of the custodial parent who wishes to relocate (Wallerstein, 1995; Wallerstein & Tanke, 1996), and more generally, to argue against joint custody.

Writers have noted that findings indicating a weak statistical association between the frequency of father contact and outcomes are not surprising given the significant changes in father involvement in parenting in both divorced and non-divorced families since the 1970s and 1980s, when much of the data reported in these studies was collected (King, 2006; Warshak, 1992; 2000). Reports from the early 1980s indicate that as many as 50 per cent of fathers had no contact with their children two to three years after divorce, while more recent statistics indicate a decrease (i.e., an increase in involvement) to between 18 and 26 per cent in the middle to late 1990s (Braver & O'Connell, 1998; Furstenburg, Nord, Peterson & Zill, 1983; Maccoby & Mnookin, 1992; Smyth, 2005). Further considerations include the fact that frequency does not capture the quality of parenting or the duration (length) of each contact (Kelly, 2007). As previously noted, methodological limitations are likely to contribute as well, given that important variables like remarriage and the presence of a stepfather are less frequently studied (Ahrons, 2007; King, 2006; White & Gilbreth 2001).

Similar to findings related to parental conflict, it is the quality of father involvement, not the frequency or duration of contact, that is most relevant when assessing short- and long-term outcomes (Stewart, 2003). In their meta-analysis[6] of 63 studies, Amato and Gilbreth (1999) found a positive impact on children's adjustment when non-residential parents remain actively involved, are competent, and provide authoritative parenting. These findings are consistent with earlier research unrelated to divorce on the effects of different types of parenting practices (Baumrind, 1971[7]; Simons & Conger, 2007). More specifically, active, involved and competent parenting, coupled with good and close father–child relationships, are associated with fewer internalizing and externalizing problems, lower school dropout rates, and higher academic achievement (Carlson, 2006; Clarke-Stewart & Hayward, 1996; Hetherington, Bridges & Insabella, 1998; Maccoby & Mnookin, 1992; Menning, 2006).

More recently, studies have examined various elements of father involvement. Elements of parental involvement include: (a) emotional closeness; (b) monitoring and discipline; (c) communication; (d) guidance; (e) social, recreational; and (f) school and education. King and Sobolewski (2006) studied dimensions of father involvement, including how important the father appears to be in the child's life, how often the father considers the child's viewpoint and explains reasons for parental decisions, and how likely the child would be to talk to the father if the child were depressed. These dimensions were associated with positive social, academic, and behavioural adjustment. The researchers note that while leisure activities constitute contact—even warm and supportive contact—they may not allow for sufficient responsive and authoritative parenting practices linked to positive child outcomes. Others have also reported that leisure activities alone do not have an impact on child adolescent adjustment (Amato & Gilbreth, 1999; Stewart, 2003).

In another recent study that relied on two waves of data collected in the middle to late 1990s by the National Longitudinal Study of Adolescent Health, Menning (2006), found that non-resident fathers' involvement that increased over time—especially discussion of schoolwork, grades and other activities at school—predicted less school failure and better academic performance among adolescents. Similar findings have been reported by others (Carlson, 2006; Simons & Conger, 2007; Stewart, 2003). Although the quality of contact is more predictive than frequency/duration, some time is needed to provide opportunities for parenting and for developing and keeping healthy and long-lasting relationships (Kelly & Emery, 2003; King & Sobolewski, 2006). Contact, then, is necessary but not sufficient to ensure a positive impact on adjustment.

Menning (2006) further reported that adolescents who are completely uninvolved with their fathers may fare better than those who experience low or even moderate levels of involvement. These results may support findings indicating that parental conflict and other dynamics relating to the parents' relationship are important risk/resiliency factors. Other studies report that when parental conflict is low, frequent and regular contact is associated with more positive adjustment (Amato & Rezac, 1994; Carlson, 2006; Wallerstein & Kelly, 1980), while in high-conflict situations frequent contact is associated with poor adjustment (Buchanan, Maccoby & Dornbush, 1991; Johnston, 1995).

However, Fabricius and Luecken (2007) found that young adults who had more time with their non-resident fathers had better long-term relationships irrespective of the level of parental conflict, low or high. More specifically, more time with fathers was beneficial in both high and low conflict conditions, while more exposure to parental conflict was harmful (i.e., distress about their parents' divorce and quality of relationship with the father) irrespective of the amount of time, low or high with fathers. In addition, these negative effects were associated with poorer physical health in young adults. These researchers suggest that the combined effect of high conflict and minimal time with fathers is likely to be more of a risk factor for long term physical problems than either one of these factors alone.

Fabricius and Luecken go on to emphasize the challenge these findings present for policies based on the simple conclusion that high parental conflict warrants minimal contact with the non-custodial parent, usually the father. In the researchers' views, this conclusion ignores the more complex interplay between two important variables—parental conflict and time with the non-custodial parent. They posit that while having less time may lower exposure to conflict and thus counter any impact of high conflict, the benefits of reduced conflict might be cancelled out by less time. They further note that studies have reported that conflict dissipates over time, while compromised relationships between divorced fathers and their children continue into adulthood.

In addition, this conclusion that higher levels of parental conflict warrant minimal contact with the non–custodial parent assumes that more time necessarily means more exposure to high conflict. While this may be true in some situations, it is not true in others. In Part II, we elaborate on practical considerations for developing parenting time schedules, including situations with moderate to high conflict.

Another consideration is that a good and close relationship with the less involved non-custodial parent may buffer the impact of a compromised relationship with the custodial parent that results from marginal parenting or mental illness (King & Sobolewski, 2005; Hetherington & Kelly, 2002). Similar findings have been reported in married families (Simons & Conger, 2007). More specifically, a poor mother–child relationship accompanied by strong ties to the non-custodial father are associated with fewer internalizing problems and less acting out in school, compared to those who have weaker ties with both parents.

Notwithstanding the small effect size (differences between the two populations) and the resiliency noted for the overwhelming majority of those in the separation and divorce group, expressions of loss and longing for more time with their fathers, as well as feelings of helplessness and loss of control, have been reported both at the time of separation and years later in retrospective accounts of young adults (Ahrons & Tanner, 2003; Amato, 1987; Fabricius & Hall, 2000; Hetherington, Cox & Cox, 1982; Laumann-Billings & Emery, 2000; Parkinson, Cashmore & Single, 2005; Parkinson & Smyth, 2004; Wallerstein & Kelly, 1980). Emery (2004) notes that these results demonstrate that ongoing distress and painful feelings and resiliency are not mutually exclusive, and furthermore that adversity is not necessarily equivalent to pathology. Kelly (2003) also notes that the presence of painful feelings about divorce have been interpreted and in her view misinterpreted as pathology. She notes that children will necessarily face challenges and adversity and it is in fact the experience of these that assists them to learn how to cope more effectively with life.

Smith, Taylor and Tapp (2003) reported that while half (52 per cent) of the children they interviewed thought the frequency of time with their non-custodial parent was "just right", the other half wanted to see that parent "more often" (34.7 per cent) or "a lot more often" (11 per cent). These researchers noted that children valued "affection, emotional support and their parents taking an interest and an active involvement in their lives in meaningful ways." Further, sources of the children's anger and hurt included resentment for the non-residential parent's lack of input into their lives and feelings of rejection.

In a large retrospective study of 820 college students, 70 per cent wished they had spent more time with their fathers, believing that equal or near-equal time would have been preferable to what they had (Fabricius, 2003; Fabricius & Hall, 2000). These results were replicated in a second sample of low-income young adults not attending college. Those who had and did not have an equal time residential schedule reported similar sentiments. The 30 per cent who did not want equal time believed children should have a substantial number of overnights. The more time children have had with their fathers, the closer they felt to them (Fabricius, 2003).

Similarly, other studies report that adult children who had more time with their fathers felt closer to them, perceived more emotional support, had less intense feelings of loss and abandonment (Laumann-Billings & Emery, 2000), and received more financial support (Fabricuis, Braver, & Deneau, 2003). In addition, studies indicate an association between payment of child support and positive child outcomes (Fabricius, Braver & Deneau, 2003; Selzer, 1994). Those with less time reported more painful and negative memories coupled with feelings of blame towards their fathers for the divorce, and anger towards their mothers, whom they blamed for their having had insufficient time with their fathers. Fabricius (2003) notes that adolescents who felt closer to their non-custodial fathers also felt closer to their custodial mothers, reinforcing the evidence that the relationship the child has with one parent is intertwined with the relationship the child has with the other parent.

Schwartz and Finley (2005) and Finley and Schwartz (2007) reported similar findings in their study of 1,989 ethnically diverse young university students. The fathering variables studied were: nurturing involvement; expressive involvement; instrumental involvement; and mentoring/advising involvement. The young adults from divorced families indicated less nurturing by and involvement with their fathers compared to those from the non-divorced group. Furthermore, the majority of those from divorced families expressed a desire for more father involvement than they had received, and in particular, for more instrumental involvement (e.g., day-to-day tasks, discipline, monitoring schoolwork, and protection). The researchers note that determining parenting time schedules for children and adolescents of divorce needs to take into account the "voices" of young adults from several studies revealing sentiments of "emotional longing" and "missed opportunities" where their fathers are concerned.

A good and cooperative relationship between mothers and fathers is associated with more and better-quality father involvement and, in turn, positive outcomes—including feelings of closeness to their fathers—in children, adolescents, and adult children of divorce (Ahrons & Tanner, 2003; Aquilino, 2006; Buchanan, Maccoby & Dornbush, 1996; Maccoby & Mnookin, 1992; Pruett et al., 2003; Sobolewski & King, 2005; Whiteside & Becker, 2000). Consistent with the studies of maternal gatekeeping[8] in married families, where the more mothers perceive fathers as incompetent, the more they exhibit gatekeeping behaviours (Allen & Hawkins, 1999; Fagan & Barnett, 2003), positive maternal attitudes toward father involvement are associated with better child adjustment (Pruett et al., 2003). When fathers feel the support of the children's mothers, they are more likely to be involved, develop parenting competence, and to remain involved in their children's lives (Buchanan, 2006; Maccoby & Mnookin, 1992; Pruett et al., 2003). When fathers do not feel marginalized as parents and spend more time with their children, they are more likely to remain committed to their children, not only in terms of emotional and practical involvement but also through financial contributions (Aquilino, 2006; Fabricius, Braver & Deneau, 2003; Gunnoe & Braver, 2001; Maccoby & Mnookin, 1992). Furthermore, fathers who remain involved at the time of separation are more likely to remain involved than fathers not as involved when separation occurs (King, 1994; King & Heard, 1999; Juby, Le Bourdais & Marcil-Gratton, 2005).

The Overnight Debate

More than 50 per cent of children born to parents who divorce are six years old or younger. Three quarters of these children are younger than three years old (Emery, 1988). Parenting time schedules are the focus of much conflict for some parents, in turn placing children, and especially young children, at risk for psychosocial problems (Cummings & Davies, 1994; Grych, 2007; Johnston, 1995; Kelly & Emery, 2003; Leon, 2003).

One of the most challenging tasks for both legal and mental health professionals is assisting our clients to develop "best interest" parenting time schedules for young children, especially those younger than three years old. Surveys indicate that more than one-third of children younger than two years old spend nights away from their usual ("primary") parent, typically the mother (Maccoby & Mnookin, 1992). Still, confusion and insufficient information about child development and the effects of separation and divorce on children are common, and consequently the benefits and risks of overnights for young children are hotly debated.[9] Blanket restrictions against overnights (Warshak, 2000), even for families not considered high conflict, while now less common, linger and carry considerable influence in the courts (Kelly, 2007). While there is and should be no "cookbook" to determine best interest parenting time schedules, the social science literature points to various considerations that can inform the advice and guidance we provide our clients and our recommendations to the court (Kelly, 2007).

Historical Perspective and Early Research on Attachment

As noted in Chapter 1, the strongly held belief that young children need their mothers more than they need their fathers is relatively recent in the larger historical perspective. Up until the early 1900s, fathers retained the rights to custody of their children, who were deemed their property. Subsequently, in response to the demands of industry and the need for fathers to work away from their homes, mothers remained at home to care for the children; the paternal preference was replaced by a maternal preference based on the tender years doctrine (Kelly, 1994).

Interestingly, this initial preference for mothers was considered temporary until children reached the age of seven, when they were to be returned to the rightful custodians, their fathers (Kelly, 1994).

By the 1970s, both the father's rights and feminist movements, together with the gradual breakdown of traditional gender roles within the family and the paid workforce, paved the way for what was intended to be a gender-neutral, best interest standard. Most agree that this standard, by moving away from a gender-biased, one-size-fits-all approach, is a much needed improvement. Notwithstanding this concession to its necessity, as previously discussed, most would also agree that the best interest standard is not without significant limitations, given that it is vague and difficult to apply (Emery, 1999; Kelly, 1997).

Theories of attachment (Bowlby, 1969, 1973) and child development, in particular psychoanalytic theory, paved the way for the solidification of the tender years doctrine and the belief that children need one primary psychological attachment figure (referred to as "the psychological parent") before they can subsequently attach to others (Goldstein, Freud & Solnit, 1973, 1986).

Typically, parenting time schedules for children and their non-custodial parents—usually fathers—arising out of the tender years doctrine amounted to every other weekend, irrespective of the individual child's needs (Kelly, 2007). Interestingly, this traditional schedule was not limited to high-conflict disputing families (Kelly, 1997). Kelly notes that children who shared warm and loving relationships with their fathers, usually seeing them daily, were now limited to having contact two out of every 14 days. Furthermore, the biweekly schedule was frequently applied to families where domestic violence and abuse had occurred, with the rationale that if the perpetrator, usually the father, had not abused the children, then parent–child contact should continue (Jaffe, Crooks & Bala, 2005). This schedule remained the standard for some time after fathers began to be studied in the 1970s (Kelly, 2005); during the 1980s, it was often supplemented with additional midweek contact, although not necessarily overnights (Kelly, 2005; Kelly & Emery, 2003).

The 1980s saw a proliferation of guidelines for parenting time schedules. These guidelines relied upon by assessors, mediators and the courts, indicated that overnights before children were three years old, and in some cases five years old, were harmful due to disruptions in attachment, stability and continuity, and consequently should be avoided (Adler, 1988; Awad & Perry, 1980; Baris & Garrity, 1988; Hodges, 1986; Ricci, 1980; Skafte, 1985; Stahl, 1994).[10] The next wave of guidelines included the possibility of overnights for children once they had reached 18 months, but not before (Hawkins, 1991; McDonough & Bartha, 1999; Stahl, 1999). We will return to current guidelines later in this chapter.

A closer look at the theories and research underlying the belief that children need their mothers more than they need their fathers is informative. The groundbreaking and seminal work of John Bowlby led to the single attachment theory, known as monotropy, indicating that children have a biological need to develop a primary attachment to one individual. This first and primary attachment was believed to be necessary to permit the healthy development of subsequent attachments and future adaptive functioning. Psychoanalytic theory stressed the need for one "psychological parent," and further claimed that the designated parent should retain sole legal custody, most notably including the authority to determine a child's contact with the other parent (Goldstein, Freud & Solnit, 1973, 1986). Later, the work of Mary Ainsworth and her colleagues provided further support to this theory, espousing the need for one primary attachment figure.

These earlier and important theories must be put into context. Early studies of attachment included only mothers, making it impossible to know the importance of fathers on children's development. Furthermore, Bowlby studied the effects of *deprivation and neglect* on institutionalized children taken from *both* their mothers and fathers.[11] Warshak (2000) notes that the negative effect on these infants was due to trauma reactions associated with prolonged institutional and inadequate care, and not separation from mothers or maternal deprivation per se. In addition, Warshak states that referring to these early inquiries as maternal deprivation studies is a misnomer since these infants were separated from their mothers *and* their fathers.

Bowlby's work was instrumental in putting in place future policies ensuring that children raised in institutions received adequate care. This context, however, is not comparable to divorce, where a child is cared for alternately by two parents to whom he/she is securely attached. Several years after its publication and in response to the misapplication of his research, Bowlby wrote that the danger of separating children from their mothers had been overstated. He noted that there could be enduring attachments between children and their fathers.

Ainsworth's research, based on the "Strange Situation" paradigm, which we discussed in Chapter 3, is also not transferable to the divorce context. The "Strange Situation" involves separating the child from one parent—the mother—while the child is placed in an unfamiliar situation without, more importantly, another attachment figure. Here attachment (i.e., secure, insecure or disorganized)[12] is measured by observing the child's reaction to the separation from the primary caregiver mother while remaining in an unfamiliar environment, followed by the child's and mother's behaviour when reunited. Like Bowlby's deprivation studies, the "Strange Situation" model is not comparable to a child being taken from one parent to spend time with the other familiar parent with whom the child shares a warm and loving relationship.

Attachment Applied to Parenting Time Schedules and the Overnight Debate

The impact of separating children from their mothers in these "deprivation" and "strange" situations was extrapolated to separation and divorce. As a result, "blanket" restrictions (Warshak, 2000) on overnight contact between the less involved parent and children under three years of age (and in some cases under five) were imposed (Kelly & Lamb, 2000; Warshak, 2000), despite the absence of empirical research indicating that overnight contact would be harmful. It is interesting to note that overnight separations from mothers purportedly put children at risk, while separations from her during the day to be with fathers, nannies, daycare or other caregivers (where children also slept) were of no concern (Warshak, 2000). Some of these children were permitted and even required (encouraged) to sleep overnight at their grandparents' homes or with other caregivers when both parents went on vacation.

On the basis of a single study by Solomon and George (1999), Solomon and Birigen (2001) strongly recommended that overnights not begin before children turn three years old. Solomon and George reported that children between 12 and 18 months who had overnights with their fathers were less likely to have secure attachments and more likely to have disorganized (or unclassified) attachments with their mothers (the primary parent) than children who had no overnights and who remained with two parents.

Opponents have noted several concerns with this single correlational (not causal) study (Warshak, 2002; Lamb & Kelly, 2001; Pruett, Ebling & Insabella, 2004). These commentators note that no differences were reported in the proportions of secure attachments in the groups of infants who had overnights with their fathers and those who did not.[13] Children who had overnights with their fathers were compared with children who, while not having overnights, remained with two parents. Furthermore, many of the children who exhibited insecure-type attachments had experienced repeated and prolonged separations from their fathers, some never having lived with their fathers. Some of the children had pre-existing insecure attachments with their mothers (Lamb & Kelly, 2001; Warshak, 2000). These circumstances, then, are not comparable to those involving children who separate from one parent to spend time with the other, both of whom the children are securely attached to. The relevant comparison group for further study needs to be children without overnights whose parents live separately (not one-home, two-parent families).

More recently, Marsha Pruett and her colleagues reported results from their empirical and longitudinal study examining the psychological impact of overnights on two groups of children less than six years of age (one-to-three and four-to-six years old) from 132 divorcing families (Pruett, Ebling & Insabella, 2004). This is the only study that compares young children with separated parents who have overnights with those who do not. The researchers note that their study is correlational, not causal, and as such the results should be treated as preliminary and provide a basis for further research and hypothesis testing. In addition to age and gender, the study examined various previously identified family-process variables, including the number/frequency of overnights, number of caregivers, schedule consistency, quality of the parent–child relationships, and the parents' communication and cooperation.

Excluding families where there was substance abuse and domestic violence, the results indicated that children between four and six years old who had overnights (one or more) with their fathers showed better adjustment than those who did not. No relationship was found between overnights and adjustment for the younger group; however, parents reported that their children were less withdrawn and had fewer social and attention problems than those with no overnights. In addition, girls in the younger group, and not boys, exhibited better adjustment and more benefit from the overnights and multiple caregivers. These gender differences were attributed to the tendency for younger girls to be verbal, more mature and to have more developed social skills than boys of the same age.

Pruett and her colleagues further reported that consistent schedules (the same days each week) predicted better adjustment for the younger group (one- to three-year-olds), whose mothers reported fewer socializing and internalizing problems. Consistent days every week did not have the same significance for the older group. A related finding indicates an interaction effect: children who had pre-existing difficulties were likely to experience more changes and inconsistencies in scheduling and parenting, in turn exacerbating their existing difficulties and poorer adjustment. The researchers concluded that it is not the overnights per se, but rather the quality of the parent–child relationship, and to a lesser extent the degree of parental conflict, that were the best predictors of children's adjustment.

Although we have very few empirical studies on the direct impact of overnights, the social science literature summarized at the beginning of this chapter is replete with studies and meta-analyses on the impact of separation and divorce on children, adolescents and adults, and this research can be applied to decisions about the merits of overnights. In addition, Biller's earlier studies on father absence laid the foundation for a proliferation of research beginning in the 1970s on the role of fathers in children's development, dispelling the single attachment figure theory as well as elucidating the benefits of father involvement in children's adjustment and development (see Biller, 1993 for a summary of his earlier research), as previously outlined in this chapter.

The abundant research on fathering more generally and not specific to separation and divorce indicates that fathers can and do parent as well as mothers, albeit differently, and furthermore, that children benefit from both types of parenting (Lamb, 2004; Pruett, 2000). More specifically, fathers tend to provide more physical stimulation, play, and opportunities for exploration and autonomy—skills that tend to relate more to the external world—while mothers tend to be more protective, soothing, safety-conscious, limit-setting, and involved in day-to-day practical and instrumental details of child care. Also, children who live with fathers have been reported to do as well as children who live with their mothers and similarly to those in non-divorced families (Bauserman, 2002).

Studies indicate that children become attached to both parents by six or seven months of age, even when one parent, usually the father, has been less involved than the mother (Kelly & Lamb, 2000; Lamb, 1997). In addition, daycare studies demonstrate that young children become attached to others when these individuals have been regularly available and responsive to their needs (Bray, 1991; Kelly & Lamb, 2000; Warshak, 2000). Daycare during the first year of children's lives does not prevent secure attachments from developing with the mother, even though it involves brief separations from the child's usual caregiver, who is typically the mother. What affects children's adjustment and attachment, rather, is the quality of the daycare coupled with the quality of parenting.

Research further indicates that there is usually a hierarchy of meaningful attachments, with young children developing preferential relationships with their usual or primary caregiver (typically the mother). These preferences may become more pronounced in times of stress, fatigue, or illness (Kelly & Lamb, 2000). These writers note that any preference for one parent does not mean that there is not also a secure and important attachment with the other parent, and possibly with others not as involved with the child. Stated differently, just because a child has a primary attachment to one parent does not mean that their less developed attachment to the other parent is unimportant or should not be fostered. Furthermore, preferences usually dissipate when children are between 18 and 24 months old (Kelly & Lamb, 2003; Lamb, 1997).

In addition, developing and sustaining meaningful relationships requires the experience of *functional* parenting in a variety of contexts, such as bedtime and waking rituals and routines, responding to night-time awakenings, soothing, feeding, toileting, play, guidance and limit-setting, assistance with homework, supervision of peer relationships, drop-offs and pickups from school/daycare, etc. (Kelly & Lamb, 2000; Lamb, Sternberg & Thompson, 1997; Warshak, 2000). Overnights are associated with many of these parenting experiences, which would not be possible without the opportunity for them (Lamb & Kelly, 2001; Warshak, 2000), leading these writers to conclude that research indicates that overnights may strengthen rather than harm attachments (Kelly, 2006; Kelly & Lamb, 2000; Warshak, 2000). Writing on behalf of 18 experts, Lamb, Sternberg and Thompson (1997) state:

> To maintain high-quality relationships with their children, parents need to have sufficiently extensive and regular interactions with them, but the amount of time involved is usually less important than the quality of the interaction that it fosters. Time distribution arrangements that ensure the involvement of both parents in important aspects of their children's everyday lives and routines—including bedtime and waking rituals, transitions to and from school, extracurricular recreational activities—are likely to keep nonresidential parents playing psychologically important and central roles in the lives of their children. (p. 400)

Additional justification for children to have more time with their fathers may be found in the previously reported retrospective reports of young adults, who wanted more time with their fathers and expressed feelings of abandonment and lack of closeness (Fabricius, 2003; Fabricius & Hall, 2000; Kelly & Emery, 2003; Laumann-Billings & Emery, 2000; Parkinson, Cashmore & Single, 2005; Warshak, 2000).

The Approximation Rule, Primary Parent Presumption, Continuity and Stability

The American Law Institute (2002) adopted the "approximation rule" to address the ambiguity inherent in the best interest standard and the resulting uncertainty in its application. This rule proposes that parenting time schedules should approximate the proportion of time each parent spent performing direct caretaking functions for the children prior to the separation or, if the parents never lived together, before the filing of an action. The "approximation rule" is designed to resolve disputes when parents are unable to reach an agreement and provides a backdrop for negotiations (Kelly & Ward, 2002). Purporting to be gender neutral, with its rationale based on children's needs for stability, predictability and consistency (Scott, 1992), the approximation rule is explicitly and implicitly justified by reference to attachment theory and to research and data on the impact of shared or joint custody on children (Kelly & Ward, 2002; Riggs, 2005). Proponents of the rule maintain that it is a useful presumption that will minimize parental conflict and consequently will benefit children (Emery, Otto & O'Donohue, 2005; Kelly & Ward, 2002).

Critics question the merits of the approximation rule on several grounds (Greenberg, Gould-Saltman, & Schnider, 2006; Kelly, 2005; Riggs, 2005; Warshak, 2000). They warn that this rule is another iteration of the primary parent presumption, in effect a reincarnation of the tender years doctrine and maternal presumption. They further assert that the rule cannot possibly meet the varied and individual needs of children. Those who caution against any rules and presumptions, including the approximation rule, note that while these may simplify matters and reduce conflict for some families, the opposite is true for others. Gould-Saltman and Schnider (2006) maintain that no empirical studies compare the litigation rates or levels of conflict before or after presumptions and that in turn supports positive outcomes for children. They maintain that while presumptions may discourage litigation and reduce conflict for some, they are likely to escalate conflict for others by shifting the focus of conflict to areas not addressed by the presumption, or to areas that might either prove or overturn the presumption. For example, it is not uncommon for assessors to observe parents fighting to stay in the marital home or to hear the less involved parent claiming to quit their job to compete with a primary parent presumption or the approximation rule.

The most significant concern with the approximation rule is that it assumes that the *quantity* of time spent providing care is indicative of both the quality of parenting (parenting ability) and the quality of the attachment (secure vs. insecure). This assumption arises from yet another assumption, that is, that there is likely to be a strong relationship between the amount of direct caretaking and the development of secure attachments (Kelly & Ward, 2002). Quantity of time, however, does not ensure the development of a secure attachment (Riggs, 2005). Furthermore, the rule does not take into account the secure attachment children often have with the less involved parent (Kelly, 2005; Riggs, 2005). As previously discussed, although some time is necessary to have the opportunity to develop attachments, children can and do form multiple attachments, even with those with whom they spend less time (Lamb, 1997).

As discussed in Chapter 3, attachments can be secure or insecure[14] (Ainsworth, Blehar, Waters & Wall, 1978; Main & Solomon, 1986). Attachment occurs because of the caregiver's ability to respond sensitively to the signals and needs of the infant. Secure attachments allow infants to alternately explore their environments and seek comfort when they feel threatened or stressed (Bowlby, 1969). In addition, secure attachment allows for independence and future adaptive functioning, and is associated with various indices of positive adjustment, while insecure attachment poses a risk for maladaptive adjustment (Cassidy & Shaver, 1999). Attachment patterns, however, are not immutable and can shift with environmental changes; secure attachments may become insecure, while insecure ones may become secure (Riggs, 2005).

Riggs (2005) notes that the approximation rule is at odds with 35 years of attachment research to the extent that the quantity of parenting is equated with having secure attachments. It is not the level or strength of the attachment that is of import, but rather, the attachment quality in terms of degree of security. A strong attachment does not necessarily mean it is a healthy (secure) attachment. A parent can be over-involved, smothering, and/or enmeshed with a child, who in turn has a strong but insecure attachment accompanied by adjustment difficulties. This child may feel a need to appease and care for the preferred parent and/or have difficulties separating from that parent. Alternatively, a child may have a strong but unhealthy attachment with an abusive parent. This child may cling to the abusive parent, identify with the aggressor, and/or reject the other parent. Given that these problematic attachments (insecure types) and unhealthy relationships frequently do not meet the legal threshold of abuse or neglect, they may not be recognized in the approximation rule (Kelly & Ward, 2002; Riggs, 2005). In addition, attachments and affinities ebb and flow throughout development, sometimes based on age and gender. The approximation rule fails to take into account age and changing developmental needs.

The approximation rule emphasizes physical care, time spent, and continuity. Emotional care and the quality of care are not necessarily addressed when speaking of direct caretaking functions (Riggs, 2005), although these are clearly important to attachment and parenting. In addition, critics of the rule question the feasibility of quantifying caretaking functions, which are but one component of parenting. Is the desired parent the one who has spent more time with the child, nurturing and providing acceptance? Alternatively, is it the parent who has done more of the housecleaning, car maintenance, financial planning, provision of economic support, or shop for groceries and other necessary items? Domestic tasks, while important, do not necessarily involve direct contact with the child. In addition, attachment is not only about physical care, but also about emotional care and fostering self-esteem, autonomy, and moral and intellectual development. These writers note that even if you could quantify caretaking—say, for example, that one parent did 60 per cent while the other did 40 per cent—a difference in time is only relevant if it predicts future child adjustment. Warshak (2000) notes we simply do not have empirical data that allows us to make these predictions.

Continuity, one of the values underlying the approximation rule, refers to continuing the pattern of caretaking that existed before separation or divorce; direct physical and emotional care, transportation to school and activities, helping with homework, bedtime and waking routines, etc. (Kelly, 2005). It is impossible, though, to implement full continuity after separation and divorce, given the numerous and unavoidable changes that occur. These include the declining quality of both parents' parenting (due to stress, time issues, litigation, conflict, etc.), mothers returning to work and being less available to their children, fathers becoming more involved with their children, economic changes, residential and school moves, loss of contact with extended family, repartnering, and so on (Kelly, 2005). Even in joint physical custody arrangements, the roles and involvement of both parents necessarily change. While mothers do more than fathers in both divorced and non-divorced partnerships, whatever complementarities existed before the separation are likely to shift afterwards when each parent assumes all, and not only some, of the parenting tasks when the children are in their care. Some believe the approximation rule biases fathers, whose role is marginalized (Riggs, 2005; Warshak, 2000). Although both parents may have agreed that the father assume the breadwinner role to allow the mother to remain home with the children, the approximation rule has the effect of punishing fathers for what was frequently a mutual decision (Riggs, 2005). Riggs notes that some fathers may have preferred to remain home while some mothers may have preferred to return to work, but economic realities dictated otherwise.

For many, *stability* is about preserving one home-base and preventing children from having to move back and forth between two homes and sleep in two beds. To maintain *relationship continuity* after parents separate, however, children will necessarily have a less stable environment, in that they will henceforth be spending time in two places rather than just one. For most children, continuity and stability of *relationships* are more important than continuity and stability of *environment*, given the reality that children change locations while going to activities or sleeping in different places, such as grandparents' homes, daycares, cottages, and friends' homes; they also move around in strollers or in their parents' arms, and manage to function in unfamiliar settings while on vacation. More important for positive child adjustment is having reliable, available and responsive attachment figures. This is achieved through *predictability*, which allows a sense of trust that one's needs will be responded to and met. Any short-term transition problems will need to be evaluated in the context of meeting the children's longer-term needs, to avoid loss and to develop and sustain existing attachments and loving relationships (Kelly, 2007).

While some researchers believe that rules and presumptions are likely to minimize conflict and legal disputes (Emery, Otto & Donahue, 2005), others (Riggs, 2005; Warshak, 2000) maintain that they lend little incentive for parents to cooperate, often leaving one parent with the upper hand. Kelly (2007) explains that not all couples who are characterized as "high conflict" involve two equally dysfunctional, competing and hostile parents. Legal and mental-health practitioners have frequently observed that one parent may be more emotionally disengaged and desirous of avoiding litigation and conflict, while the other parent remains more heavily invested in vengeance, anger, control and pursuit of litigation (Friedman, 2004; Kelly, 2007). Rules and presumptions may motivate these conflict-engaging parents to instigate conflict and/or to claim there is more strife than actually exists. Critics are doubtful that the approximation rule will reduce conflict for the 10 per cent who tend to engage in high conflict over parenting time arrangements, such as in cases involving pathological alienation and relocation. Despite this debate, determining parenting arrangements requires careful examination of the specific needs of each family. A discussion of the various considerations relevant to determining best interest parenting time schedules follows in Part II of this chapter.

Empirical data on the direct risks and benefits of overnights for children away from one parent is scant. We have, however, the benefit of a vast body of social science literature that includes longitudinal and empirical data relating to separation and divorce, risk and resiliency, child development, father absence, and attachment, all of which inform best interest parenting time schedules. Neither blanket restrictions against, nor mandatory rules in favour of, overnights for younger children are indicated by the literature. Instead, overnight visits are perceived as an option for consideration in the complex interplay of the many factors previously summarized. Clearly, further research is needed that not only examines the frequency/duration of overnights but also explores, from both parents' perspectives, how parenting time is spent (Smyth, 2005a, 2005b).

PART II: PRACTICAL CONSIDERATIONS FOR PARENTING TIME SCHEDULE OPTIONS

Relevant Factors

Determining best interest parenting time schedules requires consideration of numerous factors (Bray, 1991; Garon, Donner & Peacock, 2000; Gould & Stahl, 2001; Kelly, 1994). These include the child's age, cognitive, memory and language abilities as well as temperament and personality, all of which affects the duration of time the child can manage separations from each parent as well as the child's ability to cope with change. The child's social and emotional adjustment is important to consider. Children who are more vulnerable and those with special needs (developmental, medical, educational, emotional or social) may require more environmental stability and different parenting time schedules (Bray, 1991; Kelly, 2005).

The social science literature points to additional factors requiring consideration, including:

(a) the pre-separation parent-child relationship;

(b) involvement in parenting (e.g., physical caretaking, soothing, comforting, fostering self-esteem, providing stimulation, encouraging autonomy, supporting academic achievements);

(c) parenting strengths and weaknesses;

(d) the quality of the attachments;

(e) each parent's adjustment and parenting ability (challenges and strengths);

(f) the ability and willingness of the parent who has participated less in parenting to learn parenting skills and behaviours;

(g) the fit between each parent and the child's needs;

(h) the parents' emotional health and adjustment, and in particular how this impacts parenting;

(i) relationships with siblings and extended family;

(j) the parents' ability to communicate and cooperate with each other;

(k) the nature and intensity of parental conflict and how the parents involve their children in the conflict; and

(l) and the presence of domestic violence and abuse.

As previously discussed in Chapter 3, children's wishes and preferences are also important considerations. These must be interpreted and weighed in light of any potential undue influence exerted by parents and other adults.

Garon, Donner and Peacock (2000) provide a useful framework outlining a developmental needs assessment to assist families.[15] This needs assessment is divided into the following 10 areas requiring assessment or consideration, each of which has several components:

(1) child's personality;

(2) child's understanding of parental separation/divorce;

(3) parent–child relationship;

(4) provisions for child's supervision and safety;

(5) child's health;

(6) other relationships;

(7) current activities;

(8) educational needs;

(9) child's living arrangements; and

(10) co-parental relationships.

As previously noted, separation and divorce involves many changes, as well as secondary losses (residential moves, changes in school, daycare, caregivers, losses, and new relationships, changes in parents' work schedules, new partners and their children, etc.). The effects of stress (change) are cumulative, not additive (Rutter, 1979). Accordingly, being cautious is prudent, and rather than making abrupt and substantial changes all at once, consider phasing them in gradually. A gradual approach is likely to benefit most children, especially those with temperaments and personalities that predispose them to experience difficulties coping with change. We move now to a discussion of various practical considerations for developing parenting time schedules. Appendix 12 provides a summary of these considerations.

Younger Children

Transition difficulties for children ranging from 15 to 36 months are developmentally expected and usually indicate healthy maturation and attachment. In fact, separation anxiety is a hallmark of development, indicating the presence of object constancy.[16] For some, transitions remain problematic until the child becomes school age. These difficulties do not necessarily mean the other parent is incompetent or that the child does not want to be with that parent. Transition difficulties are usually short-lived and especially so when children are united with another positive attachment figure.

As a result of their limited memory, verbal capacity and conceptualization of time, infants and toddlers require frequent contacts of a shorter duration with each parent, ensuring they are not apart from either parent for too long (Kelly, 2005; Kelly & Lamb, 2000) while also attempting to ensure that schedules are as predictable as possible (Pruett, Ebling & Insabella, 2004).[17] To illustrate this point, note that spending time with one parent every other weekend is unlikely to give the younger child any sense of predictability for that relationship if the child is unable to conceptualize that span of time. Split weekends are an option worthy of consideration, especially for younger children (under three years) when overnights are first introduced. A 24-hour period every weekend may be a stepping-stone to implementing alternating weekends. In this way, children are not apart from either parent for too long. In addition, a more regularly occurring or frequent weekly overnight stay may assist children to acclimatize more quickly as opposed to having to wait 12 days for the next one. Although split weekends are likely to meet the needs of younger children, some parents object because this arrangement prevents them from going away on the weekends, which may or may not include visiting family. While this is an important consideration, children's needs must remain paramount. The split weekend arrangement is usually a short-term measure to ease children into longer durations of time with one parent and correspondingly longer absences from the other. Split weekends will also afford one parent time for weekly personal and domestic tasks in the absence of having to care for children.

In an effort to minimize changes when adding in overnights, the best method is to combine these with the usual schedule (for instance, add a Saturday overnight to the Saturday 10-to-5 contact). Some younger children do better when they have had a day to settle in with the parent prior to the overnight as opposed to having the transition to that parent occur an hour or two before bedtime. Consideration should be given to introducing overnights when there will be a natural change, such as over a holiday period. Initially, and for children under two or three, preference should be given to the most important holidays, leaving the others to fall as they do with a view to minimizing frequent changes to the usual schedule.

Children's nap frequency and times are important though overlooked considerations when developing parenting time schedules. Including naps in parenting time allows children to gradually become familiar with their new and less familiar home environment. These usually involve shorter separations from the other parent than an overnight would involve. The beginning and ending of the parenting time are likely to have an impact on the smooth implementation of the usual nap times as well as the night-time sleeping routines. For example, returning the child prior to a nap may be problematic if the child falls asleep in the car and/or, in the case of a longer drive, the child's usual bedtime is pushed forward. This is likely to disrupt the child's waking time and routines, thereby frustrating the receiving parent, who may now have good reason for wanting to limit time with the other parent. Consideration should be given to returning the child to the other parent after as opposed to before a nap, but not too close to the usual bedtime.

Breastfeeding is often cited as a reason overnights should be postponed. Many factors need to be considered with regard to this issue, including the child's age. Bottle supplements given by mothers and caregivers are not uncommon for nursing children, during both the day and night. Once breastfeeding is established and after the first few months, breast milk can be expressed and subsequently provided to the child in a bottle by the father. Reducing, by several, the total number of breast feedings in a week will not necessarily compromise the benefits of breast-feeding for children (or the ability of the mother to nurse), and may assist with the development of the child's relationship with the other parent.

Unless there is good reason to suspend contact with one parent, a child after separation has one life and, in most cases, two homes. Some change and disruption are inevitable, no matter how much time children spend with each parent. While it is possible that more time will promote greater comfort, what is important is that parents are proactive in making their children feel as comfortable as possible in both homes, regardless of the amount of time spent in each—even if as little as 10 per cent. Various tools and strategies can be implemented to assist younger children in the adjustment to maintaining lives in two homes. For example, Wallerstein and Blakeslee (1989) suggest having different-coloured lunch boxes depending on which parent picks up the child on any given day. Similarly, a colour-coded calendar placed in each home to identify mom and dad days is likely to assist younger children whose thinking is concrete and who have yet to master the concepts of time—the day after tomorrow, next week, etc. Usually, children are six or seven years old when they begin to comprehend the meaning of a week or a month. Allowing children to take familiar possessions, blankets and toys (i.e., transitional objects) to each home is likely to provide a sense of continuity and increase the familiarity of the environment, in turn assisting with their comfort, settling-in and adjustment (Solomon, 2005). In addition, repeated sequences or rituals around separations and reunions, by virtue of their familiarity, are likely to comfort and reassure all children, and especially the pre-verbal child (Solomon, 2005).

Continuity of care within and between homes is particularly important for infants and younger children. Parents need to be encouraged to communicate about this care and routine, just as they must when they return from work and relieve a babysitter or nanny. If direct communication proves problematic, an email communication log is often easier to maintain, supplemented by a journal that travels with the children in order to record time-sensitive information. Parents who have difficulty staying focused on their children's needs may benefit from a more structured communication protocol. For example, relying on headings such as "bedtime routines," "school," "activities," "medical/health," "requests for temporary changes," "major accomplishments/setbacks," and so on, as well as other rules relating to parental communication (e.g., response time, frequency of emails, etc.) may provide the needed structure and focus.[18] Some parents require further micromanaging of their communication do's and don'ts in terms of acceptable tone (no sarcasm), language (no insults and name-calling), and content to be avoided (no blame and criticism of the other's personality and parenting).

For parents with children less than five or six years of age, it may be helpful to develop parenting time schedules in six-month blocks that allow for a period of familiarization when required, coupled with periodic meetings with a mediator, child development consultant or parenting coordinator. These meetings provide a forum for the parents to communicate and share relevant information about their children's adjustment, developmental changes, accomplishments, challenges and the various and frequently changing routines and rituals related to sleeping, eating, toileting, health/illness, etc. In addition, these meetings may provide education with respect to child development, parenting and effective communication.

Holidays, Special Days and Vacations

Here we refer to any days that would require changes to the regular parenting time schedule.[19] Typical inclusions are Christmas, Easter, Thanksgiving, March Break, summer vacation, Jewish holidays, long weekends and professional development days, as well as Hallowe'en and family birthdays. Usually, these days take precedence over the usual schedule, and the changes they necessitate need to be noted explicitly in the plan to avoid interpretation difficulties. Parents may choose to alternate whole holiday periods every other year, share specific weekends every year (e.g., one parent always has the children over Thanksgiving, while the other always has them over Easter), or split each one every year. The latter may involve too many transitions over a short time period, and may be especially difficult for children in high-conflict situations. Children usually benefit from continuing with traditions to which they have become accustomed while also developing new traditions. Communicating about details around organizing the children's birthday parties, or attending their friends' parties (who takes the children to the party, can the non-resident parent accompany them, who buys the gift, etc.), may help preempt parental conflict.

The number of consecutive days children can vacation with each parent will depend on all of the previously noted factors and considerations that apply to the regular schedule. The specific times for advance notification of summer vacation dates, sometimes with the parents alternating the right of first option, also needs to be addressed in the parenting plan. As periods such as summer vacation tend to be longer, the child's age and ability to manage time away from the other parent are important considerations. Having older siblings present is likely to facilitate a younger child's adaptation. It is also easier for the younger child, who may struggle with a week's absence from one parent if the change is inserted into the usual schedule, to adapt to one or two longer vacation periods typically filled with fun and stimulation. Telephone calls to the non-vacationing parent may be important for younger children. Details for smooth implementation of such calls need to be specified in advance.

Of utmost importance for both predictability and minimizing of parental conflict is the identification of both beginning and ending dates of these vacations and holidays. For example, can a usually scheduled weekend be added to a two-week vacation? The times and locations of the transitions and the responsibility for delivering and picking up the children must be explicit. The parents will need to determine what happens to the regular schedule after a holiday period. Does the usual rotation continue as before, which might mean that for a two-week vacation the children would have three consecutive weekends with the vacationing parent, or do the children spend the first weekend after the vacation with the non-vacationing parent, after which the weekends alternate, in effect changing the usual rotation?

Moderate to High Levels of Conflict[20]

Children need to be protected from parental conflict while also having, where possible, meaningful relationships with both parents. While cooperative parenting is preferable, children can do reasonably well when their parents remain disengaged and function in a parallel fashion independently (Hetherington & Kelly, 2002; Johnston, 1995; Kelly, 2005; Lamb, Sternberg & Thompson, 1997; Maccoby & Mnookin, 1992; Whiteside, 1998). In the absence of domestic violence, efforts towards structuring parenting and employing conflict-reduction strategies should be a first step before concluding that a child should not have time with both parents (Kelly, 2007). The greater the parental conflict, the more structure and specificity required in the parenting plan, in order to enable the parents to disengage and, in effect, to parent parallel to one another.

Regardless of the schedule, a protocol for transitions, including neutral locations (e.g., at school, daycare, friend's home, third party, etc.), is advised for parents unable to control their anger and frustration towards the other parent in front of the children. Neutral transitions are also likely to benefit children whose parents express their hostility indirectly in non-verbal language or by the absence of a simple hello and goodbye. This protocol needs to lay out in no uncertain terms the pickup and drop-off times, the parent (or parent's delegate) responsible for the transportation, and in some cases when there is no other alternative than a transition between the parents, rules regarding parental behaviour at the transition (e.g., cordial exchanges only, absolutely no talking about the children, waiting at the curb, etc.). Children may benefit from having the parent they are with at the time taking them to the other parent. In this way, the children's activities do not need to be interrupted. Furthermore, taking the children to the other parent is likely to signal one parent's support of the children's relationship with the other parent; this may be especially helpful when children are reticent about making the transitions and/or spending time with that parent.

Other questions relevant to parenting time to ask and address in the parenting plan are: Who will care for an ill child in the morning, or pick them up and care for them if the school calls in the middle of the day? When will the regular schedule resume? Which parent will attend school field trips? Will one parent have the first option of caring for the child when the other parent is unavailable? How long must the parent in question be unavailable before this option must be offered to the other parent, who, of course, is not obliged to accept the responsibility? These are a few of the many questions that need to be addressed, especially in situations where parents have difficulty communicating without conflict and where they tend to involve their children in this conflict.

Invariably, it is not until the parenting plan is implemented that parents become aware of the inherent problems. For example, whose weekend is it after a two-week vacation? Which parent is called if the child becomes ill at school? Developing an annual calendar based on the parenting plan is most helpful, especially for higher-conflict families. This is often one of the first tasks for the mediator or parenting coordinator involved in assisting the family with the implementation of their parenting plan. Putting the plan into calendar form will identify in advance ambiguities, interpretation differences, and oversights, thereby preempting conflict close to the time of the event, when emotions are running high. In addition, having the calendar laid out in advance provides some security and predictability for children, and allows parents to plan for the times when they have and do not have the children.

Competing Needs of Children

The younger child's needs for frequent and regular contact with both parents necessarily involves multiple transitions, which may compete with the child's need to be protected from parental conflict. Including a Sunday overnight may protect the child from parental conflict and loyalty binds (while also allowing parent participation in school drop-offs); however, children who are younger, immature and/or have special needs may find four as opposed to three days[21] away from the other parent difficult to manage.

The conundrum of children's competing needs becomes evident when considering the frequently used terms of continuity, stability, and consistency that we discussed in Part 1 of this chapter. The courts place significant weight on the status quo, believing that it provides children with both stability and continuity during the upheaval of separation and divorce. Taking the conservative approach, the courts tend to convey the oft-heard maxim, "If it's not broken, don't fix it." The notion of status quo is problematic, however, to the extent that it fails to recognize the inevitability of children's changing needs. The significant weight placed on the status quo discourages parents from acknowledging the fluidity of their child's needs by agreeing to interim schedules or timetables that apply to a specific duration of time, for example six to twelve months. This is usually set in place with a view to gradually increasing the parenting time with the non-custodial parent, taking into account how the child fared during the previous period. We know that these arrangements are often not only reasonable, but are likely best for younger children who, as they mature and internally regulate, will eventually be able to manage longer separations from one parent accompanied by more time with the other. Moreover, parenting schedules and plans often need to be fine-tuned and/or revised because of other changes, including remarriage and repartnering, relocation, the birth of new siblings, changes in work locations and schedules, and school changes.

The parents' work schedules and the distances between each parent's home, workplace, and the schools must be considered in parenting time schedules. In general, maximizing the children's time with the parents when each is available is advisable. The Sunday overnight may not be possible if the school is far away from the parent's home, necessitating a prematurely early morning wake-up and, sometimes, a doubling-back commute for the parent.

Many parents choose to have their nannies move back and forth with the children between the two homes. This may provide further stability and continuity of care, and is especially important for younger children, providing the parents are able to keep the caregiver out of their conflict, which seems to be a challenge for many of our higher-conflict parents. Other parents may choose to implement a "nesting" arrangement, usually on an interim basis, whereby the children stay put and the parents move in and out of the home for their parenting time. This may require considerable financial resources if each parent has to maintain an additional residence.

PARENTING TIME OPTIONS

Table 14 lists several resources that provide various parenting time options.[22] Models of parenting time options tend to exist on a continuum that calls for the consideration of numerous relevant factors, effectively cautioning against a prescriptive, one-size-fits-all approach.

Table 14

Parenting Time Schedule Resources

- www.coloradodivorcemediation.com/family/parent_plans.asp (Joan Kelly)

- http://emeryondivorce.com/parenting_plans.php (Robert Emery)

- www.coloradodivorcemediation.com/family/schedules.asp

- www.afcc.net.org (Planning for Shared Parenting: A Guide for Parents Living Apart)

- www.supreme.state.az.us (Arizona Model Parenting Time Plans)

- www.state.ak.us/court/forms/dr-475.pdf (Alaska Model Parenting Agreement)

The Arizona guidelines provide suggestions for three types of plans (A, B and C), reflecting a continuum of parent involvement before the separation as well as the involvement desired after the separation. Plan C includes the possibility of overnights for some children 12 months of age and older. All plans include overnights for children between three and five years old, with Plan C providing for equal parenting time.

Robert Emery's model provides different parenting time options based on three divorce styles ("angry," "distant," and "cooperative") across six age groups, ranging from infancy to 18 years of age. More traditional parenting time options are provided for the "angry divorce," more integrated options for the "distant divorce," and more closely integrated options for the "cooperative divorce." Emery's model provides for overnights beginning when most children reach 18 months, leaving open the possibility of overnights for children younger than 18 months if the baby is able to tolerate them well. This guideline implies trying overnights, and points to the "organic" nature of parenting time schedules.

Joan Kelly's model provides eight different parenting time options for children ranging from five to seventeen years of age, and outlines the benefits and risks of each option. She notes that her model does not include guidelines or prescriptions but rather options for consideration. Kelly states that although the traditional every-other-weekend schedule may be indicated for some families, depending on the history of parent involvement and the presence of domestic violence, it is problematic for many children to go as many as 12 days without contact with the non-residential parent. In addition, she notes that the traditional schedule provides little relief for the other parent. Kelly advises that depending upon the parenting history, the child's age and the other relevant factors, the traditional schedule could be implemented initially, with a view to increasing time as the child's relationship with the more unfamiliar parent develops and as that parent develops more skill and experience. Like that of Emery and others, Kelly's approach underscores the ever-changing nature of parenting time schedules and the importance of implementing these schedules in a gradual and child-focused manner.

Kelly states that frequent contacts of shorter duration are recommended for infants and toddlers, the ideal being daily or every other day across varied functions and parenting domains. By two years old, children can manage longer separations, and many manage well with two consecutive overnights; longer separations of five to seven days should be avoided. Many preschool-aged children can manage three or four days of separation (extended weekends, plus mid-week overnights), with exceptions made for isolated vacation periods that may be as long as one week. School-aged children five years of age and older can often manage separations of five to seven days that occur in the shared physical custody schedule known as 5-5-2-2 or a week on/week off schedule. Children though may have difficulty with a one-week separation, without contact with the other parent. Isolated vacations of longer periods of up to two weeks may be fine for most children this age. At six or seven and older, children may be ready for alternating weeks with each parent (the 7-7 schedule, "week about"). Most adolescents can cope well with longer stretches of time apart from each parent, and sometimes prefer alternating two-week periods to limit the number of transitions and the frequent movement of their belongings.

Planning for Shared Parenting: A Guide for Parents Living Apart was sponsored by the Massachusetts Chapter of the Association of Family and Conciliation Courts (AFCC),[23] and represents the collaborative effort of a task force comprising both the legal and mental-health communities. This guide is informative and practical. It summarizes normal child development and the effects of separation and divorce at various age levels. The guide elaborates various developmentally relevant considerations for designing parenting time schedules for each of the following eight age ranges:

(1) infants (birth to nine months);

(2) babies (9 to 18 months);

(3) toddlers (18 to 36 months);

(4) preschoolers (three to five years old);

(5) early school-aged children (six to nine years old);

(6) later school-aged children (10 to 12 years old);

(7) early adolescents (13 to 15 years old); and

(8) late adolescents (16 to 18 years old).

Unlike other models, the guide breaks down the child's first 18 months into two periods, thus providing valuable information for this debated age range. Overnights in familiar settings may be indicated at this stage when parents have shared parenting tasks, the non-custodial parent has been active and involved prior to the separation, and the parents are willing and able to communicate effectively about the baby's routines and needs, thereby permitting continuity of care.

Appendix 13 provides 10 parenting time options (over a two-week cycle), with an analysis of each that takes into account six factors: duration of time away from each parent; number of days where contact occurs (including morning drop-offs at school); number of overnights; number of transitions (will vary depending on how transition is defined and counted); location of transitions; opportunity for varied parenting experiences across contexts (e.g., homework, attendance at school, bedtime and waking routines, meals, activities).

The primary objective of parenting time schedules is to allow children to develop and sustain meaningful relationships with both parents, unless good reasons show this should not occur. Determining parenting time schedules, especially those for children under the age of three, challenges mediators, lawyers, judges and mental-health professionals as they consider the competing needs of children to have meaningful relationships with both parents while at the same time being protected from parental conflict and maintaining stability, continuity and predictability. Although presumptions and rules simplify matters and to some extent reduce the ambiguity inherent in best interest criteria, a one-size-fits-all approach remains insensitive to children's varied and individual needs. The indeterminacy of the best interest standard reflects the very real and unavoidable complexities of children's lives.

Although there are a finite number of ways to divide a two-week block of time, child-focused and creative solutions for creating and implementing parenting time schedules aimed at the best possible outcome for children are available. Careful attention and specific consideration must be given to meeting the needs of children in higher-conflict families. In some of these families, the parent contact may need to be limited. In severe cases involving domestic violence, when the risks outweigh the benefits, contact may be contraindicated.[24] In many moderate- to higher-conflict families, structured and specified parenting plans, accompanied by rules of engagement and conduct, will assist parents to some extent to remain disengaged and parent in a parallel fashion, thereby protecting their children from parental conflict with the objective of developing and maintaining meaningful parent-child relationships.

In this chapter, we addressed the formulation of parenting plans in two parts. In Part 1, we summarized the social science literature on the impact of separation and divorce and discussed mitigating factors. The historical view of attachment theory as it relates to the overnight debate was reviewed as well as the approximation rule and primary parent presumption as these relate to the principles of continuity, stability and predictability. In Part II, we examined various considerations for the development of parenting time schedules, with an emphasis on higher conflict families. Checklists and parenting time options were provided in appendices to assist the assessor.

Notes

[1] (1996) 87 N.Y. 2d 727 NYCA (at p. 740).

[2] This study uses data from the 1979 National Longitudinal Survey of Youth.

[3] Studies by King, Sobolewski and Aquilino rely on the National Survey of Families and Households (NSFH), which includes data collected from adolescents and mothers as well as child outcomes.

[4] The studies by Menning and Stewart rely on the National Longitudinal Study of Adolescent Health.

[5] The Marin County Project (Wallerstein, Lewis & Blakeslee, 2000) involved a clinical study of 60 families that began in 1971 and spanned three decades. The families received counselling in exchange for their participation. Two-thirds had histories of moderate to severe psychopathology. No comparison groups of non-clinical or non-divorced families were studied, and standardized outcome measures were not used. At the 25-year mark, 26 individuals of the original sample were interviewed.

The Virginia Longitudinal Study of Divorce and Remarriage (Hetherington & Kelly, 2002), begun in the 1960s, compared divorced (72) and married (72) families and employed multiple measures. It was initially designed as a two-year study; however, the time frame and sample were expanded over the years (180 at wave 4, 300 at wave 5 and 450 at wave 6), with data gathered at two months, one, two, six, eleven and twenty years following divorce. The children ranged from four to 24 years of age. The cumulative sample was 900 from divorced, non-divorced and remarried families, with 61 adult children followed from the original sample.

The Binuclear Family Study (Ahrons, 2007) began in 1979 and randomly selected 98 divorced mothers and fathers from public divorce records. Interviews with both parents occurred at one, three and five years post-divorce. New partners and step-parents were interviewed in the second and third waves of interviews. A 20-year follow-up was conducted with 173 adult children, representing 89 of the original 98 families.

[6] Meta-analyses are commonly used and refer to conducting a survey of many studies and then analyzing the aggregate data.

[7.] Using the dimension of parental control, Baumrind (1971) identifies three styles of parenting: permissive (indulgent), authoritative and authoritarian. This was expanded by Maccoby and Martin (1983), who added responsiveness as a second dimension. Parents who are high on both dimensions are categorized as authoritative. Warmth and support with enforcement of rules and use of consequences when necessary characterize these parents. Studies consistently indicate that children do better when parented with an authoritative style compared with an authoritarian or permissive style.

[8.] Mothers are typically identified as the gatekeepers, given their primary role in caring for children (see Pleck, 1997). Gatekeeping refers to attitudes and behaviours that either facilitate or limit the other parent's opportunity to parent and develop close relationships with their children.

[9.] See Overnights and Young Children: Essays from the Family Court Review (Biringen et. al. 2002; Lamb & Kelly, 2001; Kelly & Lamb, 2000; Pruett, Ebling & Insabella, 2004; Solomon & Biringen, 2001; Warshak, 2000, 2002). Marsha Pruett's editorial introduction to this special issue provides a good overview of this debate (Pruett, 2005). In addition, see Gould & Stahl (2001), Kelly (2005), Kraft (2004), and Whiteside (1998).

[10.] See Freeman (2000) for an overview of articles and resources providing parenting time options.

[11.] Bowlby extended the research on motherless monkeys conducted by Harlow in the 1950s (Harlow, 1958). Although these studies were initially interpreted to support the maternal deprivation hypothesis, it is now recognized that the adverse effects and dysfunctional behaviour noted in the monkeys were caused by deprivation and social isolation, not a dysfunctional mother–infant relationship.

[12.] Reviews of attachment theories and types can be found in Ainsworth (1979), Ainsworth, Blehar, Waters & Wall (1978), Bryne, O'Connor, Marvin & Whelan (2005), and Riggs (2005).

[13.] In addition, Pruett, Ebling and Insabella (2004) note that the effects of overnights were limited to an examination of attachment behaviours, while there are many additional indices of child adjustment.

[14.] Insecure attachments may be categorized as three types: insecure-avoidant, insecure-resistant or ambivalent, and insecure-disorganized (an unusual mixture of avoidant and ambivalent behaviours).

[15.] This framework is one of the resources Family Solutions has relied on to develop their Family Needs Consultation, a team intervention used to assist separating and divorcing families (Fidler, Chodos, Horowitz, Radovanovic & Schloss, 2007, unpublished manuscript).

[16.] This is a Piagetian term used to describe children's cognitive ability, in this case knowing that the parent exists even when the child cannot see that parent.

[17.] See section entitled *Parenting Time Options* for further elaboration of general guidelines for schedules by age.

[18.] The website info@ourfamilywizard.com provides software parents can use for sharing information and communicating about parenting schedules, routines, requests for temporary changes, and communication.

[19.] It may be preferable to make a planned change to the regular schedule after a holiday/vacation period when a change to the schedule would have occurred anyway.

[20.] See Appendix 14 Parenting Plan Checklist For High Conflict Families, at the end of this chapter.

[21.] Assumes Friday morning and Monday after-school transitions vs. Friday morning until Sunday evening.

[22.] In a recent article, Dember and Fliman (2005) provide parenting time options for children from birth to 18 years of age. These options arose out of a seven-person multidisciplinary task force (comprising lawyers, mediators, a magistrate of domestic relations, social workers and psychologists) formed to revise the Standard Order of Visitation in Ohio (Hamilton County). This standard order called for the child, irrespective of age, to spend every other weekend (Friday to Sunday evening) and one weekly three-hour period of contact with the non-residential parent, with overnights beginning at 12 months.

[23.] Available from www.afccnet.org (email afcc@afccnet.org) for US$3, this guide is a most informative resource for parents and legal and mental–health practitioners alike.

[24.] We address the issue of domestic violence in custody assessments more fully in a separate chapter in our companion book, *Special Topics in Child Custody Assessments.*

References

Adler, R. *Sharing the Children: How to Resolve Custody Problems and Get on with Your Life* (MD: Adler & Adler Publishers, Inc. , 1988).

AFCC Task Force on Parenting Coordination "Parenting Coordination: Implementation issues" Family Court Review 41 (2003), 533–564.

Ahrons, C.R. "Family ties after divorce: Long-term implications for children" Family Process 46:1 (2006), 53–65.

Ahrons, C.R. & Tanner, J.L. "Adult children and their fathers: Relationship changes 20 years after parental divorce" Family Relations 52 (2003), 340–351.

Ainsworth, M.D.S. "Infant-mother attachment" American Psychologist 34 (1979), 932–937.

Ainsworth, M.D.S., Blehar, M.C., Waters, E. & Wall, S. (Eds.) *Patterns of Attachment: A Psychological Study of the Strange Situations* (Hillsdale, NJ: Lawrence Erlbaum, 1978).

Allen, S.M. & Hawkins, A.J. "Maternal gatekeeping: Mothers' beliefs and behaviors that inhibit greater father involvement in family work" Journal of Marriage and the Family 61 (1999), 199–212.

Amato, P. "Family processes in one-parent, stepparent and intake families: The child's point of view" Journal of Marriage and the Family 49 (1987), 327–337.

Amato, P.R. "The consequences of divorce for adults and children" Journal of Marriage and Family Therapy 62:1 (2000), 269–288.

Amato, P.R. "Children of divorce in the 1990s: An update from Amato and Keith (1991) meta-analysis" Journal of Family Psychology 15 (2001), 355–370.

Amato, P.R. "Reconciling divergent perspectives: Judith Wallerstein, quantitative family research, and children of divorce" Family Relations 52 (2003), 332–339.

Amato, P.R. & Afifi, T.D. "Feeling caught between parents: Adult children's relations with parents and subjective well-being" Journal of Marriage and Family 68 (2006), 222–235.

Amato, P.R. & Booth, C. "A prospective study of parental divorce and parent-child relationships" Journal of Marriage and the Family 58 (1996), 356–373.

REFERENCES

253

Amato, P.R. & Cheadle, J. "The long reach of divorce: Divorce and child well-being across three generations" Journal of Marriage and Family 67 (2005), 191–206.

Amato, P.R. & Gilbreth, J. G. "Non-resident fathers and children's well-being: A meta-analysis" Journal of Marriage and the Family 61 (1999), 557–573.

Amato, P.R. & Keith, B. "Parental divorce and the well-being of children: A meta-analysis" Psychological Bulletin 110:1 (1991), 26–46.

Amato, P. & Rezac, S. "Contact with residential parents, interparental conflict and children's behaviour" Journal of Family Issues 15 (1994), 191–207.

American Law Institute. *Principles of the Law of Family Dissolution: Analysis and Recommendations* (Newark, NJ: LexisNexis, 2002).

Aquilino, W.S. "The noncustodial father-child relationship from adolescence into young adulthood" Journal of Marriage and Family 68 (2006), 929–946.

Awad, G.A. & Parry, R. "Access following marital separation" Canadian Journal of Psychiatry 25:5 (1980), 357–365.

Ayoub, C., Deutsch, R. & Maraganore, A. "Emotional distress in children of high-conflict divorce: The impact of marital conflict and violence" Family and Conciliation Courts Review 37:3 (1999), 297–313.

Baumrind, D. "Current patterns of parental authority" Developmental Psychology Monograph 4:1 (1971), Part 2.

Baris, M.A. & Garrity, C.B. *Children of Divorce: A Developmental Approach to Residence and Visitation* (Asheville, NC: Blue Ridge Printing Co., 1988).

Bauserman, R. "Child adjustment in joint-custody versus sole-custody arrangements: A meta-analytic review" Journal of Family Psychology 16:1 (2002), 91–102.

Biller, H.B. *Fathers and Families: Paternal Factors in Child Development* (Westport, CT: Auburn House, 1993).

Biringen, Z., Greve-Spees, J., Howard, W., Leith, D., Tanner, L., Moore, S., Sakoguchi, S. & Williams, L. "Commentary on Warshak's 'Blanket restrictions: Overnight contact between parents and young children'" Family Court Review 40:2 (2002), 204–207.

Block, J., Block, J. & Gjerde, P. "Parental functioning and the home environments in families of divorce" Journal of the American Academy of Child and Adolescent Psychiatry 27 (1988), 207–213.

Bowlby, J. *Attachment* and *Loss: Vol. 1 Attachment* (London: Hogarth, 1969).

Bowlby, J. *Attachment and Loss: Vol. 2 Separation: Anxiety and Anger* (New York: Basic Books, 1973).

Bray, J.H. "Psychosocial factors affecting custodial and visitation arrangements" Behavioral Sciences and the Law 9 (1991), 419–437.

Buchanan, C., Maccoby, E. & Dornbusch, S. "Caught between parents: Adolescents' experience in divorced homes" Child Development 62 (1991), 1008–1029.

Bumpass, L.L., Martin, T.C. & Sweet, J.A. "The impact of family background and early marital factors on marital disruption" Journal of Family Issues 12 (1991), 22–42.

Byrne, J.G., O'Conner, T.G., Marvin, R.S. & Whelan, W.F. "Practitioner review: The contribution of attachment theory to child custody assessments" Journal of Child Psychology and Psychiatry 46:2 (2005), 115–127.

Carlson, M.J. "Family structure, father involvement, and adolescent behavioural outcomes" Journal of Marriage and Family 68 (2006), 137–154.

Cherlin, A.J., Furstenberg, F.F., Jr., Chase-Lansdale, P.L., Kiernan, K.E., Robines, P.K., Ruane Morrison, and D., Teitler, J.O. "Longitudinal studies of effects of divorce on children in Great Britian and the United States" Science 252 (1991), 1386–1389.

Cassidy J. & Shaver, P.R. (Eds.) Handbook of Attachment: Theory, Research and Clinical Applications (New York: Guildford Press, 1999).

Clarke-Stewart, K.A., Vandell, D.L., McCartney, K., Owen, M.T. & Booth, C. "Effects of parental separation and divorce on very young children" Journal of Family Psychology 14:2 (2000), 304–326.

Cummings, E.M. & Davies, P.T. Children and Marital Conflict (New York: Guildord, 1994).

Dember, C. & Fliman, V. "Tailoring parental visitation orders to the developmental needs of children of divorce" in Gunsberg, L. & Hymowitz (Eds.) A Handbook of Divorce and Custody: Forensic, Developmental and Clinical Perspectives (Hillsdale, N J: The Analytic Press, 2005), 249–257.

Emery, R. E. "Interparental conflict and the children of discord and divorce" Psychological Bulletin 92 (1982), 310–333.

Emery, R. Marriage, Divorce, and Children's Adjustment (Newbury Park, CA: Sage, 1988).

Emery, R.E. "Changing the rules for determining child custody in divorce cases" Clinical Psychology: Science and Practice 6 (1999), 323–327.

Emery, R. The Truth about Children and Divorce: Dealing with Your Emotions So You and Your Children Can Thrive (NY: Penguin, 2004).

Emery, R.E., Otto, R.K. & O'Donohue, W.T. "A critical assessment of child custody evaluations" American Psychological Society 6:1 (2005), 1–29.

Fabricius, W.V. "Listening to children of divorce: New findings that diverge from Wallerstein, Lewis & Blakeslee (2003)" Family Relations 52 (2003), 385–396.

Fabricius, W.V. & Hall, J. "Young adults' perspectives on divorce: Living arrangements" Family & Conciliation Courts Review 38:4 (2000), 446–461.

Fabricius, W.V., & Luecken, L.J. "Postdivorce living arrangements, parent conflict, and long-term physical health correlates for children of divorce." Journal of Family Psychology 21:2 (2007), 195-205.

Fabricius, W.V., Braver, S.F. & Deneau, K.A. "Divorced parents' financial support of their children's college expenses" Family Court Review 41:2 (2003), 244–241.

Fagan, J. & Barnett, M. "The relationship between maternal gatekeeping, paternal competence, mothers' attitudes about the father role, and father involvement" Journal of Family Issues 24 (2003), 1020-1043.

Fidler, B.J., Chodos, L., Horowitz, T., Radovanovic, H. & Schloss, J. "Pathways to Solutions for High-Conflict Separation and Divorce: The Family Needs Consultation" (paper submitted for publication).

Finley, G. E. & Schwartz, S. J. "Father involvement and young adult outcomes: The differential contributions of divorce and gender" Family Court Review (in press).

Freeman, R. "Parenting Plans: Making Decisions in Children's Best Interest" Special Lectures 2000: Family and Law, A colloquium on 'Best Interests of the Child': New Perspectives on the Resolution of Custody Disputes" (Toronto: The Law Society of Upper Canada, Department of Education, 2000).

Friedman, M. "The so-called high-conflict couple: A closer look" The American Journal of Family Therapy 32 (2004), 101-117.

Furstenberg, Jr., F.F. & Cherlin, A.J. Divided Families: What Happens to Children When Parents Part? (Cambridge, MA: Harvard University Press, 1991).

Furstenberg, Jr., F.F., Nord, C.W., Peterson, J.L. & Zill, N. "The life course of children of divorce: Marital disruption and parental contact" American Sociological Review 48 (1983), 656-658.

Garon, R., Donner, D. & Peacock, K. "From infants to adolescents: A developmental approach to parenting plans" Family and Conciliation Courts Review 38:2 (2000), 168-191.

Garrity C. & Baris, M. Caught in the middle: Protecting the Children of High-conflict Divorce (Toronto: Maxwell Macmillan Canada, 1994).

Goldstein, J., Freud, A. & Solnit, A J. Beyond the Best Interests of the Child (New York: Free Press, 1973).

Goldstein, J. Freud, A. & Solnit, A.J. In the Best Interests of the Child (New York: Free Press, 1986).

Gould, J.W. & Stahl, P. "Never paint by the numbers" Family Court Review 39:4 (2001), 372–376.

Greenberg, L.R., Gould-Saltman, D.J. & Schnider, R. "The problem with presumptions – A review and commentary" Journal of Child Custody 3:3/4 (2006), 139–172.

Grych, J. H. "Interparental conflict as a risk factor for child maladjustment: Implications for the development of prevention programs" Family Court Review 43:1 (2005), 97–108.

Grych, J. & Finchman, F. "Marital conflict and children's adjustment: A cognitive-contextual framework" Psychological Bulletin 108 (1992), 267–290.

Gunnoe, M. & Braver, S.L. "The effects of joint legal custody on mothers, fathers, and children" Law and Human Behaviour 25:1 (2001), 25–43.

Harlow, H.F. "The nature of love" American Psychologist 13 (1958), 673–685.

Hawkins, G. Age Appropriate Access (Tucson, AZ: Family Center of the Conciliation Court, 1991).

Hetherington, E.M. "An overview of the Virginia Longitudinal Study of Divorce and Re-marriage with a focus on early adolescence" Journal of Family Psychology 7 (1993), 39–56.

Hetherington, E.M., Bridges, M. & Insabella, G.M. "What matters? What does not? Five perspectives on the association between marital transitions and children's adjustment" American Psychologist 53 (1998), 167–184.

Hetherington, E.M., Cox, M. & Cox, R. "Effects of divorce on parents and children" in M.E. Lamb (Ed.) Nontraditional Families: Parenting and Child Development (Hillsdale, NJ: Lawrence Erlbaum, 1982), 233–288.

Hetherington, E. M., Cox, M. & Cox, R. "The long-term effects of divorce and remarriage on the adjustment of children" Journal of the American Academy of Child Psychiatry 24 (1985), 518–530.

Hetherington, E. M. & Kelly, J.B. For Better or for Worse: Divorce Reconsidered (New York: Norton & Company, 2002).

Hetherington, E.M. & Stanley-Hagan, M.M. "The effects of divorce on fathers and their children" in M.E. Lamb (Ed.) The Role of the Father in Child Development (Third edition) (New York: Wiley, 1997), 191–211; 360–369.

Hodges, W.F. Interventions for Children of Divorce (New York: Wiley Press, 1986).

Jaffe, P., Crooks, C.V. & Bala, N. Making Appropriate Parenting Arrangements in Family Violence Cases: Applying the Literature to Identify Promising Practices (Ottawa: Department of Justice Canada, 2005).

Johnston, J.R. "Children of divorce who refuse visitation in nonresidential parenting" in C. Depner and J. Bray (Eds) *New Vistas in Family Living*. Newbury Park, CA: Sage, 1993).

Johnston, J.R. "High-conflict divorce" in *The Future of Children: Children and Divorce* (Los Altos, CA: David and Lucille Packard Foundation, 1994), 165–182.

Johnston, J.R. "Research update: Children's adjustment in sole custody compared to joint custody families and principles of custody decision-making" Family and Conciliation Courts Review 33:4 (1995), 415–425.

Johnston, J.R. "Building multidisciplinary professional partnerships with the court on behalf of high-conflict divorcing families and their children: Who needs what kind of help?" Presented at the "Children of Embattled Divorce Symposium" (Arkansas, 1999).

Johnston, J.R. & Roseby, V. *In the Name of the Child: A Developmental Approach to Understanding and Helping Children of High-conflict and Violent Families* (New York: The Free Press, 1997).

Juby, H., Le Bourdais, C. & Marcil-Gratton, N. "Sharing roles, sharing custody? Couples' characteristics and children's living arrangements at separation" Journal of Marriage and Family 67 (2005), 157–172.

Kelly, J.B. "Current research on children's adjustment: No simple answers" Family and Conciliation Courts Review 31:1 (1993), 29–49.

Kelly, J.B. "The determination of child custody" in *The Future of Children: Children and Divorce* (Los Altos, CA: David and Lucille Packard Foundation, 1994), 121–142.

Kelly, J.B. "The best interests of the child: A concept in search of meaning" Family and Conciliation Courts Review 35:4 (1997), 377–387.

Kelly, J.B. "Children's adjustment in conflicted marriage and divorce: A decade review of research" Journal of the American Academy of Child and Adolescent Psychiatry 39 (2000), 963–973.

Kelly, J.B. "Psychological and legal interventions for parents and children in custody and access disputes: Current research and practice" Virginia Journal of Social Policy and Law 10:1 (2002), 129–163.

Kelly, J.B. "Changing perspectives on children's divorce adjustment following divorce: A view from the United States" Childhood 10:2, (2003), 237–254.

Kelly, J.B. "Developing beneficial parenting plan models for children following separation and divorce" Journal of American Academy of Matrimonial Lawyers 19:2 (2005), 237–254.

Kelly, J.B. "Children's living arrangements following separation and divorce: Insights from empirical and clinical research" Family Process 46:1 (2007), 35–52.

Kelly, J.B. & Emery, R. "Children's adjustment following divorce: Risk and resilience perspectives" Family Relations 52 (2003), 352–362.

Kelly, J.B. & Lamb, M.E. "Using child development research to make appropriate custody and access decisions for young children" Family and Conciliation Courts Review 38:3 (2000), 297–311.

Kelly, J.B. & Lamb, M.E. "Developmental issues in relocation cases involving young children: When, whether and how?" Journal of Family Psychology 17:2 (2003), 193–205.

Kelly, R.F. & Ward, S.L. "Allocating custodial responsibilities at divorce: Social science research and the American law institute's approximation rule" Family Court Review 40:3 (2002), 350–370.

King, V. "Variation in the consequences of nonresident father involvement for children's well-being" Journal of Marriage and the Family 56 (1994), 176–189.

King, V. "The antecedents and consequences of adolescents' relationships with stepfathers and nonresident fathers" Journal of Marriage and Family 68 (2006), 910–928.

King, V. & Heard, H.E. "Nonresident father visitation, parental conflict, and mother's satisfaction: What's best for child well-being?" Journal of Marriage and Family 61 (1999), 385–396.

King, V. & Sobolewski, J.M. "Nonresident fathers' contributions to adolescent well-being" Journal of Marriage and the Family 68 (2006), 537–557.

Kisthardt, M.K. & Fines, B.G. "Evaluator in child custody disputes" Family Court Review 43:2 (2005), 229–232.

Kline, M., Johnston, J.R. & Tschann, J.M. "The long shadow of marital conflict: A model of children's post divorce adjustment" Journal of Marriage and the Family 53 (1991), 297–309.

Kraft, M. "Rethinking access for children under age 3" Canadian Family Law Quarterly 37 (2004), 37–54.

Lamb, M.E. "The development of father-infant attachments" in M.E. Lamb (Ed.) The Role of the Father in Child Development (3rd ed.) (New York: John Wiley, 1997), 104–120, 332–342.

Lamb, M.E. "Non-custodial fathers and their impact on the children of divorce" in R. Thompson & P. Amato (Eds.) The Post-divorce Family: Research and Policy Issues (Thousand Oaks, CA: Sage, 1999).

Lamb, M.E. "Noncustodial fathers and their children" in C.S. Tamis-LeMonda & N. Cabrera (Eds.) Handbook of Father Involvement: Multidisciplinary Perspectives (Mahwah, NJ: Erlbaum, 2002), 169–184.

Lamb, M.E. (Ed.) The Role of the Father in Child Development (4th Ed.) (NY: Wiley, 2004).

Lamb, M.E. & Kelly, J.B. "Using the empirical literature to guide the development of parenting plans for young children: A rejoinder to Solomon and Biringen" Family Court Review 39 (2001), 365–371.

Lamb, M., Sternberg & Thompson, R. "The effects of divorce and custody arrangements on children's behaviour, development, and adjustment" Family and Conciliation Courts Review 35:4 (1997), 393–404.

Laumann-Billings, L. & Emery, R.E. "Distress among young adults in divorced families" Journal of Family Psychology 14 (2000), 671–687.

Lee, M. "Post-divorce interparental conflict, children's contact with both parents, children's emotional processes, and children's behavioural adjustment" Journal of Divorce and Remarriage 27:3/4 (1997), 61–82.

Leon, K. "Risk and protective factors in young children's adjustment to parental divorce. A review of the research" Family Relations 52 (2003), 258–270.

Maccoby, E. E. & Martin, J. A. "Socialization in the context of the family: Parent-child interaction" in P. Mussen (Ed.) Handbook of Child Psychology (New York: Wiley, 1983), 1–101.

Maccoby, E.E. & Mnookin, R.H. Dividing the Child: Social and Legal Dilemmas of Custody (Cambridge, MA: Harvard University Press, 1992).

Main, M. & Solomon, J. "Discovery of a new, insecure-disorganize/disoriented attachment patterns" in T.B. Brazelton & M. Yoogman (Eds.) Affective development in infancy (Norwood, NJ: Ablex, 1986), 95–124.

McDonough, H. & Bartha, C. Putting Children First: A Guide for Parents Breaking Up (Toronto: University of Toronto Press, 1999).

McLanahan. S.S. "Father absence and the welfare of children" in E.M. Hetherington (Ed.) Coping with Divorce, Single Parenting, and Remarriage: A Risk and Resiliency Perspective (Hillsdale, NJ: Erlbaum, 1999), 117–145.

Menning, C. L. "Nonresident fathering and school failure" Journal of Family Issues 27:10 (2006), 1356–1382.

Parkinson, P., Cashmore, J. & Single, J. "Adolescents' views on the fairness of parenting and financial arrangements after separation" Family Court Review 43:3 (2005), 429–444.

Parkinson, P. & Smyth, B. "Satisfaction and dissatisfaction with father-child contact arrangements in Australia" Child and Family Law Quarterly 16:3 (2004), 289–304.

Pruett, K. Fatherneed: Why Father Care is as Essential as Mother Care for Your Child (New York: The Free Press, 2000).

Pruett, M.K. "Applications of attachment theory and child development research to young children's overnights in separated and divorced families" Guest editorial notes in *Overnights and Young Children: Essays from the Family Court Review* (2005), 5–12. Available online at www.afcc.net.org.

Pruett, M.K., Williams, T.Y., Insabella, G. & Little, T.D. "Family and legal indicators of child adjustment to divorce among families with young children" Journal of Family Psychology 17 (2003), 169–180.

Pruett, M., Ebling, R. & Insabella, G. "Critical aspects of parenting plans for young children: Interjecting data into the debate about overnights" Family Court Review 42:1 (2004), 39–59.

Ricci, I. *Mom's House, Dad's House: Making Shared Custody Work* (New York: Collier Macmillan Publishers, 1980).

Riggs, S.A. "Is the approximation rule in the child's best interests? A critique from the perspective of attachment theory" Family Court Review 43:3 (2005), 481–493.

Rutter, M. "Children's responses to stress and disadvantage" in M.W. Kent & J.E. Rolfe (Eds.) *Primary Prevention of Psychopathology, Vol. 3* (Hanover, NJ: University Press of New England, 1979), 49–74.

Rutter, M. "Psychosocial resilience and protective mechanisms" American Journal of Orthopsychiatry 57 (1987), 316–331.

Schwartz, S.J. & Finley, G.E. "Fathering in intact and divorced families: Ethnic differences in retrospective reports" Journal of Marriage and Family 67 (2005), 207–215.

Scott, E.S. "Pluralism, parental preference, and child custody" California Law Review 80 (1992), 615–672.

Selzer, J. A. "Consequences of marital dissolution for children" Annual Review of Sociology 20 (1994), 235–266.

Simons, L. G. & Conger, R. D. "Linking mother-father differences in parenting to a typology of family parenting styles and adolescent outcomes" Journal of Family Issues 28:2 (2007), 212–241.

Skafte, D. *Child Custody Evaluations* (Beverly Hills, CA: Sage, 1985).

Smyth, B. "Time to rethink time? The experience of time with children after divorce" Family Matters 71 (2005), 4–10.

Sobolewski, J.M. & King, V. "The importance of the coparental relationship for nonresident fathers' ties to children" Journal of Marriage and Family 67:5 (2005), 1196–1211.

Solomon, J. "An attachment theory framework for planning infant and toddler visitation arrangements in never-married, separated and divorced families" in Gunsberg, L. &

Hymowitz (Eds.) *A Handbook of Divorce and Custody: Forensic, Developmental and Clinical Perspectives* (Hillsdale, New Jersey: The Analytic Press, 2005), 259–279.

Solomon, J. & Biringen, Z. "Another look at the developmental research" Family Court Review 39:4 (2001), 355–364.

Solomon, J. & George, C. "The effects on attachment of overnight visitation in divorced and separated families: A longitudinal follow-up" in J. Solomon & C. George (Eds.) *Attachment Disorganization* (New York: Guilford, 1999), 243–264.

Stahl, P. *Conducting Child Custody Evaluations: A Comprehensive Guide.* Thousand Oaks, CA: Sage Publications, 1994).

Stahl, P. *Complex Issues in Child Custody Evaluation* (New York: Sage Publications, 1999).

Stewart, S. D. "Nonresident parenting and adolescent adjustment" Journal of Family Issues 24 (2003), 217–244.

Wallerstein, J.S. "Amica Curiae Brief of Dr. Judith S. Wallerstein, Ph.D" filed in Cause No. SO46116 in re Marriage of Burgess, Supreme Court of the State of California, (December 7, 1995).

Wallerstein, J.S. & Blakeslee, S. *Second Chances: Men, Women and Children a Decade after Divorce* (New York: Hyperion, 1989).

Wallerstein, J.S. & Kelly, J.B. "The effects of parental divorce: Experiences of the child in later latency" American Journal of Orthopsychiatry 46:2 (1976), 256–269.

Wallerstein, J. & Kelly, J. *Surviving the Breakup: How Children and Parents Cope with Divorce* (New York: Basic Books, 1980).

Wallerstein, J.S., Lewis, J. & Blakeslee, S. *The Unexpected Legacy of Divorce: A 25-Year Landmark Study* (New York: Hyperion, 2000).

Wallerstein, J.S & Tanke, T. "To move or not to move" Family Law Quarterly 30:5 (1996), 1–18.

Warshak, R.A. *The Custody Revolution: The Father Factor and the Motherhood Mystique* (New York: Poseidon Press, 1992).

Warshak, R.A. "Blanket restrictions: Overnight contact between parents and young children" Family and Conciliation Courts Review 38L4 (2000), 422–445.

Warshak, R.A. "Who will be there when I cry in the night? Revisiting overnights – a rejoinder to Biringen et al." Family Court Review 40:2 (2002), 208–219.

Whiteside, M. "Custody for children age 5 and younger" Family and Conciliation Courts Review 36:4 (1998), 479–502.

Whiteside, M.F. & Becker, B.J. "Parental factors and the young child's postdivorce adjust-
      ment: A meta-analysis with implications for parenting arrangements" Journal of Family
      Psychology 14 (2000), 5–26.

Zill, N., Morrison, D.R. & Coiro, J.J. "Long term effects of parental divorce on parent-child
      relationships, adjustment and achievement in young adulthood" Journal of Family
      Psychology 7 (1993), 91–103.

Appendix 12

Considerations For Parenting Time Schedule Options

1. RELEVANT FACTORS: child's age, temperament, adjustment, special needs; pre-separation parent–child relationships, involvement in parenting, and attachment quality and history; each parents' adjustment and parenting abilities; the children's relationships with siblings and extended family; the ability and willingness of the parent who has participated less in the child's upbringing to learn parenting skills and behaviours; the fit between each parent and the child's needs; the parents' ability to communicate and cooperate with each other, including the nature and degree of any conflict; the presence of domestic violence and abuse; the children's wishes and preferences. Phase in changes gradually. Attend to practical considerations relating to distances between homes, schools, and workplaces.

2. COMPETING NEEDS: Frequent contact vs. frequent transitions, including exposure to parental conflict.

3. YOUNGER CHILDREN:
    a. Split weekends as a stepping stone to full weekends
    b. Napping
    c. Colour-coded calendar, lunchboxes
    d. Communication logs (for continuity of care)
    e. Interim schedules (e.g., six-month blocks), use of consultant

4. MODERATE TO HIGH-CONFLICT SITUATIONS:
    a. Disengage parents
    b. A structured and specified parenting plan (transition times, location, parent responsible for transportation, behaviour at transitions) should be put in place.
    c. Other important clauses should be included in the parenting plan (e.g., when child ill in the morning or at school; identify parent who arranges for and takes child to routine dental and medical appointments).
    d. An annual calendar combining usual and holiday schedules should also be considered.

5. HOLIDAYS, SPECIAL DAYS AND VACATIONS:
    a. Holidays take precedence over the regular schedule.
    b. Continue with similar traditions while starting new ones as well.

   c.   Details regarding starting/ending periods, transportation, notification dates, manner of choosing dates, telephone calls with non-vacationing parent, how usual schedule combines with holiday schedule, etc. should be specified.

Appendix 13

Parenting Time Schedule Options

Parenting time schedule options, as shown in tables below, indicating:

1. duration of time away from each parent[1]

2. number of days where contact occurs (includes morning drop-offs to school)

3. number of overnights

4. number of transitions, indicated by double entry

5. location of transitions, parent responsible

6. opportunity for varied parenting experiences (e.g. homework, attendance at school; bedtime and waking routines; meals; activities, etc.)

I: ALTERNATING WEEKENDS FRIDAY TO SUNDAY; WEEKLY WEDNESDAY OVERNIGHTS

MON	TUES	WED	THURS	FRI	SAT	SUN
A	A	A B	B A	A	A	
A	A	A B	B A	A B	B	B A

1. two nights of no contact with A; seven days and six nights separation from B

2. seven out of 14 days contact with B; 13 out of 14 days contact with A

3. nine out of 14 overnights with A; four out of 14 overnights with B

4. five transitions (four from parent B to/from school or daycare; one parent to parent)

5. school/daycare during the week; between parents Sunday evenings

6. limited opportunities for parenting across contexts

II. ALTERNATING WEEKENDS FRIDAY TO MONDAY; WEEKLY WEDNESDAY OVERNIGHTS

MON	TUES	WED	THURS	FRI	SAT	SUN
B		A	B			
	A			A	A	A
A		B	A			
		A	B	A		
A	A				B	B
		B	A	B		

1. four days and three nights separation from A (assumes parent A works outside the home; otherwise three days separation); seven days, six nights separation from B

2. 12 out of 14 days contact with A; eight out of 14 days contact with B

3. nine out of 14 overnights with A; five out of 14 overnights with A

4. six transitions (from B to/from school or daycare)

5. school/daycare

6. some, but limited variety of parenting experiences

III. ALTERNATING WEEKENDS FRIDAY TO SUNDAY; ALTERNATING MONDAY AND THURSDAY OVERNIGHTS*

MON	TUES	WED	THURS	FRI	SAT	SUN
			A	B	A	
A	A	A				A
			B	A		
A	B			A		B
		A	A		B	
B	A			B		A

1. no more than three nights and four days separation from A; no more than two nights and three days separation from B

2. 13 out of 14 days contact with A; seven out of 14 days contact with B

3. 10 out of 14 overnights with A; four out of 14 overnights with B

4. six transitions (five parent B to/from school or daycare, one parent to parent)

5. school/daycare; between parents Sunday evening

6. moderate opportunity for parenting experiences across contexts

* Alternating Monday and Thursday overnights alleviates seven days and six nights of no contact in Schedules I and II; however, this arrangement may require more cooperation regarding activity scheduling.

IV. ALTERNATING WEEKENDS FRIDAY TO MONDAY; ALTERNATING MONDAY AND THURSDAY OVERNIGHTS

MON	TUES	WED	THURS	FRI	SAT	SUN
B			A	B		
	A	A			A	A
A			B	A		
A	B		A	A		
		A			B	B
B	A			B		

1. no more than three nights and four days separation from A; no more than three nights and four days separation from B;

2. 12 out of 14 days contact with A; eight out of 14 days contact with B

3. nine out of 14 overnights with A; five out of 14 overnights with B

7. six transitions (B to/from school/daycare)

4. school/daycare

5. moderate opportunity for parenting experiences across domains

V. ALTERNATING WEEKENDS FRIDAY TO SUNDAY (OR MONDAY); TWO EVENINGS PER WEEK*

MON	TUES	WED	THURS	FRI	SAT	SUN
A		A		A		B
	A		A		B	
B 3–4 hrs		B 3–4 hrs		B		A
A		A				

A	A B 3–4 hrs A	A	A B 3–4 hrs A	A	A	A

1. no more than two nights and two days separation from A; no more than four days and three nights separation from B

2. 13 out of 14 days contact with A; seven out of 14 days contact with B

3. 12 out of 14 overnights with A; two out of 14 overnights with B

4. nine transitions (13 from parent to parent if A picks up children from school or daycare before they go with parent B, 10 if B picks up children from school or daycare; note frequency of transitions within several hours during the week)

5. school/daycare; between parents

6. limited opportunity for parenting experiences across domains, including school and nighttime routines

* Can be adapted to include a Sunday overnight, in which case the analyses below would differ.

VI. ALTERNATING WEEKENDS FRIDAY TO MONDAY; WEEKLY THURSDAY OVERNIGHTS

MON	TUES	WED	THURS	FRI	SAT	SUN
B A	A	A	A B	B A	A	A
A	A	A	A B	B	B	B

1. no more than four nights, five days separation from A; no more than seven days, six nights separation from B;

2. 11 out of 14 days contact with A; seven out of 14 days contact with B

3. nine out of 14 overnights with A; five out of 14 overnights with B

4. four transitions (B to/from school)

5. school/daycare

6. moderate opportunity for parenting experiences across contexts

VII. SPLIT WEEKS AND WEEKENDS: 4–4–3–3 (SHARED PHYSICAL CUSTODY)

MON	TUES	WED	THURS	FRI	SAT	SUN
		A				B
A	A	B	B	B	B	A a.m.
		A			B	
A	A	B	B	B	A p.m.	A

1. no separation of more than four days and four nights away from A or B (may be stepping stone to different shared parenting time schedule)

2. nine out of 14 days contact with A and B

3. seven out of 14 overnights with A and B

4. four transitions (two school/daycare, two parent to parent—may be problematic if a high level of conflict exists)

5. school/daycare, parent to parent

6. good opportunity for parenting experiences across contexts

VIII. 2–2–3–2–2–3 (SHARED PHYSICAL CUSTODY)*

MON	TUES	WED	THURS	FRI	SAT	SUN
B		A		B		
	A		B		A	A
A		B		A		
A		B		A		
	B		A		B	B
B		A		B		

1. no separation more than four days and three nights from A and B (may be stepping stone to different shared parenting time schedule)

2. 10 out of 14 days contacts with A and B

3. seven out of 14 overnights with A and B

4. six transitions (change of homes)

5.   school/daycare

6.   good opportunity for parenting experiences across contexts

* Inconsistent midweek days with each parent makes planning for children's activities and parents' own work/personal pursuits more challenging. Compare with 5–5–2–2 below, which is less challenging, although children must go for six days without contact as opposed to four.

IX.: 5–5–2-2 (SHARED PHYSICAL CUSTODY)*

MON	TUES	WED	THURS	FRI	SAT	SUN
B		A		B		
	A		B		A	A
A		B		A		
		A				
A	A		B	B	B	B
		B				

1.   no separation more than six days and five nights from A or B (may be stepping stone to different shared parenting time schedule)

2.   nine out of 14 days contacts with A and B

3.   seven out of 14 overnights with A and B

4.   three transitions (change of homes)

5.   school/daycare

6.   good opportunity for parenting experiences across contexts

* Consistent midweek days with each parent makes planning for children's and parents' own work/personal activities easier.

X. ALTERNATING WEEKS; 7–7 (SHARED PHYSICAL CUSTODY)*

MON	TUES	WED	THURS	FRI	SAT	SUN
B						
	A	A	A	A	A	A
A						
A						
	B	B	B	B	B	B
B						

1.   no separation of more than eight days from A or B

2.   eight out of 14 days contact with A and B

3. seven out of 14 overnights with A and B

4. two transitions (change of homes)

5. school/daycare

6. good opportunity for parenting experiences across contexts

* Some children under six or seven may benefit from midweek overnights with the other parent. Arranging for activities, given the alternating week schedule requires cooperation between parents.

---

1. A drop-off in the morning or pickup in the evening is counted as one day.

Appendix 14

Parenting Plan Checklist For High Conflict Families

Assessors may wish to structure their Parenting Plan recommendations for high-conflict families using the following headings. Examples of the specific areas that would typically fall under each heading are provided.

PARENTING GUIDELINES AND PRINCIPLES

- Various parenting guidelines, principles and aspirations relating to good parenting, promoting children's relationships with the other parent, supporting the parenting plan, not denigrating the other parent, not involving the children in conflict, respecting the other parent's privacy, not raising issues at transition times when children are present, etc.

- Relevant and appropriate child-rearing practices (e.g., degree of consistency regarding various routines such as bedtime, napping, dietary restrictions, homework, etc.).

PARENTAL COMMUNICATION

- Rules of engagement for the parents' communication and behaviour in and out of the children's presence.

- Detail regarding the parents' communication: how, when, where, how frequently, the required response time, etc.

REGULAR PARENTING TIME SCHEDULES

- Clearly delineated parenting time with each parent

- When does parenting time start and stop?

- What happens to the parenting time schedule when a child is ill?

- Who calls the school when a child is ill?

- When is time with the other parent forfeited because of illness?

- Exact pickup and drop-off days and times

- Rules for parental behaviour at transitions (i.e., no discussion of anything beyond cordial niceties)

- Location of transition?

- Who does the transportation?

- Punctuality rules

CHANGES TO PARENTING TIME SCHEDULES

- Rules relating to how the need for temporary changes to the parenting time will be addressed and resolved in the event of a dispute.
- How are temporary changes/requests handled?
- What is the agreed-upon response time for requests for changes?
- What is the policy regarding "make-up" time with the child/ren?
- Is there a right of first refusal? If so, what is the threshold of time allowed (e.g., four hours, eight hours, one overnight or more?)

HOLIDAYS, SPECIAL DAYS AND VACATIONS

- Specify *all* holidays clearly defined as to beginning and end of period, location of transitions, who provides transportation, etc.
- Agreement that these days take precedence over usual schedule
- How are summer vacation dates determined? Who gets first choice? How much notice is given?
- Is there a rule that the one-week holiday (seven days) must include a usually scheduled weekend?
- If not, what happens to the usual weekend rotation?
- Does the statutory day add to the seven days to make eight days?
- What happens to the usual schedule when the holiday schedule ends?
  - Does the usual rotation continue or change?
  - Does one parent get three weekends in row, or do the parents split one week and resume the usual alternation of weekends?
- What about professional development school days?
- Children's birthday parties:
  - Who pays?
  - Who attends?
  - How are the gifts divided?

CHILDREN'S CONTACT WITH NON-RESIDENT PARENT

- Is there unlimited telephone contact between the child and the

non-resident parent, or are there rules (e.g., frequency of calls
in a week, time of day, who initiates the call, etc.)?

EXTRACURRICULAR ACTIVITIES

- How are extracurricular activities decided upon?
- Is consent or notice only required when such activities overlap
  the other parent's time?
- Can both parents (and family members) attend all activities, only
  some (e.g., special final events), or none?

CHILDREN'S CLOTHING & BELONGINGS

- What are the rules around clothing: washing; returning; number
  of changes provided to the parent who pays child support; loss;
  breakage?
- Which are Section 7 expenses, and which come out of child
  support?

DAY-TO-DAY DECISIONS

- Who takes children to routine medical/dental appointments?
- Can both parents attend such appointments?
- What, how and when will child-related information be shared?
- Who is the librarian of documents: health card; immunization;
  etc.?
- Which parent attends at parent–teacher meetings?
- Which parent accompanies the child/ren on field trips?
- Which parent is responsible for the children's haircuts?

MAJOR DECISIONS (CHILDREN'S HEALTH/WELFARE, HEALTH, EDUCATION, & RELIGION)

- Precise protocol for how these are decided
- Exchange of information
- Details regarding the children's religious observance, if any (e.g.,
  attendance at church, Sunday school, rituals, etc.)

TRAVEL

- Notice? Consent?
- Notarized letter (rules regarding response time; number of days
  in advance of travel; who pays)

- What is in the itinerary?
- Who holds the passports?
- Phone calls with the non-resident parent during travel with the resident parent?

RESIDENTIAL MOVES

- Number of days of notice required
- Geographic boundaries/limits, or distance from each other.

JURISDICTIONAL MOVES

- Agreed to mutually; otherwise by court order

CHANGE OF NAME

- Identify restrictions as per relevant/local law

FUTURE DISPUTE RESOLUTION

- Identify future dispute resolution mechanism/method (i.e., mediation, parenting coordination, mediation/arbitration, etc.)
- Identify professional to provide services
- Identify how fees will be paid

Chapter 6

Sole, Joint And Parallel Parenting: Review Of The Social Science Literature And Practice In Our Courts

"Courts must be responsive to the winds of change. In today's society, the break-down of the traditional family is increasingly common, *and new ways of de-fining post-divorce family structures are desperately needed."*
Justice Boland[1]

REVIEW OF THE LITERATURE

Reliable statistics on the frequency of joint and sole custody are difficult to obtain, and those available are open to interpretation. Joint legal and physical custody are not always differentiated, and what's more, the living arrangements that exist on paper frequently do not reflect what is actually occurring in the families so described. Marcil-Gratton and Le Bourdais (1999) noted that although 69 per cent of respondents reported that they had obtained a shared physical custody order, only a small number of children actually lived under a shared arrangement. Notwithstanding these exceptions, it is clear that the incidence of joint custody and shared parenting arrangements has increased over the years, with Canadian and American statistics noting about a 20-per-cent rise from 1988 to 1998 (Nord & Zill, 1996; Statistics Canada, 1998). Joint legal custody accounts for about 11 per cent of all custody determinations (Payne & Payne, 2006). Statistics with respect to joint physical custody are much lower, although we see considerable variability across jurisdictions. In some areas of the United States, rates are as low as five per cent, while in California they are as high as 27 per cent (Braver & O'Connell, 1998; Maccoby & Mnookin, 1992; Selzer, 1998). Reported rates of shared physical custody in Australia range from six to eleven per cent (Parkinson & Smyth, 2003; Smyth, 2004).

Notwithstanding the surge in joint and shared custody orders beginning in the 1980s, to date we have few well controlled studies comparing the effects of joint and sole custody. Mixed results accompanied by two opposing viewpoints are evident. One view is that joint custody benefits children, encourages parents to communicate better, and keeps both parents involved (Ahrons, 1980; Bender, 1994; Benjamin & Irving, 1989; Luepnitz, 1986; Roman & Haddad, 1978; Shiller, 1986; Steinman, 1981). The other view is that joint custody places children at risk because of increased transitions and instability and the accompanying potential for being exposed to parental conflict (Goldstein, Freud & Solnit, 1973).

The mixed and oftentimes polarized nature of these findings may be attributed to methodological problems, including but not limited to cross-sectional designs, small and different samples, different measurements, and the lack of distinction between joint legal and joint physical custody. In addition, selection factors make it difficult to know if the frequently reported parent and child satisfaction and positive adjustment are due to the joint custody itself, or to other factors related to the fact that these families chose joint custody. Further complicating the picture is the fact that researchers have typically defined joint physical custody as a parent having approximately 33 to 50 per cent of the custodial time. The lower end of this range is similar to what occurs in many sole-custody families (every other weekend and one overnight per week), thus making it difficult to interpret the findings with respect to the presence or absence of differences between sole and true shared/joint physical custody arrangements.

Many studies and literature reviews indicate that adjustment to separation and divorce is unrelated to custody arrangement, be it joint or sole (mother-headed or father-headed) (Camera & Resnick, 1988; Coysh, Johnston, Pear, Beck, Hauser, Clark & Whitney, 1984; Fidler, 1986; Hess & Camara, 1979; Kline, Tschann & Wallerstein, 1989). Reviewing six studies, Johnston (1995) reported that children fared neither better nor worse in joint physical and legal custody compared with sole maternal or paternal custody. Consistent with the more general divorce-adjustment literature comparing divorced and non-divorced families, outcomes are related to what are referred to as the family-process variables, that is, what occurs in these families (i.e., parent-child relationship, parenting capacity, parental conflict, and cooperation).

However, when there is an extremely high level of parental conflict, children in joint physical and legal custody arrangements exhibited more adjustment problems than those not exposed to significant conflict (Johnston, 1995; Johnston, Kline & Tschann, 1988; Kline, Tschann, Johnston & Wallerstein, 1989). These adjustment problems were attributed to frequent access and the accompanying frequent transitions. Poorer adjustment was found in families where conflicting parents have to maintain contact, make decisions jointly, and coordinate parenting, the latter especially relevant for young children. These findings have led to recommendations that frequent contact and joint residential schedules are contraindicated in families where domestic violence has occurred, and further, in some high-conflict families where an increase in verbal and physical aggression may occur, especially at transitions.

Weak support for joint legal custody, independent of the impact of pre-separation conflict, was reported by Gunnoe and Braver (2001). Children in joint legal custody were reported by their mothers to show fewer impulsive behaviours than children in sole maternal custody; no differences were found, however, on the seven other measures examined. In addition, higher rates of maternal dissatisfaction with joint custody were found. While noting only weak support for joint custody, these researchers state that their study did not support critics who maintain that joint custody predicts greater problems for children compared with sole custody. Thus, while this study does not lend strong support to the claim that children in joint custody are better adjusted than those in sole custody, it does provide some evidence supporting other studies indicating that there are no substantial differences between the two groups.

However, a meta-analysis conducted by Bauserman (2002) of 33 published, unpublished and doctoral dissertations conducted between 1982 and 1999 reported support for joint physical and legal custody over sole custody, independent of the degree of parental conflict. These studies included 1,846 sole (maternal) custody children and 813 joint legal or physical custody children. With parental conflict controlled, children in joint physical and legal custody were found to be better adjusted than those in sole maternal custody across multiple measures and outcomes, including family relationships, self-esteem, emotional and behavioural adjustment, and academic achievement. These findings of more positive adjustment were consistent across reports from mothers, fathers, children, teachers, and clinicians. Furthermore, the noted positive adjustment was comparable to children living in non-divorced, two-parent families. In addition, children in joint legal custody arrangements tended to spend more time with their fathers than those living in sole maternal custody arrangements, a finding consistent with that reported by others (Arditta, 1992; Aquilino, 2006; Gunnoe & Braver, 2001; Selzer, 1998).

Bauserman notes the possibility of selection factors being responsible for the findings, to the extent that some of the families are likely to have chosen joint custody arrangements and that these families may have had better relationships prior to or during the divorce process. He further notes that while parental conflict was not a predictor of adjustment in joint custody, it may not be preferable in all situations, in particular those involving extreme parental conflict, violence and/or serious mental health problems on the part of the parents. He goes on, however, to say that joint custody may be indicated in families with moderate conflict. Finally, the meta-analysis included correlational studies, and consequently it cannot be said that joint custody caused the positive outcomes in the children's adjustment.

Joint custody is more common when both parents have higher education and are employed outside the home, and when fathers have higher incomes (Braver & O'Connell, 1998; Cancian & Meyer, 1998; Juby, LeVourdais & Marcil-Gratton, 2005; Maccoby & Mnookin, 1992). In addition, data indicate that shared or joint custody is more likely when mothers perceive fathers as competent caregivers (Juby et al., 2005; Pruett et al., 2003), a finding consistent with Amato's data indicating that increases in father involvement, parenting experience and confidence are associated with fathers maintaining positive ties with their children following divorce (Amato & Gilbreth 1999).

Further research is needed to better understand the impact of different custody arrangements on child and adolescent adjustment. Studies need to be carefully designed so that joint legal custody is distinguished from joint physical custody. Reliance on court documents alone, without cross-checking to ensure that what is written is in fact what is actually occurring in practice, is insufficient. In addition, research designs need to control for pertinent factors, such as the nature and extent of parental conflict and how children are involved, the nature and extent of parent involvement, the extent of parental cooperation, parental adjustment and so on, before, during and after the separation. Of particular interest would be a comparison of children from families where joint custody was chosen voluntarily and those on whom it was court-imposed.

Moreover, careful consideration must be given, not simply to the definition of the custody arrangement, but what it actually entails for the children. For instance, joint physical custody does not necessarily involve multiple transitions or more transitions ("bouncing back and forth") than sole custody. An alternating-week schedule involves one transition, while a more traditional schedule of alternate weekends and one overnight during the week involves many more transitions. Furthermore, it is possible that one transition per week between warring parents negatively affects a child in the same or similar way that three or four such transitions do. Thus, as previously noted, parenting plans for high-conflict families need to provide provisions for disengaging parents and protecting children from parental conflict. In Chapter 5 we addressed various strategies and suggestions for doing so with respect to parenting time and most importantly, the implementation of this time. We now move to a discussion of the decision-making components of parenting plans.

Sole Legal, Joint Legal and Parallel Parenting

Legal custody refers to a parent's ability to make major child-related decisions, primarily relating to residence, health and welfare, education, and religion. Typically, recommendations for legal custody would be for either sole or joint custody. More recently, parallel parenting orders have been issued in various Canadian provinces as a type of joint legal custody.

Sole custody affords one parent the authority to make major child-related decisions, which are for the most part limited to health and welfare, education and religion. Notwithstanding the law in the strictest sense, sole custody orders and/or parenting plans to that effect often, although not always, include provisions noting that the authority to make final decisions must be exercised after a consultation process and a full sharing of relevant information with the non-custodial parent. In the event the parents are unable to come to a mutual agreement, the parent with sole custody would make the final decision.[2]

Joint legal custody (as distinguished from joint physical or shared custody) requires parents to come to mutual agreements about major child-related decisions. Where applicable, and particularly for heath care and education, these parents are likely to rely on professional opinions obtained from physicians, teachers, psychologists and other relevant professionals. The future-dispute-resolution mechanism available in virtually all parenting plans addresses instances when the parents are unable to come to a mutual decision, and typically calls for participation in mediation before returning to court, or alternatively mediation/arbitration or parenting coordination.

The imposition of sole custody against the objection of one parent may be necessary for some families; however, it is usually insufficient, especially for moderate- to high-conflict families. These families typically have conflicts over day-to-day matters and the implementation of the parenting plan that are unrelated to the major child-related decisions over which the parent with sole custody has authority. Similarly, the designation of joint custody is insufficient as it neither elucidates *how* parents are to arrive at decisions mutually nor provides a protocol for consultation and exchange of information.

It is surprisingly uncommon for parents, even those characterized as being in moderate to high conflict, to argue about major child-related decisions. Typically, major decisions do not arise very often, and when they do they are (with the exception of religion) typically resolved by professional opinion, or if there are different opinions, a consensus of professional opinion. Parents are far more inclined to routinely and often vociferously argue about day-to-day decisions, most of which do not fall under the auspices of the major child-related decisions defined by the law and thus under the authority of the sole-custody parent. These day-to-day decisions, which seem endless, may include such issues as:

(a) transportation of children between parents;

(b) where, how and when transitions occur;

(c) how holidays are shared and alternated;

(d) exchanging of travel information;

(e) homework routines;

(f) what the children should eat/not eat;

(g) what and how much television the children should watch;

(h) child discipline practices;

(i) pets, toys and clothing going back and forth between homes;

(j) how, when, and what child-related information is exchanged;

(k) parent–teacher meetings;

(l) school and field trips;

(m) how changes to accommodate special events/holidays are made;

(n) peer birthday parties;

(o) haircuts and body-piercing;

(p) childcare when the resident parent is unavailable ("the right of first refusal");

(q) telephone contact between parent and child; and

(r) non-compliance with orders.

While extracurricular activities may be related to a child's health and welfare, and thus considered by some to be an instance of a major child-related decision that can be determined by the sole custody parent, in most cases one parent cannot control what the other parent does with the child when the child is in that parent's care. Decisions pertaining to extracurricular activities, then, stand distinct from other major health care decisions, such as surgery, to the extent that the sole-custody parent can in fact make such decisions and furthermore ensure that they are implemented, even if the event decided upon is to occur during the other parent's scheduled time with the child.

Parallel parenting in the social science literature refers to a co-parenting style of disengagement and limited communication between the parents (Kelly, 2007; Maccoby & Mnookin, 1992). Studies have identified three types of post-divorce parenting relationships (Hetherington & Kelly, 2002; Maccoby & Mnookin, 1992). The Conflicted Relationship (less than 25 per cent) is characterized by ineffective communication, lack of dis-engagement by one or both parents, and continued conflict. Cooperative Parenting (25 to 30 per cent) is characterized by coordination, joint planning and consultation, give-and-take, and providing support to the other parent when needed. Parallel Parenting comprises the largest group (greater than 50 per cent) and is characterized by low conflict, low communication and emotional disengagement.

To the extent that parents remain disengaged, children are protected from parental conflict; as previously noted, children do best when they maintain good relationships with two parents who keep the children out of their conflict. The absence of conflict, however, does not necessarily mean that parents are able to parent cooperatively, and in many cases may mean that they remain disengaged. While cooperation and effective communication and conflict resolution are preferred, if parents are unable to achieve these goals the next best scenario for children is for the parents to remain disengaged (Maccoby and Mnookin, 1992). Children can do well when their parents each parent adequately in a parallel, disengaged manner (low-conflict); these children also do better than those who are actively involved in their parents' disputes (Hetherington & Kelly, 2002; Maccoby & Mnookin, 1992).

While these researchers note that over time most parents become disengaged, even those with shared parenting arrangements, some parents will ultimately achieve cooperative parenting. Still, the goal is to protect children, not necessarily to improve parental communication, a bonus if it occurs at all. Although we have no empirical data on this point, it makes sense that if cooperative parenting is at all possible, it is more likely to occur from a place of distance and disengagement than from the throws of conflict. As previously noted, the greater the parental conflict, the more structure and specificity required in any parenting plan, regardless of whether it is for sole, joint or parallel parenting (see Appendix 14, Parenting Plan Checklist For High Conflict Families).

At a rate of approximately 15 to 20 per cent, high-conflict parents represent a minority of separated/divorced couples. Many are mired in intractable legal disputes, ongoing conflicts over parenting practices, hostility, physical threats, and intermittent violence (Johnston, 1994). Additionally, as many as 60 per cent of these parents are likely to have personality disturbances and/or disorders, substance-abuse problems, and/or mental illness (Ayoub, Deutsch & Maraganore, 1999; Emery, 1999; Johnston & Roseby, 1997, Roseby & Johnston, 1998; Siegal & Langford, 1998). A disregard for authority and non-compliance are high in this group of parents, many of whom also suffer from narcissistic characteristics and the inability to separate their own needs and feelings from those of their children.

It is important to recognize, as we have noted previously, that high-conflict families do not always involve two high-conflict parents. It is not uncommon to find that one parent has achieved emotional disengagement and works hard to avoid conflict and litigation, while the other parent remains embroiled in anger and revenge, often manifested in repeated motions to the court (Friedman, 2004; Kelly, 2003).

It is noteworthy that although the courts may have stated otherwise, cooperation is not the intention, or even the ultimate goal, of parallel parenting. In both theory and practice, *parallel parenting* runs counter to the principles inherent in joint legal custody to the extent that its ultimate objective is to disengage parents and provide a framework that makes their communication unnecessary, thereby minimizing conflict and decreasing risk to children (Johnston, 1995). In fact, parallel parenting (plans) pre-empt the need for the parents to communicate, and in effect deter failed cooperation when there is risk of conflict, thereby minimizing, but not eradicating, risk to children. While parallel parenting and joint custody may share some components, they are fundamentally very different. We have concerns, therefore, that by identifying parallel parenting orders as a subtype of joint legal custody, courts are not making the necessary distinctions (Birnbaum & Fidler, 2005), and consequently, misconceptions abound. For example, five of the seven points listed as differentiating parallel parenting orders by Justice Trussler in *Broder v. Broder* (1998),[3] are actually common to both sole and joint custody, and are not in fact exclusive to parallel parenting.[4]

Notwithstanding the potential of parallel parenting to disengage parents and minimize their conflict, opponents of parallel parenting orders raise provocative questions regarding their practicability and the probability of achieving their stated goals. Epstein & Madsen (2004) state:

> While perhaps well intentioned, parallel parenting is deeply flawed, reflecting less of a concern with the best interests of children than judicial resistance to the imperative to 'choose' between parents, a narrow and formal conception of parental equality, and an unstudied faith in the ability to compel cooperation between hostile litigants.

In reply to the opponents of parallel parenting orders (as a subtype of joint custody), who correctly note the negative impact of parental conflict on children, one should keep in mind from our earlier discussion that it is not parental conflict per se or even the *extent* of it that is predictive of children's adjustment. Rather, it is the extent of the *children's involvement* in the parental conflict: the *form* of the conflict coupled with *how* the children are involved in it by their own volition and/or more directly by one or both of their parents' overt or covert behaviour. Relevant to understanding the impact of conflict on children is the extent to which they observe their parents' conflict, and especially that related to them—such as scheduling conflicts. Also relevant is the manner and extent to which parents involve children in the conflict by asking for their opinion, telling them to talk to the other parent about certain issues, and/or attempting to get them on side one way or the other. If children are afforded an opportunity to experience healthy problem solving and conflict resolution through parental role modelling, they are less likely to be at risk.

A parallel parenting plan provides a methodology for parents to resolve the types of problems previously listed. Even if the courts choose one parent over the other by avoiding joint legal custody or a parallel parenting order that is a subtype of joint legal custody, disputes pertaining to the innumerable day-to-day and implementation issues are likely to continue. Orders for sole legal custody are not likely to abate to any significant extent most of the disputes in which high-conflict parents tend to engage. Clearly, children are at less risk under the terms of a parallel parenting order (not necessarily joint legal custody) that includes sufficient detail around scheduling, day-to-day decision-making, and implementation issues than they would be without such a plan or with a more simplistic order for sole legal custody.[5]

Parallel parenting plans are not necessarily the same as *parallel parenting orders*, just as parallel parenting is not necessarily equivalent to joint legal custody. In practice and social science theory, we observe two types of parallel parenting; by delineating and distinguishing these two types, we hope to clarify the evident confusion. One type of parallel parenting is a subcategory of joint custody, while the other clearly is not.

In the first type of parallel parenting, each parent is allocated a different domain of decision-making. In such cases, parallel parenting involves each parent having final decision-making authority (i.e., equal status in a general sense) in a certain domain, in effect affording each parent sole legal custody for their respective domain (i.e., unequal status specifically). For example, one parent may have authority to make major decisions about education (e.g., school or change of school, psycho-educational testing), but not make day-to-day decisions, such as attendance at field trips or parent-teacher meetings. One may decide upon school events while the other does the same for major health care decisions, such as surgery, but not for routine medical or dental appointments during the other's parenting time or when a child becomes ill. Consistent with the words of J.A. Laskin in *Lefebvre v. Lefebvre*[6], "The parents are given equal status, but exercise the rights and responsibilities associated with custody independent of one another." Similarly, summarizing Justice Aston in *M. (T.J.) v. M. (P.G.)*,[7] parallel parenting orders are a form of joint custody—a sub-category—and are not dependent on cooperative working relationships or even on good communication between the parents.

In the second type of parallel parenting, one parent has sole legal custody (final decision-making authority) for all major child-related decisions; this model, therefore, should not be construed as a subtype of joint legal custody. This type of arrangement is likely to be indicated in cases of domestic violence and in some cases of high levels of conflict.[8] Still, the parenting plan and/or order may provide for parallel parenting, which is necessary in high-conflict situations irrespective of the determination of legal custody, whether sole or joint. Such plans and orders allocate other areas of decision-making (day-to-day) and parental conduct that do not fall under the auspices of legal custody relating to both parenting time and its implementation (e.g., transportation, location of transitions, parental conduct at transitions, the suspension of access due to illness) and decision-making (e.g., the sole-custody parent's responsibilities regarding the consultation process, if any, and information exchange). The above-noted details pertaining to parenting time in parallel parenting plans attempt to ensure that the child's time with both parents, as ordered and/or agreed to (and no more or less contact), does indeed occur, thereby addressing the maximum contact provision in the *Divorce Act*. Such specificity is typically required in higher-conflict cases, when by virtue of having the title of sole legal custody, one parent oversteps his/or her authority and makes arbitrary decisions regarding parenting time.

Parenting plans cannot predict every eventuality, especially in the case of high-conflict parents who invariably find a loophole in the plan, or a circumstance about which they disagree. A structured and specified parenting plan is not intended to be a disguise for joint custody. While parenting plans and parallel parenting orders are not a panacea to the struggles and turmoil that children and families endure before, during and after separation and divorce, they do provide some of the much-needed distance in protecting children from parental conflict and facilitating parent-child relationships. In addition, detailed parallel parenting plans provide a methodology for parenting after separation and divorce, thereby allowing both parents to parent (parallel to one another), albeit not necessarily cooperatively or jointly. Such plans honour each parent's respective value and contribution to the children, in turn reinforcing children's senses of self and identity, as these are intimately related to their perceptions of their parents and themselves.

PARENTING AND THE COURTS

Historically, courts have resolved parenting disputes by awarding one parent (usually the mother) custody and the other parent access. The parent granted "custody" of the child is thus empowered to make all decisions affecting the child's life and the "access" parent has no right of input in the decision-making process, except in some cases through the intervention of the court. In the past several years, however, changing societal values have been reflected in the decisions of the courts, and more recently they have begun to investigate shared parenting models such as divided custody and parallel parenting.

Custody of a child consists of an assortment of rights and responsibilities, including, but not limited to: the right to care for the child; the right to consent to medical treatment for the child; the right to make decisions regarding the child's education; and the responsibility to ensure that the child is properly fed, clothed and provided with the other necessities of life. Final custody orders tend to follow a full hearing into the best interests of the child dealing with both the short-term and long-term welfare of the child. In addition, although custody orders can be varied in the event of a material change in circumstances, they are intended to be long-term solutions to post-separation parenting.

SOLE CUSTODY

Despite changes in societal norms, the most common order continues to be sole custody to one parent with a right of access to the other. A judge who grants an order of custody in favour of one parent in all likelihood will grant access to the other parent. In *Kruger v. Kruger*,[9] the Ontario Court of Appeal held that a person who is awarded sole custody has full parental control over and ultimate parental responsibility for the care, upbringing, and education of a child, generally to the exclusion of the non-custodial parent. When making an award of access, the court envisions that the access parent may visit with the child and be kept informed of health, education and other important issues relating to the child. However, unless specifically endorsed by court order, an access parent does not have any ability to make decisions that relate to the health, education, religion, residence, and welfare of a child.

At times, the courts have placed limits on the extent of the authority of the custodial parent. While the custodial parent has the obligation to make basic decisions about the child, this does not mean that the wishes of the custodial parent govern the terms of access granted to the other parent. In *Young v. Young*,[10] Justice McLachlin held that a custodial parent did not have the right to dictate how an access parent should spend his or her time with a child; an access parent had the right to share day-to-day life with the child unless this posed a risk to the child. In *Carter v. Brooks*,[11] Justice Morden held that some decisions, such as where a child will reside, were too important to be left to one parent, and that if the parents could not agree on such an important matter, it should be referred to a judge. The custodial parent, ruled Morden, did not have the unilateral right to make the decision. Justice Abella, in *MacGyver v. Richards*,[12] while not disagreeing with the analysis in *Carter v. Brooks*, stated that in making a decision affecting an incident of custody, a judge should give great weight to the wishes of the custodial parent, as this parent was in the best position to know what was best for a child.

JOINT CUSTODY

Joint custody can mean different things to different people. Although joint-custodial parents share legal custody—that is, the ability to make significant decisions for the child—they may not necessarily share physical custody of the child. For the most part, judges and lawyers use joint custody to describe a parenting arrangement whereby the child lives primarily with one parent who has the day-to-day care and control of and responsibility for the child. The other parent has liberal contact with the child, along with the right of consultation and input in respect to all significant decisions that affect the child. Joint-custodial parents are each entitled to exercise the incidents of custody and to participate in all significant decisions affecting a child. The intention of joint-custodial parenting plans is to provide a child with frequent contact with both parents and to provide both parents an opportunity to make significant decisions concerning the upbringing of their child.[13]

Historically, in Ontario, the two leading cases dealing with joint custody are the Court of Appeal decisions in *Baker v. Baker*[14] and *Kruger v. Kruger*.[15] In *Baker v. Baker*, the trial judge ordered joint custody despite the fact that neither parent, in this bitter court battle, had requested it. In her trial judgment, Justice Boland wrote:

> Courts must be responsive to the winds of change. In today's society, the breakdown of the traditional family is increasingly common, and new ways of defining post-divorce family structures are desperately needed. It is apparent that the traditional award of custody to the mother and access to the father is the cause of many of the problems and most of the tensions between parents and children and between the parents themselves. Our courts see many cases in which the father has been deprived of access. Gradually he loses interest or finds that he cannot afford to continue his court battles, and as a result, the child is deprived of the love, influence, and financial support of its father. Joint custody would seem to be the ideal solution to present challenges and past experiences.[16]

In allowing the appeal and ordering a new trial, the Court of Appeal held that joint custody was appropriate for an "exceptional category" of parents who were "able and willing to cooperate as loving parents." The court further opined that such parents were rarely before the court in a custody dispute.

In *Kruger v. Kruger, supra* the court once again addressed the issue of joint custody. Justice Thorson, writing for the majority, expressed the opinion that joint custody orders may be appropriate where both parents are willing to cooperate with one another, but that such an arrangement should not be imposed on unwilling participants. Furthermore, continued the judge, it was inappropriate for the court to impose joint custody with the hope that it would work, as this was a "triumph of optimism over prudence."[17] The fact that there was no agreement between the parties on the issue was also a major consideration. The majority of the court stated: "The fact remains that in this case there is no agreement between the parties on the issue of joint custody. That fact, in my opinion, makes all the difference to the approach which should be taken by this court to the question whether it should now seek to impose an order for joint custody. . . ."[18]

The court refused to assume that the parents, who had been able to get along under the interim custody arrangement in place prior to trial, would continue to do so in the future. The court concluded:

> . . .Any court that is considering the making of an award of joint custody should be guided by the following precepts: if the court has before it the right combination of thoughtful and mature parents who understand what is involved in such an arrangement and are willing to try it, the court should feel encouraged to go ahead with it; but if they are not evidently willing, the court should not seek to impose it on them, because the price to be paid if it does not work is likely to be altogether too high to warrant taking the risk that is then present of trying it.[19]

There is little direction from the Court or any clear basis for deciding between sole or joint custody. For example, *Kaplanis v. Kaplanis* and *Ladisa v. Ladisa* were released on the same day by the Court of Appeal for Ontario, were not dissimilar factually, yet different parenting orders were granted by the Court. As a rule, the courts will only order joint custody, in the traditional meaning of the phrase, if there is cogent evidence that the parents can and will cooperate to promote the best interests of their children. While it may no longer be accurate to state unequivocally that the court will not order joint custody over the wishes of the primary caregiver of the child, most judges are reluctant to force joint custody on a parent in the absence of evidence that the parties can and will cooperate if ordered to do so.

Examples of Cases Where Joint Custody was Ordered

In *Charlton v. Charlton*,[20] the court ordered joint guardianship despite the judge's admission that he was not favourably disposed toward granting such orders. He found that "there is a reasonable prospect that the parties will cooperate, despite some disagreements that have arisen from time to time."[21] Similarly, in *Daoust v. Leboeuf*,[22] the Court of Appeal upheld the trial judge's decision of joint custody despite the father's opposition. The trial judge found that the parents would be able to cooperate despite their differences. In *Walsh v. Walsh*,[23] the Court of Appeal upheld the trial judge's order of joint custody despite the fact that neither parent sought joint custody at trial. Joint custody was ordered in *Griffiths v. Griffiths*[24] despite the conflict and communication problems of the parents. The court found that conflicts are to be expected as separating parents go through the "process of disengagement." However, this was not deemed sufficient reason to decline an order of joint custody, especially when the conflict was "not deeply embedded." The judge also found that, generally, the parents arranged access without incident, and neither parent had behaved inappropriately in the presence of the children. A court is not prohibited from ordering joint custody on the basis that one of the parents does not want to share the decision-making authority. If the child is thriving and is benefiting from the joint custody arrangement, a court may make such an order.[25]

In *Ladisa v. Ladisa*,[26] the Court of Appeal upheld the trial judge's decision to award joint custody despite the conflict between the parties, their communication difficulties, and the mother's objection to the order. Although the trial judge restricted the manner in which the parties could communicate with each other, he nonetheless found that the parents had the ability to cooperate on important issues involving the children's best interests.

Similarly, in another Ontario decision, *Mancini v. Mancini*,[27] the court awarded the parties joint custody over the objections of the mother. In making the order, Justice Tulloch stated:

> Despite the animosity that has existed between the parties, they have managed to make the shared custody arrangement work, as noted by the assessor. While both parties dispute that the arrangement has been working, this is consistent with their position on all matters in this trial. It is apparent that the joint custody has been more successful than the sole custody arrangement, which preceded it, at least in terms of the respondent being able to spend time with Marco [the child]. I believe that the petitioner has exaggerated the negative effects of the joint custody arrangement in an attempt to improve her claim for sole custody. . .

> The fact that the parties have managed the joint custody regime is an indication that they are able to communicate and cooperate on some level in the best interests of the child. While issues remain

between the parties, I do not see why joint parenting cannot continue
to work, as long as it is accompanied by terms consistent with high
conflict situations.[28]

Courts in other provinces have also continued to make awards of joint
custody over the objection of one of the parents. In *Haché v. Haché*,[29] the
court in New Brunswick ordered joint custody despite the evidence of
the assessor that the parties were incapable of resolving child-related
issues by themselves. In *Harper v. Carroll*,[30] Justice Kraus of the Saskatchewan Queen's Bench made an award of joint custody in spite of the
mother's argument that the parties had continual disagreements about
matters that affected the best interests of the child. The court, while
acknowledging the existence of the disagreements, held that the child
was thriving under the existing joint custody regime and that the parents'
relationship could not be described as being in enough conflict to prevent
joint custody. Similarly, Justice Mahoney of the Alberta Queen's Bench
awarded joint custody in *Johnston v. Johnston*.[31] Although the parties were
in conflict, the court found that both had something to offer the child.

Examples of Cases Where Joint Custody was Not Ordered

In determining if orders of joint custody will be granted, the courts
have analyzed the degree and nature of conflict between the parties.
While some conflict is expected, bitterness and frequent disputes may
make joint custody impracticable. The seminal cases of *Baker v. Baker*,
supra and *Kruger v. Kruger*, supra have paved the road for the rationale
that joint custody ought not to be ordered in the absence of clear evidence
that the parties can and will cooperate in the best interests of their child.

In *Coulson v. Cohen*,[32] the court held that an order for joint custody
was inappropriate despite the parties' separation agreement containing
provisions for joint custody. The court found that the parties were unable
to set aside their differences and communicate effectively. In *Johnson v.
Cleroux*,[33] the Court of Appeal for Ontario reiterated its traditional view
of joint custody, stating: "The law and common sense accord on the
matter of joint custody – it requires a high degree of cooperation between
the parents and ought only to be awarded where the parents have demonstrated the ability to cooperate."[34] The Court of Appeal decided that
joint custody was not appropriate as the parents had conflict over parenting issues.

Similarly, in *Kaplanis v. Kaplanis*,[35] the Court of Appeal for Ontario
set aside a decision for joint custody and remitted the matter back to
trial, determining that the trial judge erred in making such an order. The
parties could not communicate with each other in a civilized fashion and
there was no evidence before the court that the parents were capable of

working together for the sake of their child. The Court of Appeal, however, did clarify that in certain situations, an order for joint custody may be appropriate. Justice Weiler, speaking for the court, stated:

> The fact that one parent professes an inability to communicate with the other parent does not, in and of itself, mean that a joint custody order cannot be considered. On the other hand, hoping that communication between the parents will improve once the litigation is over does not provide a sufficient basis for the making of an order of joint custody. There must be some evidence before the court that, despite their differences, the parents are able to communicate effectively with one another. No matter how detailed the custody order that is made, gaps inevitably occur, unexpected situations arise, and the changing developmental needs of a child must be addressed on an ongoing basis. When, as here, the child is so young that she can hardly communicate her developmental needs, communication is even more important. In this case there was no evidence of effective communication. The evidence was to the contrary.[36]

The principles outlined in *Kaplanis* were applied in *Cameron v. MacGillivray*.[37] In this case, the father was found to be threatening and exhibiting bullying behaviour towards the mother. This behaviour raised doubts as to whether a joint custody arrangement would be workable, even though the parties had demonstrated that they could cooperate on some level. Justice Aiken was concerned that the father would be able to prevail over the mother, because of his bullying, to the detriment of the child's best interests. The court granted the mother sole custody, with the father having some input into significant decisions such as medical treatment, schooling, and extracurricular activities. To minimize the conflict, the court awarded the mother final say in instances of disagreement.

In *Trendle v. Trendle*,[38] the court refused to make an order for joint custody even though the evidence clearly showed that both parents had excellent relationships with the children. The parents, however, could not communicate appropriately with each other.

In *Aguilera v. Reid*,[39] the court refused to grant joint custody where the father was unable to put his children's interests before his own. Additionally, there was considerable domestic violence for which the father refused to take any responsibility. Similarly, in *Berzins v. Straughan*,[40] the court refused to order joint custody in circumstances where the father had been convicted of an assault on the mother.

Shared Custody

Unlike the concept of joint custody, where the ability to make significant decisions on behalf of children is key, the motivating force behind shared custody is the ability to exercise a full role in physical parenting. Historically, courts have dealt with shared custody claims in the same manner as claims for joint custody. The primary question in most judges' minds is whether or not the parents cooperate to the extent necessary to make the parenting arrangement work. In *B. (P.J.) v. B. (M.M.)*,[41] the court awarded shared custody to ensure that each parent continued to play an active role in the children's lives. The court found that the potential negative consequences for the children from moving back and forth between their parents' homes were offset by the positive benefits of nurturing and maintaining a consistent relationship with both parents. In *Emerson v. Emerson*,[42] the child alternated between the parents' homes on a weekly basis. The mother moved to change the arrangements, alleging that the father did not maintain the child's health treatments. The father acknowledged his shortcomings and took steps to remedy the difficulties. The court found that the child was thriving under the shared parenting arrangement and that it was in the child's best interests for the order to continue.

While the parents' level of cooperation is an important consideration in determining whether a shared custody arrangement will be awarded, the children's ability to manage such a regime must also be given great weight. In *MacArthur v. MacArthur*,[43] the court terminated a shared parenting arrangement and granted custody to the mother. The court found that the disruptions surrounding the children's weekly residence changes were detrimental to the children's well-being.

Parallel Parenting

The increasing trend towards parallel parenting in family law disputes has been met with considerable discussion and debate.[44] As previously discussed, in recent years, some judges have imposed "parallel parenting" arrangements as a type of legal custody in high-conflict cases. The term has been utilized by the courts to describe a variety of parenting arrangements, but most frequently, each involves very detailed rules that govern the responsibilities and rights of each parent. Typically, each has the ability to make day-to-day decisions when the child is with him or her, but decision-making with respect to significant matters that affect the health and welfare of a child is commonly divided. For example, one parent may be responsible for all schooling decisions and the other for medical ones. Typically, in cases where parallel parenting has been ordered, the parents' ability to communicate with one another is strained and as a result, the parents are encouraged to communicate through a communications book or by email only.

For many practitioners, including the courts, *parallel parenting orders* have been identified as a subcategory of joint legal custody orders (Epstein & Madsen, 2004). In *M. (T.J.) v. M. (P.G.)*,[45] Mr. Justice Aston provided an apt description of parallel parenting:

> . . . "parallel parenting" orders have become a form of joint custody, a sub-category if you will, which does not depend upon cooperative working relationships or even good communication between the parties. The concept (consistent with subsection 20 (1) of the *Children's Law Reform Act*) is that the parents have equal status but exercise the rights and responsibilities associated with "custody" independently of one another. Section 20 (7) of the *Children's Law Reform Act* provides clear authority for the court to deal separately and specifically with "incidents of custody." The form of a "parallel parenting" order addresses specific incidents of custody beyond a mere residential schedule for where the children will reside on a day-to-day basis.[46]

In *St. Pierre v. St. Pierre*,[47] Justice Aston awarded joint custody, which involved a parallel parenting arrangement, although the parents found it difficult to communicate with each other except with a communications book, which the judge found to be effective communication. Similarly, in *Bernardi v. Bernardi*,[48] the Ontario Superior Court made a parallel parenting award, stating that it was in the best interests of the children in the circumstances. Each parent was allowed to make independent decisions for the children while they were in their respective care.

Parallel parenting can be an appropriate disposition even in cases where parents are openly hostile and uncooperative; the challenge for the courts is to design detailed orders as "parallel parenting" rather than "cooperative parenting."

Mol v. Mol[49] is one of the early decisions that awarded joint custody under a parallel parenting regime. Justice Kruzick, relying heavily on his interpretation of Justice Wilson's dissent in *Kruger v. Kruger, supra*, found that a joint custody plan was workable despite the mother's express unwillingness to consider such an arrangement. He stressed that the principles codified in the *Divorce Act* allowed him to make an order for joint custody "if the best interests of the children are to be truly served."[50] These principles are: (a) children's best interests are the only consideration in custody matters; (b) the court ought not to consider past conduct, unless relevant to the ability of a person to parent a child; and (c) children must have as much contact with each parent as is consistent with the best interests of the child. Justice Kruzick also found that the mother's hostility towards the father was "not justified" and that for the sake of her children, "she must be less rigid."[51]

In *Dagg v. Pereira*,[52] the court revisited the issue of parallel parenting. In this case, there was intense conflict throughout the marriage, conflict that at times became physical. On one occasion following such an altercation, charges were laid against both parents for assault "while the be-wildered children witnessed their parents being taken to the police station."[53] By the time of trial, the parties were barely speaking to one another. Justice Bellamy found that the father was very caring and involved in the care of all four children. She expressed concerns about the mother, although she found her to be a tireless advocate on behalf of her children. In the end, the judge designed an extremely detailed parenting arrangement that she called joint custody but which was, essentially, a parallel parenting order. Each parent was given authority over day-to-day decisions while the children were in their care. Additionally, the father was awarded final authority over educational and health-related decisions for the children. Justice Bellamy also noted that orders such as the one she awarded maximized contact and would reduce the likelihood of parental alienation.[54]

Parallel parenting is also an option where the court is concerned that the primary caregiver will force the other parent out of the children's lives, and that the relationship is too conflicted for joint custody (in its usual usage) to work. In *Cox v. Stephen*,[55] the trial judge awarded the father custody of the child to address, amongst other things, alienation by the mother even though the child had always resided with her. The mother appealed. The appellate court, in overturning the trial decision, created a form of parallel parenting to address the concerns of parental alienation; the parents were to have equal status but to exercise the rights and responsibilities associated with custody independent of one another. The child was to remain in the primary care of the mother, thus protecting the child's sense of stability, and the father was granted joint custody, thereby reducing the possibility of alienation. Next the Court of Appeal dismissed the father's appeal and affirmed the decision of the first appellate judge; however, it did not address the issue of parallel parenting.

Similarly, in *South v. Tichelaar*,[56] joint custody resembling a parallel parenting arrangement was ordered, largely to compel the father to involve the mother as much as possible in the children's lives. The father for the most part controlled the situation by dictating the circumstances under which the mother would have contact with the children. Requests for additional access by the mother were regularly denied. Justice Heeney held that a joint custodial model, while recognizing the importance of their father, would provide the children with more meaningful contact with their mother.

In *Bernardi v. Bernardi*,[57] the court made a parallel parenting award stating that this was in the best interests of the children in the circumstances. In this case, each parent was permitted to make independent decisions based on the children's best interests while the children were in their care.

In *M. (T.J.) v. M. (P.G.)*,[58]Justice Aston rejected the mother's argument that the imposition of joint custody in their circumstances would only increase the conflict between the parents. The judge found that there was no evidence that the children were adversely affected by their parents' conflict and that, in fact, the children were happy and thriving. Justice Aston ordered joint custody under the parallel parenting model.

In *Hildinger v. Carroll*,[59] the trial judge varied a joint custody order and granted sole custody to the mother, primarily because of the highly conflictual relationship of the parents. The father appealed and sought joint custody on the parallel parenting model. Justice Laskin held that:

> assuming without deciding that parallel parenting is now a viable option where the parties are uncooperative, I see no justification for it in this case. The overwhelming evidence accepted by the trial judge pointed to but one conclusion: granting Ms. Hildinger sole custody was very much in Nancy Mae's best interests.[60]

The appeal was dismissed.

In *Roy v. Roy*,[61] the Court of Appeal for Ontario clarified its position on joint custody orders akin to parallel parenting. The court stated: "The Supreme Court of Canada and this court have consistently held that joint or parallel custody should only be ordered where the parents can cooperate and communicate effectively."[62] Although the court awarded sole custody to the mother, it did not vary the residential arrangements whereby the parents had the children in their care equal amounts of time.

In *Andrade v. Kennelly*,[63] the parties separated after a seven-year marriage. Following separation, the three children of the marriage resided with their mother in Toronto, who refused to allow unsupervised access to the children outside of her home. It was not until the father sought the assistance of the court that the mother consented to unsupervised access. After the making of that order, the father exercised access to the children on alternate weekends and one night during the week. The mother subsequently brought a motion seeking permission to relocate to Ottawa with the children in order to pursue employment. The court dismissed this motion and granted an order for joint custody in the parallel parenting mode, with the children residing with their father. The court held that it was in the children's best interests to have maximum contact with both parents, and the mother would not support the children's relationship with their father.

The Ontario Court of Appeal was provided with another opportunity to deal with parallel parenting in *Ursic v. Ursic*.[64] In this case, the trial judge ordered that the parents share "joint custody in the parallel parenting mode." He set out a detailed parenting schedule under which the child was to live with each parent about half of the time. The mother appealed, contending that the trial judge erred in failing to award her sole custody of the child. Relying heavily on *Mol v. Mol, supra* and *M. (T.J.) v. M. (P.G.), supra*, the Court stated,

> The trial judge did not merely order joint custody. He included with it a parallel parenting order. Many trial courts have recognized that joint custody under a parallel parenting regime may be suitable where both parents love the child and should play an active role in the child's life, yet have difficulty communicating or reaching a consensus on the child's upbringing. The trial judge viewed parallel parenting to be suitable in this case, and I am not persuaded that he erred in ordering it.[65]

The Court affirmed the trial judge's order with minor adjustments to the summer access schedule.

CONCLUDING REMARKS

In this chapter, we discussed the legal and mental health distinctions between sole and joint, shared and parallel parenting by reviewing the social science literature as well as the case law. The preceding cases, though, do not purport to be a comprehensive list of all the relevant case law that has come out of the Canadian courts in recent years, nor do they purport to be the definitive view of the judiciary in the area of parenting orders. They are, however, a representative sampling of the diverse nature of the decisions made by the Canadian judiciary. What becomes clear upon a closer analysis of the cases is that the terminology in this area of law is not consistent. Judges and lawyers use terms interchangeably and inconsistently, and at times without any regard to the correct definitions. It is submitted that rather than clarifying appropriate parenting arrangements for children, the cases themselves raise significant questions. Is parallel parenting a sub-type of joint custody? Can parallel parenting be a good solution for children if parental communication is conflict-laden or non-existent? Are shared custody, joint custody, and parallel parenting part of the same parenting regime? Should there be a presumption in favour of joint custody, and if so, what evidence is necessary to rebut this presumption? The list of questions goes on. What is evident is that the questions continue to remain unanswered and that the cases continue to be inconsistent, thus creating even more uncertainty for the children we serve.

Notes

[1.] *Baker v. Baker* (1978), 1978 CarswellOnt 244, [1978] O.J. No. 711, 3 R.F.L. (2d) 193, 1 Fam. L. Rev. 226 (Ont. H.C.) at p.197 [R.F.L.], reversed (1979), 1979 CarswellOnt 367,

[1979] O.J. No. 4074, 8 R.F.L. (2d) 236, 95 D.L.R. (3d) 529, 23 O.R. (2d) 391, 2 Fam. L. Rev. 69 (Ont. C.A.)]

2. These provisions for consultation and efforts to come to a mutual decision with the other parent may not be included, for example when the non-custodial parent has abandoned the child, or when there has been a finding of violence and/or child abuse. Notwithstanding such exclusions, in these situations the non-custodial access parent would by law (*CLRA*) be entitled to make enquires and receive full information about major decisions, unless indicated otherwise in the order.

3. [1998] A.J. No. 1046, 1998 CarswellAlta 878, 42 R.F.L. (4th) 143, (sub nom. *J.E.B. v. C.B.*) 238 A.R. 187 (Alta. Q.B.).

4. The seven points are: (1) parent assumes responsibility for child during the time the child is with that parent (occurs in sole and joint legal and physical custody); (2) parent has no say or influence over the actions of the other parent while child is in the other parent's care (occurs in sole and joint legal and physical custody); (3) no expectation of flexibility or negotiation (occurs in joint custody, generally not in sole custody or parallel parenting); (4) parent does not plan activities for child during the other parent's time (required in sole and joint custody); (5) contact between parents is minimized (occurs in parallel parenting and in some sole and joint parenting); (6) child not to deliver verbal messages between parents (invariable and frequently ordered or recommended in sole, joint and parallel parenting); and, (7) child-related information about school, health, vacations, etc., shared in writing (typical in parallel parenting, not uncommon in sole and joint custody depending on level of conflict).

5. See *Ganden v. Kovalsky*, 2003 CarswellAlta 891, [2003] A.J. No. 793, 2003 ABQB 20 (Alta. Q.B.). Justice Park declined to make a parallel parenting order. Although aware that the parallel parenting model was developed for high-conflict situations, the justice believed that in the case at hand, the inevitability of the parents' continued bickering and interference in each other's parenting when the child was in the other's care would preclude the efficacy of parallel parenting. The court concluded that the child would be raised more effectively by granting one parent sole custody. We note, however, that while it is likely that having one parent make the final decisions regarding major issues may have been indicated to the extent that this arrangement protects the child from parental conflict, it remains unclear how such an order addresses the bickering and interference surrounding day-to-day parenting issues.

6. (2002), [2002] O.J. No. 4885, 2002 CarswellOnt 4325, 167 O.A.C. 85 (Ont. C.A. [In Chambers])

7. (2002), 2002 CarswellOnt 356, [2002] O.J. No. 398, 25 R.F.L. (5th) 78 (Ont. S.C.J.),

8. See *Broder v. Broder* (1998), [1998] A.J. No. 1046, 1998 CarswellAlta 878, 42 R.F.L. (4th) 143, (sub nom. *J.E.B. v. C.B.*) 238 A.R. 187 (Alta. Q.B.). This is an example of a parallel parenting order where the residential schedule was highly detailed (to ensure implementation of access in the face of evidence that one parent was attempting to obstruct it) and a communication protocol ("rules of engagement") are delineated. This parallel parenting order is not an instance of joint legal custody and in effect is equivalent to a sole legal custody order, as the mother was afforded final decision-making authority for all non-emergency medical and dental circumstances, as well as for major issues relating to education and religion.

9. (1979), 1979 CarswellOnt 299, 25 O.R. (2d) 673, 11 R.F.L. (2d) 52, 2 Fam. L. Rev. 197, 104 D.L.R. (3d) 481 (Ont. C.A.).

10. [1993] S.C.J. No. 112, EYB 1993-67111, 1993 CarswellBC 264, 1993 CarswellBC 1269, [1993] 8 W.W.R. 513, 108 D.L.R. (4th) 193, 18 C.R.R. (2d) 41, [1993] 4 S.C.R. 3, 84 B.C.L.R. (2d) 1, 160 N.R. 1, 49 R.F.L. (3d) 117, 34 B.C.A.C. 161, 56 W.A.C. 161, [1993] R.D.F. 703 (S.C.C.).

11. (1990), 1990 CarswellOnt 317, [1990] O.J. No. 2182, 41 O.A.C. 389, 2 O.R. (3d) 321, 77 D.L.R. (4th) 45, 30 R.F.L. (3d) 53 (Ont. C.A.).

12. (1995), [1995] O.J. No. 770, 1995 CarswellOnt 90, 11 R.F.L. (4th) 432, 22 O.R. (3d) 481, 123 D.L.R. (4th) 562, 84 O.A.C. 349 (Ont. C.A.).

13. *Beaven v. Beaven* (1994), 1994 CarswellBC 1542 (B.C. S.C.).

14. (1979), 1979 CarswellOnt 367, [1979] O.J. No. 4074, 8 R.F.L. (2d) 236, 95 D.L.R. (3d) 529, 23 O.R. (2d) 391, 2 Fam. L. Rev. 69 (Ont. C.A.).

15. *Supra*, note 9.

16. *Baker v. Baker* (1978), 1978 CarswellOnt 244, [1978] O.J. No. 711, 3 R.F.L. (2d) 193, 1 Fam. L. Rev. 226 (Ont. H.C.) at p. 197 [R.F.L.], reversed (1979), 1979 CarswellOnt 367, [1979] O.J. No. 4074, 8 R.F.L. (2d) 236, 95 D.L.R. (3d) 529, 23 O.R. (2d) 391, 2 Fam. L. Rev. 69 (Ont. C.A.).

17. *Supra*, note 9 at p. 681.

18. *Supra,* note 9 at p. 679.

19. *Supra*, note 9 at p. 681.

20. (1980), 1980 CarswellBC 16, 19 B.C.L.R. 42, 15 R.F.L. (2d) 220 (B.C. S.C.).

21. *Ibid.,* p.223.

22. (1998), 1998 CarswellOnt 76, 35 R.F.L. (4th) 143, 107 O.A.C. 73 (Ont. C.A.).

23. (1998), 1998 CarswellOnt 2893, [1998] O.J. No. 2969, 111 O.A.C. 118, 39 R.F.L. (4th) 416 (Ont. C.A.).

24. 2005 CarswellOnt 3209, 2005 ONCJ 235 (Ont. C.J.).

25. *Ibid.* at para. 23.

26. (2005), 2005 CarswellOnt 268, [2005] O.J. No. 276, 11 R.F.L. (6th) 50, 193 O.A.C. 336 (Ont. C.A.).

27. (2006), 2006 CarswellOnt 1080, 25 R.F.L. (6th) 137 (Ont. S.C.J.).

28. *Ibid.*, at paras. 64 & 67.

29. [2004] N.B.J. No. 318, 2004 CarswellNB 388, 2004 NBQB 301 (N.B. Q.B.).

30. 2006 CarswellSask 117, 2006 SKQB 72 (Sask. Q.B.), additional reasons at 2007 CarswellSask 337, 2007 SKQB 180 (Sask. Q.B.).

31. [2004] A.J. No. 333, 2004 CarswellAlta 336, 49 R.F.L. (5th) 82, 2004 ABQB 221 (Alta. Q.B.).

32. (1998), 1998 CarswellOnt 1817, [1998] O.J. No. 1781 (Ont. Gen. Div.).

33. (2002), [2002] O.J. No. 1801, 2002 CarswellOnt 1559, 24 R.F.L. (5th) 422, (sub nom. *J. (M.) v. C. (P.)*) 159 O.A.C. 346 (Ont. C.A.).

34. *Ibid.*, at para. 4.

35. (2005), 2005 CarswellOnt 266, [2005] O.J. No. 275, 10 R.F.L. (6th) 373, 194 O.A.C. 106, 249 D.L.R. (4th) 620 (Ont. C.A.).

36. *Ibid.*, at para. 11.

37. (2005), 2005 CarswellOnt 8095, (sub nom. *D.L.C. v. R.J.M.*) [2005] O.J. No. 5500 (Ont. S.C.J.).

38. (2003), 2003 CarswellOnt 5358, 50 R.F.L. (5th) 440 (Ont. S.C.J.), additional reasons at (2004), 2004 CarswellOnt 600 (Ont. S.C.J.), affirmed (2004), [2004] O.J. No. 5155, 2004 CarswellOnt 5385, 12 R.F.L. (6th) 225, 193 O.A.C. 192 (Ont. C.A.).

39. (2006), 2006 CarswellOnt 1227, (sub nom. *R.A. v. J.R.*) [2006] O.J. No. 810 (Ont. S.C.J.).

40. (2002), 2002 CarswellOnt 3160, [2002] O.J. No. 3661 (Ont. S.C.J.).

41. (1998), 1998 CarswellBC 1521, 163 D.L.R. (4th) 566 (B.C. S.C.).

42. (1995), 1995 CarswellOnt 4192 (Ont. Gen. Div.).

43. (1995), 1995 CarswellBC 1645 (B.C. S.C.).

44. Epstein, P. & L. Madsen, "Joint Custody with a Vengeance: The Emergence of Parallel Parenting Orders,"(2004), 22 C.F.L.Q. 1; Birnbaum, R. & B. Fidler, "Commentary on Epstein and Madsen's 'Joint custody with a Vengeance': The emergence of parallel parenting orders, (2005), 24 C.F.L.Q.

45. (2002), 2002 CarswellOnt 356, [2002] O.J. No. 398, 25 R.F.L. (5th) 78 (Ont. S.C.J.).
46. *Ibid*. at para. 20.
47. (2005), 2005 CarswellOnt 1624, [2005] O.J. No. 1669, 17 R.F.L. (6th) 347 (Ont. S.C.J.).
48. (2005), 2005 CarswellOnt 4107 (Ont. S.C.J.).
49. (1997), 1997 CarswellOnt 3693, [1997] O.J. 4060, 40 O.T.C. 1 (Ont. Gen. Div.).
50. *Ibid*. at para. 32.
51. *Ibid*. at para. 34.
52. (2000), [2000] O.J. No. 4450, 2000 CarswellOnt 4390, 12 R.F.L. (5th) 325 (Ont. S.C.J.).
53. *Ibid*. at para. 13.
54. *Ibid*. at para. 45.
55. 2002 CarswellOnt 2321, [2002] O.J. No. 2762, 30 R.F.L. (5th) 54, [2002] O.T.C. 499 (Ont. S.C.J.) affirmed (2003), 2003 CarswellOnt 4554, [2003] O.J. No. 4371, 47 R.F.L. (5th) 1, 179 O.A.C. 45 (Ont. C.A.).
56. (2001), [2001] O.J. No. 2823, 2001 CarswellOnt 2447, 20 R.F.L. (5th) 175 (Ont. S.C.J.).
57. (2005), 2005 CarswellOnt 4107 (Ont. S.C.J.).
58. *Supra*, note 45.
59. (2004), 2004 CarswellOnt 444, [2004] O.J. No. 291, 2 R.F.L. (6th) 331 (Ont. C.A.), additional reasons at (2004), 2004 CarswellOnt 1334 (Ont. C.A.), leave to appeal refused (2004), 2004 CarswellOnt 4951, 2004 CarswellOnt 4952, 338 N.R. 193 (note), 204 O.A.C. 394 (note) (S.C.C.).
60. *Ibid*. at para. 24.
61. (2006), 2006 CarswellOnt 2898, 27 R.F.L. (6th) 44 (Ont. C.A.).
62. *Ibid*. at para. 4.
63. (2006), 2006 CarswellOnt 3762, 33 R.F.L. (6th) 125 (Ont. S.C.J.).
64. (2006), 2006 CarswellOnt 3335, [2006] O.J. No. 2178, 32 R.F.L. (6th) 23 (Ont. C.A.), additional reasons at (2007), 2007 CarswellOnt 694 (Ont. C.A.).
65. *Ibid*. at para. 26.

References

AFCC Task Force on Parenting Coordination "Parenting Coordination: Implementation issues" Family Court Review 41 (2003), 533–564.

Amato, P.R. & Gilbreth, J. G. "Non-resident fathers and children's well-being: A meta-analysis" Journal of Marriage and the Family 61 (1999), 557–573.

Aquilino, W. S. "The noncustodial father-child relationship from adolescence into young adulthood" Journal of Marriage and Family 68 (2006), 929–946.

Ayoub, C., Deutsch, R. & Maraganore, A. "Emotional distress in children of high-conflict divorce: The impact of marital conflict and violence" Family and Conciliation Courts Review 37:3 (1999), 297–313.

Bauserman, R. "Child adjustment in joint-custody versus sole-custody arrangements: A meta-analytic review" Journal of Family Psychology 16:1 (2002), 91–102.

Bender, W.N. "Joint custody: The option of choice" Journal of Divorce & Remarriage 21:3–4 (1994), 115–131.

Benjamin, M. & Irving, H.H. "Shared parenting: Critical review of the research literature" Family and Conciliation Courts Review 27:2 (1989), 21–35.

Birnbaum, R. & Fidler, B.J. "Commentary on Epstein and Madsen's 'Joint custody with a vengeance: The emergence of parallel parenting orders'" Canadian Family Law Quarterly 24:3 (2005), 337–345.

Coates, C., Deutsch, R., Starnes, H., Sullivan, M.J. & Sydlik, B. "Parenting coordination for high conflict families" Family Court Review 42:2 (2004), 246–262.

Emery, R.E. "Changing the rules for determining child custody in divorce cases" Clinical Psychology: Science and Practice 6 (1999), 323–327.

Epstein, P. & Madsen, L. "Joint custody with a vengeance: The emergence of parallel parenting orders" Canadian Family Law Quarterly 22 (2004), 1–35.

Fidler, B.J. "The influence of gender, the parent-child relationship, and custody arrangement on children's adjustment following family break-up". Unpublished dissertation (1986).

Friedman, M. "The so-called high-conflict couple: A closer look" The American Journal of Family Therapy 32 (2004), 101–117.

Goldstein, J. Freud, A. & Solnit, A.J. In the Best Interests of the Child (New York: Free Press, 1986).

Gunnoe, M. & Braver, S.L. "The effects of joint legal custody on mothers, fathers, and children" Law and Human Behaviour 25:1 (2001), 25–43.

Hess, R. D. & Camara, K. A. "Postdivorce family relationships as mediating factors in the consequences of divorce for children" Journal of Social Issues 35 (1979), 79–96.

Hetherington, E. M. & Kelly, J.B. For Better or For Worse: Divorce Reconsidered (New York: Norton & Company, 2002).

Johnston, J.R. "High-conflict divorce" in The Future of Children: Children and Divorce (Los Altos, CA: David and Lucille Packard Foundation, 1994), 165–182.

Johnston, J.R. "Research update: Children's adjustment in sole custody compared to joint custody families and principles of custody decision-making" Family and Conciliation Courts Review 33:4 (1995), 415–425.

Johnston, J.R. & Roseby, V. In the Name of the Child: A Developmental Approach to Understanding and Helping Children of High-conflict and Violent Families (New York: The Free Press, 1997).

Juby, H., Le Bourdais, C. & Marcil-Gratton, N. "Sharing roles, sharing custody? Couples' characteristics and children's living arrangements at separation" Journal of Marriage and Family 67 (2005), 157–172.

Kelly, J.B. "Parents with enduring child disputes: Multiple pathways to enduring disputes" Journal of Family Studies 9:1 (2003), 37–50.

Kelly, J.B. "Children's living arrangements following separation and divorce: Insights from empirical and clinical research" Family Process 46:1 (2006), 35–52.

Kline, M., Tschann, J., Johnston, J.R. & Wallerstein, J. "Children's adjustment in joint and sole physical custody families" Developmental Psychology 25:3 (1989), 430–438.

Maccoby, E.E. & Mnookin, R.H. *Dividing the Child: Social and Legal Dilemmas of Custody* (Cambridge, MA: Harvard University Press, 1992).

Marcil-Gratton, N. & Le Bourdais, C. "Custody, access and child support: Findings from the National longitudinal Survey of Children and Youth" (Ottawa: Department of Justice, 1999).

Payne, J.D. & Payne, M.A. *Canadian Family Law: Second Edition* (Toronto: Irwin Publishers, 2006).

Pruett, M.K., Williams, T.Y., Insabella, G. & Little, T.D. "Family and legal indicators of child adjustment to divorce among families with young children" Journal of Family Psychology 17 (2003), 169–180.

Roman, M. & Haddad, W. "The case for joint custody" Psychology Today (September, 1978), 96.

Roseby, V. & Johnston, J.R. "Children of Armageddon: Common developmental threats in high-conflict divorcing families" Child Custody 7:2 (1998), 295–309.

Selzer, J. "Father by law: Effects of joint legal custody on nonresident fathers' involvement with children" Demography 25 (1998), 135–146.

Shiller, V.M. "Joint versus maternal custody for families with latency age boys; Parent characteristics and child adjustment" American Journal of Orthopsychiatry 56 (1986), 486–489.

Siegel, J. & Langford, J. "MMPI-2 validity scales and suspected parental alienation syndrome" American Journal of Forensic Psychologist 16:4 (1998), 5–14.

Smyth, B. "Parent-child contact schedules after separation" Family Matters 69 (2004), 32–43.

Steinman, S. "The experience of children in a joint custody arrangement: A report of a study" American Journal of Orthopsychiatry 51(1981), 403–414.

Conclusion

Covering every topic and issue that may arise during the assessment of custody and access disputes is difficult, if not impossible, to do in one book. We have tried to organize as much of the current social science literature and themes found in case law as possible, in order to provide the reader with a compendium of helpful information to do the work in a field that is continually changing and ever challenging.

Fortunately, our knowledge base has grown considerably from the days of child custody being determined on the parent's gender as if there is a one-size-fits-all. The best interest standard, while vague and discretionary, provides a useful framework for attending to the individual needs of children and their families. Relying on presumptions such as the approximation rule and the primary parent presumption may be simpler and reduce conflict for some parents. However, for those parents who cannot resolve parenting arrangements on their own, their conflict is likely to continue. In these situations, it is prudent for the recommendations of assessors and the decisions of the court to be made on a case-by-case basis. We need to be cautious about replacing one presumption with another, as rules and presumptions alone cannot possibly meet the complex and varied needs of children when their parents are in dispute over their parenting arrangements.

Throughout this book, we have argued that having knowledge of the social science literature, methodology, and the many aspects therein is *only* one piece of the puzzle when making parenting plan recommendations that are in a child's best interests. The child custody assessor must also be knowledgeable of the law and the rationale behind the decisions of the courts. Lawyers, in turn, must be familiar with the social science literature in order to represent their clients effectively. We hope that we have accomplished both of these goals.

While this volume provides much about the "how to" of child custody and parenting plans/assessments, we do not maintain that our methods are sacrosanct. Our suggested methodology, however, is based on all the available standards and guidelines, as well as what are considered *acceptable* methods and procedures for conducting parenting plan assessments.

When we began this process, we intended to apply the commonly accepted methods and practices to the various circumstances that often accompany custody and access disputes. For example, when one parent wishes to move away with the children; when a child is alienated from one parent; when there are domestic violence concerns; and cases when children have been conceived through the assistance of reproductive technologies. We came to the conclusion that this application was better left to a separate book.

We hope that our companion book will also be of assistance to our mental health and family law colleagues, who work with families and children in these difficult and challenging practice areas.

Index